SEEKING A FAITH FOR A NEW AGE

Essays on the Interdependence of Religion, Science and Philosophy

by

Henry Nelson Wieman

Edited and introduced by
Cedric L. Hepler

The Scarecrow Press, Inc.
Metuchen, N. J.   1975

Library of Congress Cataloging in Publication Data

Wieman, Henry Nelson, 1884-
    Seeking a faith for a new age.

    Bibliography: p.
    Includes index.
    1. Religion--Philosophy--Addresses, essays, lectures.
2. Worth--Addresses, essays, lectures. 3. Religion
and science--1946-   --Addresses, essays, lectures.
I. Title.
BL51.W585   200'.1   74-34052
ISBN 0-8108-0795-5

Copyright 1975 by Cedric L. Hepler

To

My wife and children,

Myrtle, Michele and Sean

TABLE OF CONTENTS

Preface   vii

Acknowledgments   viii

INTRODUCTION   1

PART 1: THE EMERGENCE OF A METHOD   17
Introduction   17
A Problem in Value Theory   19
Adaptive, Instrumental and Creative Interests   25
Experience, Mind, and the Concept   40

PART 2: STRUCTURE/PROCESS--QUALITY--
VALUE/GOD   53
Introduction   53
Religion in John Dewey's Philosophy   55
God and Value   71
Values: Primary Data for Religious Inquiry   89

PART 3: RELIGIOUS INQUIRY   113
Introduction   113
The Need of Philosophy of Religion   114
Commitment for Theological Inquiry   129
Empiricism in Religious Philosophy   148
What Is Most Important In Christianity?   165

PART 4: THE PERSON, SOCIETY, AND
CREATIVE INTERCHANGE   181
Introduction   181
Speech in the Existential Situation   182
Achieving Personal Stability   194
Education for Social Direction   209

PART 5: WHY RELIGION, SCIENCE, AND
PHILOSOPHY NEED EACH OTHER   225
Introduction   225
Science and a New Religious Reformation   226
Co-operative Functions of Science and Religion   242

Knowledge, Religious and Otherwise   272

BIBLIOGRAPHY   295

INDEX   305

PREFACE

The editor first approached Henry Nelson Wieman in March of 1968 about making a collection of his essays. Throughout the years Mr. Wieman has been most cooperative and helpful in the matters of verifications, editing, and structure. Mr. Wieman read several introductions for the essays by the editor. He offered significant criticisms pertaining to the interpretation of the essays in this collection. The present introduction is the outcome of taking seriously these criticisms and several rewritings of the major parts of the interpretations. It is hoped that the interpretative role of the introduction has been enhanced by the changes undertaken.

Gratitude is expressed to the following whose help has been most beneficial: Stewart A. Newman, who introduced the thought of Henry Nelson Wieman to the editor, and read several drafts of the introduction. William S. Minor read the introduction and offered suggestions about certain portions of its contents, and encouraged the editor early on to see the collection and the publication of Wieman's essays through. Wayne E. Bell, with whom, as seminarians, the editor first discussed the significance of Wieman's religious philosophy in light of the neoorthodox "captivity" of the seminaries and divinity schools in our time--the late 1950s--was helpful in several matters. John B. Cobb, Jr. read the introduction and offered some criticisms concerning the "speculative character" of Wieman's religious philosophy. The editor hopes that these men can see that he has benefited from their criticisms, insights, and support.

Cedric L. Hepler
The Library
North Carolina Wesleyan College
Rocky Mount, N. C.

February 15, 1974

ACKNOWLEDGMENTS

The author and the editor wish to thank the following publishers for permission to reprint the essay(s) that originally appeared in their publication(s):

Harper & Row, Publishers, Inc.--for "Education for Social Direction," in Perspectives On A Troubled Decade: Science, Philosophy, and Religion, 1939-1949, edited by Lyman Bryson, Louis Finkelstein, and R. M. MacIver. Copyright, 1950 by The Conference on Science, Philosophy and Religion in Their Relation to The Democratic Way of Life, Inc.

Harvard University. Harvard University Library, University Archives--for Chapter I, "Introductory" (reprinted in this collection as "A Problem in Value Theory"), and Chapter II, "Adaptive, Instrumental and Creative Interests," in "The Organization of Interests" by Henry Nelson Wieman, Doctoral thesis, 1917, Harvard University, Department of Philosophy.

The Journal of Philosophy--for "Experience, Mind, and the Concept," in Volume XXI:21 (October 9, 1924). Copyright 1924 by The Journal of Philosophy.

The Journal of Religion, The University of Chicago, publisher, --for "Religion in John Dewey's Philosophy," Volume XI: 1 (January 1931). Copyright 1931 by The University of Chicago.
--for "The Need of Philosophy of Religion," Volume XIV:4 (October 1934). Copyright 1934 by The University of Chicago.
--for "Values: Primary Data for Religious Inquiry," Volume XVI:4 (October 1936). Copyright 1936 by The University of Chicago.
--for "Knowledge, Religious and Otherwise," Volume XXXVIII:1 (January 1958). Copyright 1958 by The University of Chicago.
--for "Commitment for Theological Inquiry," Volume

XLII:3 (July 1962). Copyright 1962 by The University
of Chicago.

Macmillan Publishing Co., Inc.--for "God and Value." Re-
printed with permission of Macmillan Publishing Co.,
Inc. from Religious Realism, D. C. Macintosh, Editor.
Copyright 1931 by Macmillan Publishing Co., Inc.

Martinus Nijhoff--for "Empiricism in Religious Philosophy,"
in Philosophy, Religion, and the Coming World Civilization, Essays in Honor of William Ernest Hocking, edited
by Leroy S. Rouner. © Martinus Nijhoff's Boekhandel
en Uitgeversmaatschappij, 1966.

Quarterly Journal of Speech--for "Speech in the Existential
Situation," Volume XLVII:2 (April 1961). Copyright
1961 by the Speech Association of America (now Speech
Communication Association).

The University of Chicago Press, The University of Chicago,
publisher--for "Achieving Personal Stability," in Religion
and the Present Crisis, edited by John Knox. Copyright
1942 by The University of Chicago.

Zygon, Journal of Religion and Science, The University of
Chicago, publisher--for "Science and A New Religious
Reformation," Volume 1:2 (June 1966). Copyright 1966
by The University of Chicago.
--for "Co-operative Functions of Science and Religion,"
Volume 3:1 (March 1968). Copyright 1968 by The University of Chicago.

Gratitude is expressed also to those spirits who were
responsible for the founding of the journal, Religion in the
Making, in which "What Is Most Important In Christianity?"
appeared in 1940 in Volume I. This journal was discontinued
after several years and we know of no successor.

Mrs. Betty Schadegg of Cheney, Washington typed the
manuscript of this collection of essays. The author and the
editor gratefully acknowledge her labors on this project.

INTRODUCTION

by Cedric L. Hepler

The concern of Henry Nelson Wieman throughout his career has been to indicate that the task of religious inquiry is to seek to answer the question, "What operates in human life with such character and power that it will transform man as he cannot transform himself, saving him from evil and leading him to the best that human life can ever reach, provided he meet the required conditions?"[1] Wieman identifies creativity as that which has the character and power of transforming, saving, and leading man to the best. Creativity is the integration of diverse views creating a valuing consciousness in human life; the best is the indefinite expansion of the valuing consciousness of the individual in community with others. One condition that must be met so that creativity might function in the manner described is that man must exercise religious faith. In religious faith there are two levels, according to Wieman. In the first, commitment is guided by the knowledge, concepts, and ideas which one may have at any one time about this creativity. In the second level, "one is motivated by the intention to give himself, in the wholeness of his being so far as he is able, to what in truth does save and transform, no matter how different it may be from one's ideas about it."[2] This is "man's ultimate commitment."

Creativity and man's ultimate commitment are the constitutive processes through which life's "progressive renewal" and the "good life" are actualized.[3] There is no way, however, for the human mind to preconceive or predetermine what the nature of "progressive renewal" and the "good life" will or ought to be. The function of the second level of commitment relative to the possibilities of the transforming power of creativity beyond our present experience and knowledge is to keep us sensitive and inquiring, thereby to discover error in our ideas and concepts of creativity, to save us from fanaticism, and to keep us open to new insights. Commitment to creativity should itself do this,

1

but creativity becomes encased by and confined to the prevailing ideas and concepts of the human mind if these ideas
and concepts are not continuously analyzed by empirical
methods of inquiry.   And even when we have to admit that
our empirical methods of inquiry are unable to remove all
illusion and deception from our ideas and concepts we must
commit ourselves ultimately to what really does transform
us, in spite of how different it may be from our ideas and
concepts of it.

Wieman's religious philosophy is naturalistic and
empirical by design and purpose.   It is naturalistic and
empirical because it is commited to the assumption[4] that
man is transformed, saved, and led to the best by creativity only in and through events, and all events are temporal and spatial and, therefore, are forms of natural
existence.   Since both man's transformation, salvation, and
guidance to the best by creativity and man's giving of self
in religious faith to creativity occur in and through events,
Wieman draws the conclusion that "the empirical method is
the only possible way to distinguish events and to know what
transformation results from them."[5]   Wieman's use of the
empirical method for religious inquiry into the events of
human life which display the characteristics of creativity
and religious faith entails his theory of knowledge and his
theory of value, both of which will be discussed below.

Compared to other theological methodologies of the
twentieth century

> Wieman's procedure in describing God is unique.
> Traditional theology has used the non-rational
> methods of faith and revelation, and the rational
> methods of deduction and analogy.   This method
> is essentially idealization: God is conceived as
> the supreme case of being and value.   By contrast,
> Wieman's method is concretization: it is an ef-
> fort to state the (necessarily abstract) structure
> of the concrete creative process.   This attempt
> at 'sheer display' stems from both a philosophical
> respect for reality and a religious respect for
> God as operative in history. [6]

That Wieman's method displays a "concretization" and not
an "idealization" of the conception of God is evident from
his analyses of creativity and man's ultimate commitment
in the events of natural existence and human history.

The concrete supreme good of creativity, according to Wieman, is felt, observed, conceptualized, analyzed, and known from the data of experience just as any other natural process is, by the empirical method. Wieman emphasizes that creativity must be that one process occurring in the events of existence and human life that makes the difference between the human propensity for evil and the transformation of persons from the evil to the good. He places himself in opposition to the predominant theological practice of seeking the answer to the religious question (What actually saves man as man cannot save himself?) first in "ultimate being" and only secondarily in existence and human life. Wieman reverses this procedure:

> ... If we start with inquiry about ultimate Being, we will almost certainly fail to find the process which saves and transforms, because ultimate Being is a mystery, as Tillich and many others assert. The great exemplars of religious personality, such persons, for example, as Jesus, Socrates, Paul, Martin Luther, and Gandhi, were not metaphysicians. When and if metaphysical problems engaged them at all, these problems were quite peripheral to their central questions. The primary question for every one of them was the question about man's salvation and what operates in human life to accomplish it. ("Knowledge, Religious and Otherwise. ")*

Creativity, for Wieman, is the natural process in existence and human life that accomplishes human salvation. He asserts that it is known like any other process that is natural, i.e., temporal and spatial.

How is knowledge of a natural process obtained? Wieman does not think it adequate to answer this question with the simple reply, "Knowledge is obtained through experience." ("Experience, Mind, and the Concept.") There has to be experience before rational and cognitive knowledge comes about, but the rational process through which knowledge comes cannot be identified with the proposition that knowledge is experience. If this proposition is allowed to stand it is easy to fall into the error of saying the reverse,

---

*All such references given in parentheses are to essays by Wieman that are reprinted in this collection.

"experience is knowledge," which is not the case.

> Although there is nothing back of experience ex-
> cept more experience ... we cannot know the
> world, made up of experience in time and space,
> merely by experiencing it. We must experience
> it, to be sure; but we must do more. We must
> use concepts in order to refer beyond immediate
> experience. ("Experience, Mind, and the Con-
> cept.")

Wieman specifies "immediate experience" in the following
way: "Most of the time we live sustained and guided by
physiological processes equipped with unthinking habit and
impulse and the undiscriminated flow of felt quality."
("Knowledge, Religious and Otherwise.") It is out of this
immediate experience--physiological processes and the flow
of felt quality--that value, action, and knowledge are structured.

It is a basic principle of Wieman's empirical method
that knowledge is developed out of abstractions from "the
massive continuity of physiological processes and the flow
of felt quality." ("Knowledge, Religious and Otherwise.")
The physiological processes and the undiscriminated flow
of felt quality are first in the order of time, and then comes
knowledge. It is this affirmation as to the priority and
order concerning immediate experience and knowledge that
distinguishes Wieman's empiricism from the so-called School
of British Empiricism. [7]

The human organism does not live just within the
borders of its physiological processes or merely at the
skirts of the flow of felt quality. If it did, it would not
be human. What distinguishes it as human is that it is able
to construct intelligent action out of the encounters between
its physiological processes and the flow of quality. The
human organism attains knowledge and acts intelligently
when it selects certain data from the flow of quality by
virtue of specific interests arising to satisfy various needs,
one such need being the need to survive. The interests of
the human organism are both physical and mental, both
bodily feelings and conceptual feelings. The specific range
of the interests and the meaning derived from the data selected by these interests are determined by the categories
of thought, the significance of the past (history and culture),
and the structure of language, all of which place the person

in responsible communal relationships.   According to Wieman, the selection of these data under the guidance of the
ruling interests of the human organism creates the percep-
tual event with its meaning.

Knowledge, then, is attained when the psychophysical
organism selects certain data from both its own physiological
processes and the flow of felt quality and designates them as
having certain orders in time and space.   The human organism acts intelligently on the basis of the empirical principle that these data are designated as having certain orders
in time and space precisely because they are abstracted
from immediate experience.   Knowledge is about specified
data and their designated orders that pertain to the total
organism, inclusive of its psychological, physical, and
social dimensions.   The method by which these data are
selected and designated is called the empirical method, or
the scientific method, and it is comprised of reason, observation, experimentation, and verification/falsification.

In the attainment of knowledge one must first get an
insight into the theoretical order that the data will display
when they are selected out of physiological processes and
felt quality.   This insight is determined by the interdependence of the mind and the experienceable world.   Next, the
insight, or theory, must be applied to the observable (experienceable) world to see if it fits what is found to be
there.   Often the order provided by the theory does not fit
the actual sequence of observed events.   This means that in
the third stage the theory must be modified and observation must be redirected and controlled until some such order
does seem to appear.   If the theory never "fits the facts"
then it is abandoned, falsified.   When order does appear it
can become the basis for other insight, intuition, and imagination generating further theories of the experienceable
universe which can be observed, rationally directed, and
controlled for the benefit of human life and its world.
("Knowledge, Religious and Otherwise" and "Empiricism in
Religious Philosophy.")   Thus, knowledge, as delineated in
the epistemology of Henry Nelson Wieman, is considerably
less extensive than the massive continuity of physiological
processes and the undiscriminated flow of felt quality.
Knowledge consists of statements which articulate selected
and designated data.

A statement is an instance of knowledge if, and
only if, we (1) have had an insight, variously

called 'hypothesis,' 'theory,' or 'innovating suggestion'; (2) have put this suggestion into the form
of a statement with terms unambiguously defined;
(3) have developed the implications of this statement into a logical structure of propositions of
such sort that some of these propositions specify
what must be observed under required conditions
if the statement is to be accepted as knowledge;
and (4) have made the observations under the
specified conditions to discover if the data do appear in the order required to warrant accepting
the statement as having met the tests of probability.   ("Knowledge, Religious and Otherwise.")

Knowledge is attained in this manner of any process
in natural existence that can be selected and designated as
having certain orders in time and space.   According to the
empirical religious naturalism of Henry Nelson Wieman,
creativity also is known in this manner.   Creativity is the
integration of diverse views creating a valuing consciousness which comprehends an order of value more profound
and extensive than was possible in the situation before this
creative interaction occurred.

Wieman stresses (1) that knowledge as attained by
the empirical method does not encompass all of experience
or the potentialities and possibilities of creativity, and
(2) that knowledge is abstract and barren compared to the
fullness, richness, and intensity of the massive continuity
of physiological processes and felt quality.   What he stresses
can be ignored only at great peril.   His concern is to help
make clear the nature of the action that must be taken in
order to handle creatively the explicit threat of planetary
destruction by the devices of technological power.   It is in
stating the case for this need of action--the reordering of
priorities in the social system--that Wieman anticipated the
basic thrust of the "quality of life" and ecological concerns
of recent vintage.   The dilemma, then, consists of the following: It is only through the empirical or scientific method
that we can think and act intelligently in our technological
world.   It is only through the empirical method that conditions can be sought and provided which are most conducive
for creativity through which man is transformed and saved.
Yet, contrasted with this, it is through the empirical method that we have the technological power which, if used un-
intelligently, stands as the ultimate threat to human history
as known and lived.   Also, the abstract forms of reason

can enthrall the mind to the point that one ceases to be sensitive and aware of the concrete fullness of quality which
creates the valuing consciousness in depth and scope. [8] With
this narrowing of sensitivity and awareness, man loses the
"capacity to appreciate the 'surplusage' of experience."
("Experience, Mind, and the Concept.")

> This surplusage of experience means all those
> data, and all that unanalyzed datum, which is ir-
> relevant to our established scientific theories, but
> is indispensable to the development of any radical-
> ly new theories and the solution of very different
> and more complex problems that are bound to arise
> with an evolving civilization. It means, further-
> more, all that concrete, scientifically meaningless,
> experience which makes seven-eighths of the joy of
> living--a lover's kiss, the colors of the sunset, a
> child's soft little hand, the heart of a rose. ("Ex-
> perience, Mind, and the Concept.")

In contrast to this surplusage of experience, science

> ... vastly magnifies our efficiency in procuring
> anything we want and have the capacity to enjoy;
> but it greatly diminishes our capacity to enjoy. It
> gives us wonderful instruments of achievement, but
> narrows and distorts our vision of what is to be
> achieved. ("Experience, Mind, and the Concept.")

As man makes his way intelligently and creatively in
the world two things can be observed: (1) man's knowledge
always falls short of the concrete fullness of quality, and
(2) man's knowledge is increased by the new insights created
out of the interaction between physiological processes and
felt quality. Thus, knowledge is that which distinguishes man
as the intelligent and creative thinker and actor and makes
him able to ex-ist, stand out of the world of immediate experience. Knowledge, however, is not an end in itself; rather it should be held subject to the process of creativity
whereby the greatest structured content of physiological process and felt quality becomes appreciable to man's valuing
consciousness. It is the "creative interchange" between conscious awareness and the appreciable world that creates and
sustains human life beyond the "clear and distinct ideas" of
knowledge.

In summary, Wieman's theory of knowledge is based

on two principles: (1) the empirical method does not claim anything more than probability for the knowledge attained through observation and the formation of theory--inclusive of the "knowledge of 'God' "; (2) it is creativity that creates innovating reason and the conditions for valuing consciousness, the appreciable world and the appreciative mind. This creativity is the "divine presence" in human life because it creates and expands indefinitely the valuing consciousness of the individual in community with others. Hence, it calls for religious faith (ultimate commitment) because only it is capable of creating, sustaining, transforming, and saving human life. Creativity is found to function in these ways however different its processes may be from our concepts and ideas of it. This creativity--by nature the generative source of all value--is not limited to any particular religious doctrinal orthodoxy, to any cultural and political heritage, nor to any life style. (See both "What Is Most Important in Christianity?" and "Achieving Personal Stability.")

Wieman's epistemology is crucial not only for an understanding of his conceptions of creativity and man's ultimate commitment but also for his theory of value and the indefinite expansion of the valuing consciousness of the individual in community with others. Wieman makes his most substantial contribution to the discussion of the "God" question in his study of value. It is through his value theory that his analysis of creativity, creative interchange, comes into its sharpest focus.

Wieman's study of value is empirical. Values cannot be deduced ready-made and applied to human life and existence with no regard to the feelings and activities of persons. According to Wieman, "the highest values that are ever to be achieved must be achieved by physical operations." ("Religion in John Dewey's Philosophy.")

> So we see that knowledge of any reality consists of two parts: getting the right data and connecting them in the right way.... The data are always bits of experience that have to be put together into a pattern...We believe the factor in value which lends itself most readily to a guiding pattern or principle by which to discover, appraise, and appreciate values is appreciable activity. ("Values: Primary Data for Religious Inquiry.")

Appreciable activity is of two sorts, enjoyable and

sufferable. The meaning of value is to be found in some
critique of enjoyable and sufferable activities.

Various persons will have diverse enjoyments and sufferings because of different ruling interests and because of
the differences in their psychophysical responses to quality.
Even an individual will have diverse enjoyments and sufferings at different times about and for the same "object." The
various and diverse enjoyments and sufferings, "utterly different though they may be, can be had only when they are so
connected that they do not destroy one another." ("Values:
Primary Data for Religious Inquiry.") Value is not merely
enjoyment; rather it is the creative connection between activities and feelings that makes them mutually sustaining and
mutually meaningful with possibilities of indefinite expansion.

> When we experience enjoyment [with meaning] it is
> not merely our enjoyment that we enjoy; what we
> enjoy is a certain connection between activities even
> though we may not be conscious of that fact. And
> these connections can be extended indefinitely to
> render stable and progressive the order which we
> enjoy. Value, then, is that connection between ap-
> preciable activities which makes them mutually sus-
> taining, mutually enhancing, mutually diversifying,
> and mutually meaningful. ("Values: Primary Data
> for Religious Inquiry.")

Thus, it may be noted that there are five empirical aspects
of this system of mutuality which illustrate the supreme good
of creativity: (1) Some enjoyments involve activities which
support other enjoyable activities; (2) Appreciable activities
not only support others, in many cases they actually enhance
them; (3) When activities are connected creatively, increase
in their diversification and number can be permitted without
a threat to their mutual support and enhancement; (4) An activity may be exceedingly painful, and yet, because it is connected to other activities by the supreme good of creativity,
it becomes the carrier of wide, rich meaning; (5) Meaning
is created in and for human life when the present event is so
connected with other events and possibilities that it enables
the mind to evaluate these other events and possibilities in
terms of their relation to one another and to the present.
(See both "Religion in John Dewey's Philosophy" and "Values:
Primary Data for Religious Inquiry" for Wieman's analysis of
the empirical aspects of the system of mutuality in value.)

> Meaning is that connection between the here-and-
> now and the far-away which enables a mind that
> understands the connection to experience the far-
> away through the mediation of the here-and-now.
> This ability to transmit the far-away to the exper-
> ience of a mind by way of representation is what
> we call meaning. This ability depends on two
> things: (1) the rich connections and (2) the mind's
> understanding of these connections. ("Values: Pri-
> mary Data for Religious Inquiry.")

This system of mutuality in which the various and diverse activities and feelings are connected creatively for the
increase of value operates as a process of natural existence
and human life involving interchange between persons. This
interchange creates the valuing consciousness capable of indefinite expansion in community with others. This process
of creative interchange can be observed and analyzed by the
empirical method. Since this process can be known and articulated through the empirical method it might be asked
about its nature and its significance for human life and the
experienceable world.

> ... The process which carries highest possibility
> of value is that interaction between many factors
> which generates and promotes to the maximum com-
> munication and community... Here we have some-
> thing going on in the world which is observable;
> upon which and in which we can operate with our
> bodies, our techniques, our machines; and to which
> all the resources of science and the whole of hu-
> man life can be dedicated for the sake of the pos-
> sibilities of value which it offers. ("Religion in
> John Dewey's Philosophy.")

This body of shareable experience is not caused by human
purpose. It is not the mysterious transposition of absolute
principles from "eternity" into time. Rather, it is the consequence of an interaction that actually creates the person
and the human processes of feelings, activities, and knowledge. This interaction is itself creativity or creative interchange and it creates the appreciative mind and the appreciable world relative to such a mind. As this creativity or
creative interchange creates and works in the processes of
activities of persons it can be observed as having certain
characteristics. Not all of it can be observed because a
part operates at the subconscious level of the particular individuals.

Creative interchange is that kind of interaction between persons in which the progressive growth of value is
realized. It progressively creates the valuing consciousness
when required conditions are met.

> Creative interchange creates appreciative under-
> standing of diverse perspectives of individuals and
> peoples. It also integrates these perspectives in
> each individual participant. Thus commitment to
> creative interchange is not commitment to any given
> system of value. It is commitment to what creates
> ever deeper insight into the values that motivate hu-
> man lives. It creates an ever more comprehensive
> integration of these values so far as this is pos-
> sible by transforming them in such a way that they
> can be mutually enhancing instead of mutually im-
> poverishing and obstructive. ("Commitment for
> Theological Inquiry.")

This creative interchange creates valuing consciousness and
is that strand of existence in which the process of progressive integration of value and the unlimited growth of the connection of values takes place. In this sense it is the supreme
value. Thus for Wieman, creative interchange is the "concretization" of the concept traditionally called "God" in the
Judaeo-Christian heritage of Western civilization. Creative
interchange, creativity, is "that structure which sustains,
promotes, and constitutes supreme value." ("God and Value.") But it is not a person nor is it the absolute all-domi-
nant power against which nothing can prevail. Wieman's concept of creative interchange differs from the traditional concept of "God" especially at the point of "God's" relations to
the processes of existence and human life. For Wieman,
creative interchange is the continuous sustaining relationship
in the processes of existence and human life that transforms,
saves, and leads human life to the best that it can become.
The transcendence of creativity has to do with its functions,
not with its location outside of time and space. Creativity
cannot be unrelated to the processes of existence and life; in
fact, it is the one strand of the processes of existence and
life that "brings lesser values into relations of maximum mutual support and mutual enhancement." ("God and Value.")

Obviously, this creativity cannot be completely known
and articulated in statements through the empirical method.
But this is true of every complex process known to the human mind. There is an unknown dimension to creativity.

It is an unknown dimension, yet knowable in principle. Because this dimension is beyond our ideas and concepts of it,
it is unmanageable for human endeavors. The quality of creativity far exceeds any and all statements of knowledge about
it. Its qualitative distinctiveness has "come from" the unknown into cognitive knowledge in the sense that on the basis
of observation and analysis it has been experienced, abstracted, and known as that process of existence that human
life which has carried and is carrying the greatest content of
value that humanity has thus far attained. Furthermore, for
Wieman, creativity must be identified with that process of
existence and human life which carries the "possibilities of
greatest value," even though these possibilities are unknown
at present. These possibilities will become known as the
valuing consciousness of man is progressively created. The
word "creativity" means what actualizes possibilities which
are not known at the present time, or brings them into the
range of human vision. Thus, Wieman avoids the logical
contradiction of the "unknowable God."

The giving of the self in religious faith to whatever
in truth does transform and save man, however different its
actuality may be from our concepts and ideas about it, is
wild irresponsibility unless one has first sought and found
what all available evidence seems to indicate has this saving
power. Only after this is done is man 1) "able to, and actually does focus his interest and effort upon the unknown"
("God and Value."), and 2) able to gather further insight.
One can do this when he commits himself to creativity because creativity actualizes possibilities and generates new insights. In the absolute commitment of faith man finds personal stability and security in the quality of creativity--its
immense possibilities. In ultimate commitment man gives
up relying on all "orders of life" as final, or on "schemes
of self-sufficiency," or on any ideal as ultimate, or on
mythical beliefs understood as faith which stand beyond rational and empirical evidence. Neither does he yield to adaptations that would blend him in with whatever interest might
happen along. ("Achieving Personal Stability.")

Although the quality of creativity is more extensive
than the concepts and ideas that may be held about it, man's
ultimate commitment is given over to it in faith to the effect that it is the source of supreme value and human good.
Creativity, so far as it prevails, connects relative values
and goods into a system that brings them into relations of
maximum mutual support and enhancement.

It was pointed out above that Howard L. Parsons argues that the concepts of "God" in traditional theology exemplify "God" as the supreme case of being <u>and value</u>. Now it has been indicated throughout this introduction that Wieman considers creativity to be that strand of existence and life that "sustains, promotes, and constitutes supreme value." The present writer holds that the statements of Parsons and Wieman are not contradictory, for the following reasons. Traditional theology has conceived "God" to be the "supreme case of being and value" in the sense of "God" being Transcendental Perfection, unencumbered by the temporal and spatial processes of existence and human life, yet exercising <u>full</u> power and control over the world. Creativity for Wieman is that structure and process <u>in</u> existence and human life which generates and connects relative values and goods into a system of relations for maximum mutual support and enhancement. The concepts of traditional theology cast "God" as supernatural, beyond experience, and empirically unknowable; the creativity of empirical religious naturalism is natural, observable, and knowable.

Wieman's philosophy of creativity, indicates that: 1) religious commitment is invalid, deceptive, and evil if it is not directed to what is accessible to empirical inquiry; 2) religious commitment must be given to what creates in the person appreciative understanding of the basic values which motivate the lives of others and which integrates these values in each individual; and 3) religious commitment to this empirical actuality combines the most complete giving of the self with a mind open to inquiry and subject to correction. ("Commitment for Theological Inquiry.") With these three points the question of the distinction between good and evil is raised.

The distinction between good and evil for empirical religious naturalism does not depend on any human judgment (or statement of knowledge) but is an objective reality to be discovered by inquiry. This objective reality is the standard that good is the continued expansion of the valuing consciousness of the individual in community with others. Evil is the obstruction of such continued expansion of the valuing consciousness. But as soon as any achieved level of this expansion is set up as the standard, in opposition to the continued expansion of the valuing consciousness, there is a false standard that is self-destructive.

The insights and experimentations of Wieman's em-

pirical religious naturalism indicate that an "ontology of power" is inadequate for the world today.   ("Commitment for Theological Inquiry.") Creativity is the ultimate good, but it is not <u>almighty.</u> Creativity, therefore, is dependent upon required conditions being met by persons in relation so that its efficacy might be actualized as creative interchange.
From the perspective of empirical religious naturalism, the "ontology of good and evil" must be chosen over the "ontology of power"--but not under the illusory and speculative assumption that good by definition is what "inevitably wins in the end." There is too much historical and experiential evidence against the assumption that "good is all-powerful and triumphant in the end." Certainly we should seek to increase to the utmost the "power" that expands the valuing consciousness of the individual in creative community. Every kind of power obstructive to this creativity should be opposed. Creativity may prevail over all other powers in the far reach of history but the power of modern technology has made man responsible for providing some of the conditions under which this can occur. What is ultimate (or powerful) in the "ontology of good and evil" is that if you and I were crushed, defeated, and destroyed by those powers that oppose creativity we could yet trust that we had contributed to the conditions necessary for the increase of value and human good if we had committed ourselves over to the keeping of creativity.

Notes

1. Henry Nelson Wieman, "Intellectual Autobiography,"
    The Empirical Theology of Henry Nelson Wieman,
    Robert W. Bretall, editor (Carbondale: Southern Illinois University Press, 1969), p. 3. This work is cited as Bretall hereafter.

2. Ibid., pp. 6-7.

3. William S. Minor, "Renewal and the Good Life," Bretall, pp. 164-179.

4. What is meant by "assumption" is the distributive basic assumption of human feeling, action, and knowledge, such as Wieman speaks of on page 35 of the "original version" of "Intellectual Autobiography":
    I have not answered the claim that the empirical method rests upon assumptions which cannot them-

selves be defended by the empirical method. I
think that this claim is open to question but even
suppose we grant it, the reply is obvious. If the
empirical method does depend upon prior assumptions, these assumptions are made by every human
being because it is impossible to get the common
knowledge necessary for daily life in any other way.
Stones and trees, tables and chairs, are known in
this way. No other alleged way of knowing with its
different assumptions is wrought so inextricably into human existence. Therefore the burden of proof
rests upon him who claims that there is any other
way to knowledge. It does not rest upon the de-
fender of the empirical method because every one
practices it whether he admits it or not.

5. Wieman, Bretall, p. 3.

6. Howard L. Parsons, "The New Reformation," Bretall,
p. 122, fn 15. Other statements with regard to the
"uniqueness" of Wieman's religious inquiry are to be
found in Bernard E. Meland's "The Root and Form of
Wieman's Thought," Bretall, p. 57 and Bernard M.
Loomer's "Wieman's Stature as a Contemporary Theologian," Bretall, p. 396.

7. See how Wieman is misunderstood in his relationship to
the School of British Empiricism by Huston Smith,
"Empiricism Revisited," Bretall, and by John B.
Cobb, Jr. Living Options in Protestant Theology
(Philadelphia: Westminster Press, 1962).

8. In 1971, in response to questions posed by Cedric L.
Hepler, Wieman wrote:
Under the dominating power of modern technology,
social development has been subordinating the individual ever more narrowly to specialized social
functions. Indeed it has been this increasing suppression of the valuing consciousness of the individual to specialized social functions which has
caused rebellion against it in the form of the counter culture. This exposes the most critical point
now developing in our lives. Will the counter culture prevail in bringing the technology into the service of providing conditions most favorable for expanding the valuing consciousness of individuals in
community with one another, or will the power of

technology prevail in bringing the consciousness of
values accessible to the individual within the narrowing bounds of specialized functions prescribed by
the technology? Will future history bring technology increasingly into the service of man, or will
man be brought increasingly into the service of
technology? Will increasing economic abundance
enable each individual to develop the creative potentialities of his own consciousness in community
with others, or will it increasingly confine the consciousness of each to the increasingly narrow spe-
cialization of his social function? The counter culture expanding the individual consciousness of each
in community with others is identical with what I
call creative interchange.

PART 1:
THE EMERGENCE OF A METHOD

INTRODUCTION

This first group of essays epitomizes Wieman's religious philosophy from the vantage of its beginning. From the beginning, Wieman entered upon the task of religious inquiry by characterizing the structure of creativity and its bearing upon human interests. During this early period, Wieman initiated his study of value, considered as goal-seeking activities which mutually support, enhance, and sustain one another over the widest range of diversity. He also began his religious inquiry of God as "valued because of the immediate relations sustained with Him, and not because of any ulterior results or rewards which may follow upon these relations." (From Wieman's doctoral thesis, "The Organization of Interests," Chapter XII, "A Creative Type of Religion.")

The little known influence of the earlier literature of Freud is alluded to in the first essay. This influence, and that of the other social and behavioral scientists cited in the second essay, were important for the development of Wieman's understanding of the self, personality, creative interchange, "the constitutive structure of reality: the mind and the universe," and "the valuing consciousness of the individual capable of indefinite expansion in community with others." The second essay illuminates Wieman's early apprehension of the need for required conditions to be present before creativity can work unobstructively. The adaptive, instrumental and creative interests of this essay became the intrinsic, instrumental and creative values of the essay in the Journal of Philosophy, XLII (March 29, 1945), pp. 180-185, and The Source of Human Good (1946).

In "Experience, Mind, and the Concept" the meanings implicit to creativity and value were gathered up and put into perspective through a tendentious analysis of the interde-

pendence of religious inquiry, science, and philosophy. However, Wieman cautioned against an overzealous adherence to
science with its narrowing of interests, its barrenness of
qualitative meaning, and its impoverishment of experience.
Wieman's <u>Religious Experience and Scientific Method</u> was published in 1926. By then he saw clearly the need for an adequate religious ruling commitment to meet the demands of
the growing power of twentieth century scientific technology.
He also saw that the religious concept of God could and
should be subjected to the closest scrutiny of science. And
"...by science we understand merely that method by which
truth and error are discriminated and knowledge verified."
(From <u>Religious Experience and Scientific Method</u> [Carbon-
dale and Edwardsville: Southern Illinois University Press,
1969], pp. 32-3.)

A PROBLEM IN VALUE THEORY*

Our problem will be to discover that organization of human interests which is most conducive to their maximum fulfilment. The object of our quest is the greatest good. The principle of organization, which we propose, we shall call creativity. Our thesis is that all interests should be so organized as to function as one; and that one should be creative interest. Interest which is directed to developing a fuller consciousness of some object, purely for the sake of experiencing that object, and not for any ulterior end, is what we call creative interest. It is creative of integrated experience. We believe that the organization which causes all the processes constitutive of human life to function in satisfying creative interest, is the organization of life which yields the most complete and continuous satisfaction.

In the struggle of living creatures to maintain their existence above the dead mass of inorganic matter on the one hand and above the internecine conflict of species on the other, there has been born that light which we call <u>attentive</u> consciousness or creative attention or intelligence. With respect to it we stand before two alternatives. Is it the purpose of intelligence to diminish the sufferings and doings of men that their lives may be more easeful; or is it the purpose of these sufferings and doings to magnify the range and intensity of attentive consciousness? Which is the end and which the means? Our purpose is to defend the latter of these two alternatives by showing that it leads to the largest measure of good.

By good we shall understand the fulfilment of any interest whatsoever. When I have a tendency to act in a certain way, that tendency is an interest; and to carry out the tendency is to satisfy the interest. If we exclude from our consideration all the effects which such an act may have upon other contemporaneous tendencies both in ourselves and in other persons, and also ignore all its future consequences,

---

*Henry Nelson Wieman, "The Organization of Interests" (unpublished Doctor's dissertation, Department of Philosophy, Harvard University, 1917), Chapter I, "Introductory."

then the accomplishment of the act is a good so far as it
fulfils that single interest under consideration.   There are
many different criteria for determining various quantities and
qualities of good; but the ultimate unit of good, to which they
all reduce in the last analysis, is satisfaction of interest.
Such a unit may well be bad from the standpoint of some
wider range of interests, but for itself it is a good.

In actual life we very rarely restrict our vision to one
isolated impulse in this manner, although at times such situations arise.   Suppose a starving man, gagged and bound.   Upon the sudden presentation of food he might be dominated by
the impulse to seize it even though he could not put it to his
mouth; and the frustration of that impulsive act by the bonds
about his wrists would be for the moment a very great evil
to him.   Even though the food were poisoned, the fulfilment
of that single tendency, excluding consideration of future consequences, would be so far a good.   When Esau sells his
birthright for a mess of pottage the act is not bad because it
satisfies his momentary hunger, but because it thwarts many
other larger interests.

The reason the fulfilment of many interests is universally pronounced bad, and rightly so, is that such particular
satisfactions make impossible, or render more difficult, a
fuller and more continuous satisfaction, either for the person
concerned or for others, or both.   Whenever the consequences
of an act tend to diminish the total number of interests which
can be satisfied, or increases the number of those which
cannot, it is generally called bad.   But the common principle
upon which all such judgments are based is that of satisfied
interest.   The thing is bad because it conflicts with the larger will of the individual or the social group or humanity or
God.   But it is always the fulfilment of some will which constitutes the good; and the will is always some organization
of interests.   So we always come back again in the end to
this ultimate unit of the good.

The term interest includes all the activities of a physical organism.   Activity is taken to include all 'readiness to
act' or 'motor attitude' as well as the gross efforts of limb
and trunk.   Thinking is activity; it is 'the lambent interplay
of motor attitudes'.   Every impulse involves a certain readjustment of the organism, however minute and imperceptible
may be the changes, and hence is activity.   Thus interest
may be expressed in various ways and appear in diverse
forms.   It is 'response of the organism to its environment';

it is 'wish', want, desire, purpose, instinct, habit, will. It
is the tendency of the organism to act in a specific manner;
to produce a definite result; to create or sustain a certain
situation. It is necessary to have some comprehensive term
to which we can reduce all the phenomena under consideration. We have adopted the word interest for this purpose,
following, as we understand it, the usage of Professor R. B.
Perry.

So, in quest of the greatest good, we will know what
we are looking for. It must be the maximum fulfilment of
interest. It must be some massing of the ultimate units of
good. But human interests are so numerous and diverse,
presenting to the casual glance such a chaos of inextricable
activities, that the types of inter-relation which might be established among them seem to be legion. Yet it is manifest
that some systems of interrelation will afford a more continuous and complete satisfaction of a larger number of interests than other systems. The greatest good will lie in that
system which gives us the most constant and ample fulfilment
of purpose.

Of course that system which contravenes the laws of
physical nature, or does not conform to the will of God, cannot be the mediator of maximum fulfilment. But we shall
not make either of these a distinct object of investigation
apart from the study of human interests. We cannot know
God's will except as we somehow find it in ourselves. If we
assert that a certain course of action is the will of God, we
mean to say that it is the right course. But by acknowledg-
ing it to be right we are recognizing that it is that which we
would do, however far from it our actual course of procedure
may be.

We cannot for several reasons make a distinct study
of that natural environment which would be most favorable to
satisfaction of human needs. Such a study would lead us too
far afield. The significance of climate, rivers, soil, sea
board, mountains, etc., it is no doubt very great, as well
as the wider cosmic processes. But every field of investigation must be more or less arbitrarily limited. So we shall
restrict ourselves to the consideration of that internal correlation of activities most conducive to satisfaction, leaving to
one side the bearing upon human interests of such factors as
time, space, fauna, flora, the dead mass of inorganic matter and the great geological changes.

Our first task will be to arrive at some classification of human interests. Viewed as an aggregation of single interests they are altogether beyond the power of our thought. We cannot think them at all except as we reduce them to a few simple categories. This task of formulating a scheme with which to deal intelligibly with the mass of human activities will constitute the first part of our work.

We shall next consider that principle of organization which has been very frequently proposed since men first began to reflect upon the conduct of human life. It is the method of reducing interests to a system in which they shall harmonize with each other. It is proposed that only then can maximum fulfilment of will be achieved when all antagonism of activities is brought to an end and the total process of life becomes a system of mutually sustaining interests. This proposal we shall submit to critical examination.

With reference to this method of coordination we shall raise the question whether it is possible to reduce the inalienable interests of human nature to a harmony. Freudian psychology has demonstrated that there are ineradicable interests which cannot be simply ignored. It is not possible to cultivate indifference with respect to them. They must find expression in some form or other. If suppressed they persist in some form of nervous irritation. In extreme cases they cause hysteria and even insanity. Now it is a highly debatable question whether all these persistent characters of human will can be brought into harmony with one another. Our conviction is that they cannot; that the effort to bring them into such a cooperative system is a hopeless task. Granted that a system can be devised which will bring a great many interests into coordinated activity, still if any ineradicable tendencies whatsoever are left outside the system however few, they may be, they will be a constant irritant. The more compact and perfect the system of coordinated interests become, and the more completely we surrender ourselves to it, the more aggravated will be the dissatisfaction of the suppressed interests. The constant pressure they exert, even though it be altogether subconscious, will eventually turn the beautiful harmony we have fashioned into gall and wormwood. This is the inevitable working of suppressed tendencies.

But when interests thwart one another and cannot possibly be coordinated, there is a way out of the difficulty, which Freud has called the process of 'Sublimation'. It consists in diverting the antagonistic interests into some process of action which will drain off their suppressed energy. The antagonism still persists but a super-interest is generated which is sustained and fulfilled by virtue of this antagonism. This process of sublimation we shall recognize as a distinct interest and shall include it under our category of 'creative interests'.

But in giving up the method of coordination as the means to the greatest good, and being forced to seek some other principle of organization, are we necessarily reverting to that which is second best? When turning our faces away from the ideal of harmony, are we leaving the greatest good which might have been for a lesser good which must be? Our conviction is that such is not the case. It is possible to organize the conflict of interests in such a way as to make the conflict yield a fuller measure of satisfaction than any harmony could ever realize.

We consider several ways in which this conflict of tendencies within the individual attains an organization which is very highly valued as an end in itself, and this by universal consent. The several types of this sort of organization which we examine are: humor, art, friendship and the relations of the individual to society. In humor, art and friendship it is the interaction of antagonistic tendencies which quickens the consciousness to a certain vivacity, emotional tension or process of idea-forming which is cherished by the person concerned as one of his most precious experiences. But it is the organized conflict of minds which is most highly valued and is most fruitful in developing all the ideas and emotions of which human nature is capable. Friction between persons is necessary in order that there be any mutual interpretation of minds. This friction is an integral part of the interpretation. Through this interaction each individual comes first to understand the purpose of the other, and then forms his own purpose in relation to this other, either as a cooperator or antagonist. The other person reacts in the same way, and there ensues a mutual creation of mind out of which has arisen that marvelous growth of idea and emotion which we call culture.

The most remarkable effect of this organized conflict of minds is a peculiar acceleration and exuberance of what we shall call secondary consciousness. Primary consciousness consists of perceptions; secondary, of the phenomena of reflection, of memory, of imagination, of conception, of desires, fears, hopes, affections. The two are inseparable and

cannot be distinguished in any clear line of demarcation, but
for our purposes we can represent them as two. In primary
consciousness we discern the nonego; in secondary the ego.
The development of secondary consciousness is the development of self-consciousness. Its growth is what we mean by
creativity.

It is the antagonism of other minds which, more than
anything else, stimulates the processes of secondary consciousness. The most striking example of this is when we
are engaged in animated conversation. There is at such time
a richness and lightning play of revivified memories, a pro-
ductivity of imagination, of conception, and growth in concreteness of idea that we do not experience at any other
time. But this experience is not restricted to conversation
strictly so called. It arises whenever we deal with other
minds, as when reading a book, contemplating a work of art
or observing the product of human efforts in any form.

Since it is the interaction of minds which offers the
most promising field for the development of organized and
valued conflict, we turn to the study of society. Here we
find an acceleration of secondary consciousness, or a mutual creativity of minds, which is of highest worth. But we
also find other tendencies in society which move in the opposite direction, and these cannot be removed from social organization. They are its necessary conditions. So, while
an ideal society would give us the largest measure of satisfaction beyond a doubt, and would do so because of the way
in which it organized the antagonism of minds, the actual societies do not do so. And because of the essential principle
of social organization they never can do so.

But since ideal society is undoubtedly the indispensable condition of our largest satisfaction, or the greatest
good, we turn to that way of life which throughout history has
claimed to lead men into such a society. We turn to religion. From all the various forms of religion we differenti-
ate that particular type which seems to uphold those postu-
lates which would most nearly fulfill this claim. We then describe the essential features of that faith in which men have
so frequently found, according to their assertions, that complete and continuous satisfaction for which we have been seeking. We do not try to demonstrate the reality of this belief.
It cannot be demonstrated and in this respect is exactly like
all the other major interests of life. It is a practical postu-
late which must be lived. One proves it by living it and
cannot prove it in any other way.

ADAPTIVE, INSTRUMENTAL AND CREATIVE INTERESTS*

Any classification is determined by the purpose for which it is made. Our purpose in formulating human interests in convenient categories is to ascertain the degree to which they attain satisfaction. But the degree to which interests may be satisfied within a given environment depends upon the manner in which they are correlated. So we shall classify interests according to the different ways in which they may be brought into relation with one another. According to our method those interests shall belong to the same class which function under the same system of organization. We shall study these fundamental types of organization with a view to adjudicating their merits as mediators of maximum fulfilment of interest.

A living thing is never satisfied by any status quo of objects; it is always some process of action on the part of the organism itself which affords satisfaction. It is not the presence of food, but the eating of it which is the demand of the organism; not the existence of food in the stomach, but the digestion of it; not the status of having blood in the arteries, but the circulation of it, etc. The satisfaction of a living being is always to be found in some process of activities; and the reason why one process is satisfying and another is not, must be because of the interrelation of the activities which compose it. Eating of the food is satisfying if the component activities in the process function properly; but it is not if saliva does not flow, or the teeth are so decayed as to expose the nerves, or even if the nasal passages are closed. Hence fulfilment of interest depends not only upon the existence of certain conditions external to the organism, but also upon a certain correlation of the activities of the organism itself. It is this correlation in its several forms which we are to study. We shall study the adjustment of interests both in the individual and in society, feeling it impossible to separate the two.

---

*Henry Nelson Wieman, "The Organization of Interests," (unpublished Doctor's dissertation, Department of Philosophy, Harvard University, 1917), Chapter II, "Adaptive, Instrumental and Creative Interests."

Our classification leads to three categories, according to the manner in which interests are adjusted to each other. We shall call them adaptive, instrumental, and creative. When we see a man going through motions of any sort we may ask: Why does he act that way? The answer might be any one of three: He is acting adaptively; or he is acting instrumentally; or he is acting creatively. These three answers represent, respectively, the three ways in which interests may be so organized as to function as one. The most significant difference between them, for our purpose, is the comprehensiveness peculiar to each. Adaptive interest, which involves perfectly coordinated activity, is limited to the fewest number of interests. Instrumental procedure takes a larger number into consideration. Creativity comprehends the greatest multiplicity and diversity of interests.

When we say that the man acts adaptively we mean that he is not conscious of the future situation to which these actions are leading. It is possible that he is wholly unconscious of the motions which attract your attention, for they are quite automatic. He is probably going through some routine habit without conscious motive and without any conscious control. Or it may be that those motions are the manifestation of certain innate mechanisms of nerve and muscle, called instinct, which function whenever the right stimulus is applied, without necessarily involving consciousness at all. He may be conscious of his actions in the sense of a certain awareness of a mass of sensations and feelings, but he has no preconceived idea, at the time, of the situation which is to result from his efforts.

All such activity, whether it is the acquired automatism of an established habit from which intelligence has lapsed, or whether it is the work of innate reflexes and instincts, is in any case satisfying because it follows a certain predetermined sequence of neural preparedness. It fulfils interest because it is coordinated. That means that there is no conflict of tendencies; no mutual interference of neural processes; no 'stasis or summation of stimuli' unable to discharge into the ordinary channels of activity. (C. J. Herrick, Introduction to Neurology) The function of such motions is to adapt the organism to its environment. The adaptation is not something which appears subsequent to the action, as its result; it is that which is sustained in the actual process of action itself. So we call this adaptive interest.

As I walk to the office I ordinarily am not conscious
of the movement of my limbs, of the pressure of the ground
against my feet, of the fact that at one moment my right
foot is foremost with my left behind, the next moment the
reverse. Walking may be regarded as one interest since all
the units of activity which compose it are integrated into one
process. But it also may be viewed as a number of interests which sustain one other, each finding fulfilment only as
it cooperates with the others. Lifting each foot off the ground
may be regarded as one interest; moving it forward, as another, etc. Or this whole process of walking may be considered as one interest forming a unit in a larger system,
of which opening the office door, hanging up coat and hat,
drawing up a chair, etc., are other units, but all automatic
and scarcely conscious. However we regard the matter we
have here a way of so correlating interests that each finds
complete fulfilment. There is no restraint, no conflict, each
functions in perfect harmony with all the others; and the
function of each is to sustain the body in a certain relation
to its environment. All interests which find satisfaction in
this manner we call adaptive.

But there was another possible answer to the question: Why does the man act that way? He is acting instrumentally. He is very well aware of what he is doing.
There is something he wants and he is trying to get it. Perhaps he will obtain it within a moment, or within an hour,
or a year; or it may be fifty or sixty years before he real-
izes the end of his endeavor. But when he does obtain it
that particular sort of action which you observe will cease
because it is only exercised in order to attain that end.

I said that I was walking. If I had the intelligence of
a fish that might be the whole truth; all my activities would
be coordinated in very much the same manner as those involved in walking. But as a fact I incorporate, simultane-
ously with my pedestrian interests, a great many others
which are not coordinated with each other. I have five interests at home which have to be clothed and fed. The reason I am walking instead of riding in an automobile is in order to bring about a greater degree of coordination between
these five interests and the activities at the office which represent three dollars and fifty cents a day. My walking is
instrumental because it is exercised as a means to an end.
The reason it is a means is because my interests are not
perfectly harmonious. If I gave to Tommy all that my interest in him demands, I would deprive Jenny. If I gave to

both all they needed, I should not be able to continue my activities at the office for lack of sufficient nutrition and cloth-
ing. The end to which my walking is instrumental is the attainment of a situation in which these several interests shall
be more harmonious with each other.   I want to reduce them
to a system in which each interest will find complete fulfilment in cooperating with the others, very much as the component activities in walking sustain and fulfil each other.   If
I could attain such an end, all my activities would become
automatic and unconscious or semiconscious.

But there was a third answer to the question: Why
does the man act that way? He is acting creatively. His interests are not coordinated. If they were, he would have,
as we have indicated, the intelligence of a fish. It is precisely the effort to bring about some degree of working harmony among these antagonistic needs which quickens his consciousness, causes schemes to appear in his mind for increasing his salary, arouses the tender emotion when he
thinks of Tommy in need of new shoes, stirs up his anger
when he sees the rich man who never works. In a word it
is precisely the uncoordinated state of his interests, and his
efforts to bring them into some kind of system, which gives
to his consciousness that vividness, variety, rapid interplay
of idea and feeling which makes it distinctively human.

Now it happens that this man has a distinct interest
in preserving and developing this type of consciousness which
characterizes humanity. He prefers it to that of the fish.
Precisely so far as he struggles with uncoordinated interests,
not merely in order to reduce them to a cooperative system,
but to apply every such system of coordinated activity as
soon as attained to some wider problem and thus increase the
range and intensity of antagonistic interests, instead of diminishing the conflict, just so far is he actuated by creative
interest.

When we consider walking by itself, it is ordinarily
adaptive. When we introduce another interest, such as the
impulse to sit down for rest, we have an antagonism which
demands some sort of adjustment. This problem engages
the mind. It transforms walking from an automatic to a conscious process. It brings the whole situation more or less
vividly to consciousness. One becomes aware of the distance
to the destination, of the urgency of the errand, of the com-
fortable resting places along the way, etc. The world of experience becomes vastly more concrete by reason of this an-

tagonism of impulses. So long as the isolated process of
walking is the only operative interest, there is no idea of
the environment at all. At the most there is nothing but a
series of sensations and feelings. And this is true no matter how numerous the operative interests may be, if they are
as perfectly coordinated and cooperative as those involved in
walking. Creative interest is interest in the concrete idea
of reality. It is interest in sustaining and increasing the
number of different elements or aspects of the world which
enter into consciousness. But the number and diversity of
aspects of any object which can enter consciousness is precisely the number of uncoordinated interests which center in
that object. Therefore creative interest is fulfilled, and can
only be fulfilled, by uncoordinated interests. It is satisfied
by dissatisfaction. It is a paradoxical interest.

It is true that after uncoordinated activities have been
reduced to a perfect system and have lapsed to subconscious-
ness, they may be again restored to the focus of attention
and the diverse aspects of the object, which this system in-
corporates, may again be brought to the light of consciousness. Furthermore, these systems of reaction, even when
subconscious, serve to modify and enrich the meaning of the
object which is being attended at any given time. The object
is more concrete, has a far more significant 'fringe' because
of these. Therefore creative interest is fulfilled in reducing
uncoordinated interests to a coordinated system, provided
these systems can be applied to a wider range and complexity of antagonistic responses. Coordination has no value for
creative interest except as it enters in to magnify the conflict of systems, and thereby make consciousness more vivid
and complicated. For it is the increasing concreteness of
the idea of reality which is the sole satisfaction of creative
interest.

One of the simplest instances of creative interest is
theoretical science. All the activities of theoretical science
are engaged in the solution of problems. It is the process
of solution, not the problem as solved, which fulfils the interest of science. After the problem has been solved it has
no value for this discipline except as it can be applied to the
solution of further 'uncoordinated interests'. It is precisely
the situation of uncoordinated responses which affords the
breath of life to science.

It is apparent that adaptive and instrumental activities
may inhere in the same process, for the latter is nothing

more than the endeavor to form new connections between the
units of adaptive response. Instrumental activity consists in
breaking down old habits and building up new ones; but the
older habits are always made up of minor habits, and the
last unit is always some established mechanism, such as a
reflex, which is adaptive as far as it goes, i. e., it tends,
so far as it extends, to protect, nourish or propagate the
organism. Instrumental interest is always directed to forming some new combination of these adaptive reactions, or
new combination between systems of adaptive reaction.

It is also manifest that adaptive and creative interests
always occur together, for the latter is precisely like instrumental in being engaged in forming new combinations between
order units of activity. But the difference between the two is
that in case of creative interest, one likes to form new combinations; the process is valued for its own sake. But when
one forms the new combination solely in order to enjoy it after its establishment, not because one enjoys the process of
making it, we have instrumental interest. Creative interest
is play; instrumental is work.

Adaptive activity is always coordinated; instrumental
and creative always involve uncoordinated, antagonistic tendencies. While adaptive and instrumental may occur together, and also adaptive and creative, there is one couple
which can never appear at the same time in the same person. The experience of uncoordinated interests, taken as a
whole state of consciousness, cannot be both satisfying and
not satisfying. If the former, it is creative; if the latter instrumental. These two cannot be simultaneous, although
they may rapidly alternate with each other.

To prove that our classification is exhaustive, we can apply a simple dichotomy. Human interests divide into those
which harmonize with each other without the need of any process
of mutual readjustment, and those that do not. The former we
call adaptive. Inharmonious or uncoordinated interests divide
again into those which yield satisfaction by virtue of their antagonism and those which do not. The former state of consciousness we call creative, the latter instrumental.

If my eyes chance to light upon a printed page and I
mechanically scan the letters without interpreting their meaning, I am indulging in adaptive interest. If I proceed to
read the page in order to present the ideas in the class
room, or apply them in my business, the actuating interest

is instrumental. I am compelled to readjust my ideas to those on the printed page. But if I read for the sake of the mental stimulus, because I enjoy the growing wealth of idea which proceeds from adjusting my thoughts to those of the writer, my reading is creative interest.

If the words spoken to me by another person are more sounds or signals causing me to react as I would to a danger sign or a clock dial, my interest in those words is adaptive. If I engage in conversation in order to induce the other person to loan me five dollars, or in order to regain his good will after having offended him, our conversation is instrumental. But if I talk to him because I love him; because the sound of his voice and the sight of his countenance stirs my emotion, and quickens my sensibilities; because contact with his mind illuminates and expands my consciousness, our conversation is creative.

The interaction of minds is the situation in which creative interest appears most commonly and most powerfully. Creativity is the development of ideas and the elaboration of emotions for their own sake. It is the interest which sustains any process because of the growing experience involved. But there is no experience in which the play of ideas and emotions is so accelerated as when minds are in converse. In this situation we have a rapidity in the development of mental processes, a diversity and multiplicity of intensely conscious responses, which no other activity affords. We have luminous flashes of revelations and kaleidoscopic changes in the vistas of emotion and idea. When this intensity and range of consciousness, with its lightning-like changes comes to the isolated individual (which is rare and generally the mark of genius), he insists that he is in converse with his muse or the Spirit of God, or Nature as Living Person, or the like.

The modern propensity for reading the primitive biological instincts into all the activities of man, has often led to attributing many phenomena of human life to such instincts when in reality they are due to creative interest. Of course if one wishes to call creative interests an instinct it may be perfectly proper to do so, but it is not an instinct in the purely biological sense. Men often engage in activities which are utterly useless. The modern tendency is to say that this is due to the persistence of some primitive instinct which has outlasted its usefulness. In some cases no doubt such is the case; but in most cases we judge that it is not.

The useless procedure is more frequently impelled by this
tendency to creativity.

It is said for instance that men often fight without
cause save that they enjoy it. They certainly do, but that is
not necessarily because they have an instinct of pugnacity
which must be satisfied. The latter hypothesis will sometimes apply, but human behavior must be explained by mul-
tiple hypotheses.

Fighting is a form of converse between two minds
when it takes place between man and man. It is highly stimulating to the consciousness, requiring the most rapid and
diverse adjustments. Of course when the two opponents are
organisms whose activities are rigidly determined by innate
mechanisms, the fighting does not involve the making of new
adjustments and the consequent creation of new experience.
But if there is in the organism any capacity at all for variation of behavior, fighting will develop it. This may be one
reason why struggle for survival has been so potent a factor
in causing variation of species. But in any case, among
men it has been competition, the antagonism of man to man,
group to group and race to race which has stimulated the ingenuity and inventive powers, that has been most fruitful in
producing new alignments, new systems of organization and
totally new modes of life. We see this very plainly in the
present war in Europe.

It is for this reason, we believe, that men love to
fight. It quickens their inventive genius, it intensifies their
attentive consciousness, it brings to them a wider range and
diversity of reality, it makes the world more concrete for
them. Fighting stimulates like wine, and men love it for the
same reason that they love wine; not for the sensations giv-
en, of pain on the one hand, of taste on the other, but for
the enlarged mental activity, the interplay of feeling and idea
engendered. Of course we are not advocating the use of either. The ultimate effects of both may be a diminished creativity. But its immediate effects are such as to warrant us,
in some cases at least, in ascribing it to creative interest.

The same is true of danger. It arouses the creative
powers. Men often seek it out. They go to the ends of the
earth to find it. Love making is another interest often ascribed exclusively to the instinct. To be sure instinct enters
in some degree, perhaps, into all love affairs, and some
love making may be wholly instinctive. But it is rarely the

sole determinant between human beings, and at times it may
be a minor element. A great deal of human love making is
pure play, sustained for the sake of that piquant mental stimulus arising out of the peculiar antagonism of the male and
female mind. They never exactly agree, they never see
things from exactly the same angle, but their disagreement
is of such a nature as to stimulate the growth of new ideas
and sentiments in each. The fascination of battle, danger
and love is not altogether a matter of biological instinct. It
is rather a testimony to the potency with us of creative interest.

Neurologists and psychologists bear us out in recognizing such a unique and fundamental interest as this.
Thorndike says that "mental emptiness must be one of man's
greatest interests. Making an ideal plan and getting a conclusion, making an imaginary person and thereby getting further imaginations of how he would act, are designated as
processes affording supreme satisfaction." But these are,
precisely, instances of that interest which we call creative.

Thorndike further testifies that the brain of man contains "many neurones, in connection with sensory neurones,
which crave stimulation--are 'readiness to conduct'--tho no
immediate gratification of any more practical want follows
their action... Novel experiences are to him (man) their
sufficient reward... It is because they satisfy this want...
that visual exploration and manipulation are the most inces-
sant occupation of our waking infancy." (Thorndike, Educational Psychology) He calls this the satisfyingness of making connections, meaning the satisfaction of making new combinations of reflexes and other automatisms and thereby developing a vast integrated complex, which Stout might call
an apperceptive system. The satisfyingness of making connections is the satisfaction of that interest which seeks one
thing and one thing only, namely, the increase of the range,
complexity and intensity of consciousness. Just so far as
this growth of the consciousness of reality, whether it be in
the form of feeling or idea, is the object of all activity, we
have what we call creative interest.

"To do something and have something happen in consequence is, other things being equal, instinctively satisfying, whatever be done and whatever be the consequent happening." This use of the term 'instinctively' by Thorndike
may not be justified if by it we mean an innate mechanism
so adapted as to produce a specific situation. But if by it

we mean a tendency which, under favorable circumstances,
invariably appears in human nature, and which, though not
adapted to produce a specific situation, is adapted to produce a specific result, namely, the indefinite increase of
consciousness of reality, then we may properly call it instinctive. "The excitability of conduction units apart from
those concerned in the more specialized instincts" is the
neurological condition necessary to creative interest of play.
It is in man that this condition is realized to an immensely
greater degree than in any other organism.

Hirn, who is quoted by Thorndike as the man who had
made the most acute study of the origins of art, lays espe-
cial emphasis on the tendency to engage in mental activity
for its own sake. He describes it as "a yearning after increased consciousness, which leads us to pursue, even at
the risk of some passing pain, all feelings and emotions by
which our sensation of life is reinforced and intensified."
His terminology is a little archaic, for of course he does
not mean by 'sensation of life' sensation in the strictly psychological sense, but rather consciousness of life in the form
of idea and feeling. This yearning is the introspective aspect of creative interest.

C. J. Herrick, in his Introduction to Neurology asserts that mere increase of consciousness in range, complexity, no matter what may be its constituent factors or
contents, may be satisfying so long as these constitute factors can be so adjusted to one another as to permit of "free
discharge of nervous energy." Such increase may be satisfying irrespective of the situation in which it is realized.
Even torture to the point of destroying the organism may be
satisfying to the human being. To get the original nature of
man as over against the monkey, one must, among other
things, "increase the intensity and breadth of the satisfyingness of mental life for its own sake." (Thorndike, Educational Psychology)

If there are any organisms which are completely under the control of innate reflexes and instincts, never acquiring new habits, such creatures are bereft of instrumental and creative interest, for the latter consist precisely in
the process of forming new habits. The functioning of such
habits, when established, is adaptive. But that period of
uncoordinated activity which transpires before the habit is
completely established, is either instrumental or creative,
according as the quickened consciousness then arising is
valued for its own sake or is not.

When an organism does acquire the capacity for forming new habits, there almost inevitably arises some conflict
between these individually acquired habits and the innate system of response racially inherited. Creative or instrumental interest, as the case may be, is that neural process
which seeks to bring about some workable adjustment between these two conflicting sets of mechanisms, the innate
and the acquired. The more acute and the more complicated this conflict becomes, the keener becomes intelligence,
the wider its range and the richer its content. It is in society, and especially when those acquired habits called social conventions and laws enter in to shape the responses
of the human organism, that this conflict reaches its
acme.

All the artificial environment brought about by civilization, to which the innate tendencies are not adapted, is
bound to increase this antagonism between innate and acquired characters. Of course the innate tendencies have
themselves been operative in determining this social structure, but they have by no means been the only factor. Instrumental (or creative) interest is the functioning of the organism to the end of producing a situation in which innate
and acquired impulses may act harmoniously. This involves,
on the one hand, the breaking down of old habits and the
building up of new, and on the other hand, the reconstruction of the environment. Such a process is not satisfying in itself, but it has value as leading to, or making
possible, those adaptive activities which are satisfying in
themselves.

Instrumental becomes creative interest when the organism adjusts these automatisms, not to the end of enabling
them to operate without conflict, but to the end of making
wider and more complicated adjustments, thereby continuously sustaining and progressively enlarging the process of adjusting. That means that consciousness becomes progressively more active, more creative. While instrumental interest always tends to restore and preserve the coordination
of adaptive response, creativity is ever breaking away from
the smooth running routine and disrupting the coordinated
system or proving it inadequate by applying it to situations
too wide and new for it. Creative interest feeds upon the
dissatisfaction of adaptive interest, while instrumental never
finds fulfilment save in the ultimate satisfaction of adaptive.

We believe that instrumental and creative interests

have been sufficiently distinguished to allow a preliminary
but definite line of demarcation between the two.   Adaptive
and creative interests will scarcely be confused.   If there is
further question with regard to their distinction, it will probably be answered in the following chapters.   But there may
still be some difficulty with regard to the difference between
adaptive and instrumental interests.   This might arise in
particular with regard to remedial and protective reflexes
and all those automatic responses which express dissatisfaction of the organism.   The whole point of difference between
adaptive and instrumental was that the former is satisfying
by virtue of the action itself.   When satisfaction is found in
the situation which appears as the result of the activity, and
subsequent to the actual process, we call it instrumental.
A reflex or an instinct may be quite automatic and perfectly
coordinated, thus meeting the requirements of adaptive interest; and yet it may be exercised in a situation which is almost unbearable to the organism.   Its function may be to
remedy, or escape from, the predicament.   Hence satisfaction will only be attained as a result subsequent to the activity.

        Let us take a concrete case.   A man in a burning
building will run and leap.   If he cannot do that he will
writhe and scream.   Are such activities satisfying?   They
certainly are.   It is more satisfying to writhe and scream
while being burned, (providing no other interest is operative)
than not to do so.   If that were not the writhing and scream-
ing which cause the dissatisfaction, it is not the sensation
of burning pain [sic].   The activity, as far as it goes, is
satisfying.   If the entire energy of the organism is given
over to these automatic contortions, there will be no ideas,
not even a clearly defined emotion.   Consciousness will be
little else than a dizzy blur largely occupied with the bare
sensation of pain.   In such a situation the human consciousness probably comes nearer to bare sensation than at any
other time.

        Thus these reactions meet the two conditions of adap-
tive interest, minimum consciousness of the objective world
and the satisfying nature of the active process.

        But suppose the writhing and screaming, or the auto-
matic frantic running and leaping, without conscious purpose,
result in delivering the man from the fire, does not the activity become instrumental?   No, the first of two criteria of
instrumental interest is that the satisfaction yielded by the

activity shall not arise from the process but from the anticipation of the subsequent result. There has been no anticipation of result in this case, the only satisfaction associated
with the activity being that experienced in the process of activity. The second criterion of instrumental interest is that
there shall be some suppressed impulses which are held in
abeyance until the desired situation shall be attained. But
in the case under consideration there has been no suppression. Every impulse has been allowed to fulfill itself to the
utmost. There has been no antagonism or conflict of tendencies.

Let us take a case of flight in a somewhat different
sense. It is a little difficult to deal with adaptive interest
in human experience in any such critical situation as that
causing fear, because in such cases instrumental or creative
interest almost invariably arises to some degree, at least,
and obscures the adaptive. But it is quite conceivable that
when I suddenly meet a bear I do not 'stop to think'. I
merely whirl about automatically and hurl myself into precipitate flight. Now just in proportion as every ounce of available energy is expended in the agony of flight, the emotion
of fear will disappear in that blurred state of consciousness
which one experiences at the moment of the very maximum
limit of physical exertion. To be sure in most cases some
degree of fear will persist because this maximum limit is
seldom reached, or, if it is reached, it is intermittent, al-
ternating with moments of lesser exertion when the 'fear',
which is nothing else than backwardness in this discharge of
energy, spurs the organism to renewed effort. Thus in this
case again flight displays the two features of adaptive interest.

But in meeting the bear I may stop to consider if he
is not a tame one, or in any case harmless. Perhaps he
will be as much afraid of me as I of him. As soon as such
mental processes occur, intelligence has entered in and instrumental interest manifests itself. I stand my ground despite the strong disagreeable feeling which impels me to flee.
My behavior is not satisfying, but I apply it experimentally
with the hope of attaining a situation in which all my interests will find fulfilment, namely the situation of the bear
fleeing from me.

Or again I may find enjoyable the quickened and intensified consciousness which arises from the stimulus of
fear. I may dare the bear. I may even make slight efforts

to attract his attention.   I look about hastily to see what
means of escape are available.   I rejoice in the quickened
sensibilities, the rapid intuitions which come to me by reason of consciousness aroused through danger.   This is creative interest.

The mutations of these three types of interest into one
another should be noted.   Instrumental activity is always an
unstable process.   It is always tending to pass over into either adaptive or creative interest.   Its very nature makes it
so.   It is never satisfying in itself; it is always undertaken
as something temporary.   It is something which is endured
only so long or so often as is necessary in order to attain
something more desirable.

Its most common transition, when under pressure of
circumstances ... long continued or frequently recurrent,
is to pass over into adaptive interest.   That means that it
becomes a routine habit.   It gives satisfaction in process because of its familiarity and the ease with which it is carried
out.   It requires an ever diminishing degree of mental activity.   It ceases to be a means and becomes valued for its own
sake because it presents the line of least resistance.   It is
the well worn groove down which one slides to comfort and
twilight consciousness.

But sometimes the opposite movement takes place.
The business or politics or teaching which one at first under-
took in order to make a living becomes a game which one develops because it increases the zest of life.   As one ampli-
fies the process under this impulsion, it constantly demands
a keener intelligence, the growing complexities call forth a
more vivid and comprehensive consciousness.   Thus it ceases
to be instrumental and becomes creative.

But as we have said before, the most common destiny
of instrumentality is, no doubt, reduction to the mechanism
of automatic habit, with the minimum of attentive consciousness.   So in the majority of cases instrumental activities can
be aligned with adaptive in tending to the utmost diminution
of consciousness.   With them intelligence is a transitory and
sometimes evanescent auxiliary; but in creative action it is
the whole teleology of the process.   In the first two feeling
and idea tend to fund themselves in automatic response; but
in creativity the overt action tends to fund itself in idea and
feeling.

Whatever adaptation may result from creativity is contingent and extraneous to its inherent purpose. Of course if such adaptive by-products do not result, the creative activity must cease or the organism perish. Men have often chosen to perish.

So we see that instrumental and adaptive interests tend to align themselves together in opposition to creative. So we have two antagonistic and mutually frustrative tendencies in human life. To this fact we trace much of that tragedy which philosophers have so generally ignored and poets and seers so keenly perceived and vividly portrayed. Perhaps the reason for this has been that philosophers have attacked the tragedy as a problem and in order to make their solutions applicable have been forced to ignore much of its more difficult features.

Of course we also shall attempt a solution, for philosophy has no other raison d'etre. The solution we propose is to make an absolute decision between the two alternatives in favor of creative interest. It is to cease all vacillation and compromise between the two and to cast all fortunes, for destruction or eternal life, on the side of creativity. Men have been known to cherish their conscious relations with reality more than anything else. Can they ultimately cherish anything else?

EXPERIENCE, MIND, AND THE CONCEPT*

Experience is an ambiguous word. It is used in so many different senses and with such diverse connotations, that we would not use it at all if another term were available. But we cannot distinguish mind from other physical objects, except in terms of experience. Neither can we define the nature of the concept except in relation to experience. But to be intelligible we must first state what we mean by the word "experience." In defining our usage we are not trying to prove anything. If another believes, as we do not, that primary and secondary qualities have a different metaphysical status, or that there is something back of experience, which is not more experience, but is the substratum, or substance, or neumenon, of which experience is the phenomenon, he is welcome to his belief. Without stopping to argue or demonstrate, we only want to make our use of the word intelligible.

I. EXPERIENCE

By experience we mean the sensuous qualities in that temporal and spatial structure that goes to make up nature. Experience consists of time-space just as much as of sense qualities. These qualities in time and space are independent of any and all experiencing subjects. In other words, the world is made up of sense qualities in space-time whether or not any organism is present to undergo the experience of those qualities. Of course, the experience cannot enter into the life of any organism unless there be an organism so situated and so constituted as to undergo the experience. But the experience is one ingredient of the objective world in the sense that if an organism were rightly situated and constituted it would undergo the experience. What is there is that which yields such experience. And what yields such experience is precisely such experience. There is nothing back of experience except more experience.

*Reprinted from The Journal of Philosophy, Vol. XXI, No. 21 (October 9, 1924), pp. 561-572.

II. MIND

If physical nature and formed experience are identical, then what is mind? Mind is, first of all, a part of physical nature; but it is also more. Mind is physical nature plus. This something more emerges in spots throughout nature and is called mind or minds. Does all physical nature have in it that something more by virtue of which it is not only physical nature, but also mind? That is a metaphysical question into which we cannot now enter, but we only mention it to say that the view of mind and nature here presented does not necessarily preclude the possibility of all nature being mind. But neither does it necessitate that view. In other words the problem of a world-mind can be treated on its own merits and is not involved in our definition of nature. If we so define nature as to involve a world-mind or God, we fall into a hopeless and vicious circle of reasoning whenever we attempt to investigate the object of religious experience.

What is this something more by which physical objects, without ceasing to be physical, become also mental? This something more is what makes life as well as mind. Life and mind are so closely connected that, for the present, we shall not try to separate them. There must be life in order to be mind, mind requiring a high degree of life in the sense of a very complex organization of organic responses and, what is perhaps a difference in kind, a progressive organization of responses. But just now we shall treat them together.

So our question becomes: What is life and mind?

The life of the organism is not merely its flesh and blood and other materials that enter into it, but a certain traffic which goes on between this flesh and blood and certain other objects past and present. Note especially that the objects are both past and present, for that is exceedingly important in distinguishing life and mind.

Physical objects interact on one another by way of many different media. They may interact through bodies of water, through vibrations of the air, through solid stone, through electro-magnetic fields and many other ways. But they can also interact on one another through the medium of an organism. Now life is this interaction of physical bodies on one another through the medium of an organism. Notice

that life is not merely interaction between the organism and
its environment, although, of course, that is included, but it
is interaction between physical bodies through the medium of
an organism. In other words, life is not merely activities
of an organism, because such activities taken by themselves
are an abstraction. They are merely segments in a total
process of interaction going on between physical bodies. The
activities of the organism are but segments of motions transmitted from one body to another through the organism and
other media. Of course, it must be remembered that motion, anywhere in nature, is the structure of certain sensory
qualities. Motion is always a form of experience. But for
brevity we must designate it merely as motion.

Now if we stopped with this there would be nothing to
distinguish the living organism from any other transmitter of
formed experience. It would be like any other medium of interaction between physical objects, itself a physical object.
There would be nothing to distinguish the living organism
from, say, an electro-magnetic field.

What is there distinctive about the transmission of motion from one physical object to another by way of an organism that makes such organic mediation qualitatively different
from every other case of mediation? For it is this qualitative difference in type of mediation which constitutes life and
mind.

The unique feature of organic mediation is that it
learns. It forms habits. In other words, it brings the experience of the past to bear upon the present and the future.
But let us not forget that all experience is physical. It enters into the constitution of some physical object. It is never
merely mental. It may be mental, and it is precisely experience as mental that we are trying now to describe. But
when mental it does not cease to be physical. A physical object becomes a participant in that total process called mind
when the experience of which it is in part constituted is
transmitted by way of an organism to some future object.
Expressing it in still other language, mental interaction between physical bodies is by way of an organism which refers
back to past objects and forward to future objects. Life and
mind perpetuate through time the experience which constitutes
past objects. In life and mind, but incomparably more in
mind, experience with its time-space structure takes on an
added form without losing its time-space structure. It rolls
up, as it were, like a snowball or a spiral, so that the past

is operative in the present and the future.   As long as an object, continuing in its proper space-time as physical, cannot
reach over intervening space-time to an object of some other
space-time and act immediately upon that remote object, we
have physical nature only.   But when this overleaping of
space-time occurs, we have life and mind.   This overleaping
of space-time does not mean in any sense the abrogation of
space-time or the transcendence of it.   It only means the addition to physical space-time of an added feature.   It means
that certain bits of experience begin to roll up like a snowball.   As soon as the uniform flow of experience in the form
of space-time throughout all nature begins to take on this
added character we have the beginnings of life and mind.

      The preceding paragraph can be summarized by saying
that as soon as learning or habit formation appears in nature
we have the emergence of life and mind.   Our only difficulty
has been to indicate just what is involved in that familiar
event called learning or habit formation.   Through the living
organism objects that are past in time or remote in space,
without ceasing to be past or remote, can act on objects that
are present in time and near in space, after a fashion which
does not occur elsewhere.   In a nutshell, when experience
not only controls the behavior of objects directly, as it does
throughout nature, but also by referring to future and past
objects, we have mind.

      Life and mind are not something apart from physical
objects, but they are physical objects when physical objects
begin to interact through the mediation of an organism in the
way described.   Physical objects become ingredients in life
and mind when they begin to interact in this way.   And there
is no life and mind, so far as we know, which is not made
up of physical objects after this fashion.

      The theory is abroad that habit formation is not pe-
culiar to life; that many other objects display it.   If that be
true, which we do not believe, then life would differ from
these other habit-forming propensities only in degree.   Our
reasoning would still hold concerning the distinctive character of life, its differentia being, however, in such case, a
matter of degree and not of kind.   Life would still be unique
in the degree to which learning was developed.   We feel sure,
however, that when habit formation is attributed to non-living
physical objects there is confusion of thought and inadequate
definition of habit, due, perhaps, to the strong desire on the
part of some to preserve the continuity of nature in passing

from the physical to the vital and mental.   But if our definition of life be correct there is no break between the physical
and the vital; there is only the emergence of a new quality.
It is now becoming common to speak of mind as an emergent.
We are trying to state a little more precisely what it is that
emerges.

We cannot go deeply into this matter of habit formation.   But the crudest instances of so-called habit may be
considered.   It has been said, for instance, that a coat forms
habits as shown by the folds it assumes when worn for some
time.   But this is a wholly different matter.   The folds are
effects of past events to be sure, just as the stone that lies
on the ground at a certain spot is the effect of past events.
It would not be there were it not for past events, but it is
not there because it has learned to hug the earth at that particular point.   Nor has the balloon learned to float in the air.
The stone sticks to the earth, and gradually settles deeper,
because of tensions and motions (experience) which flow uniformly with time-space.   The stone is not able to refer to
past and future objects of experience and thus mediate interaction between the past and future.   But this is precisely what
life and mind do.   And this is precisely what the coat does
not do.   The coat does not hold its folds because of past and
future objects, but only because of tensions that are immediately operative in it at the present moment.

Kick a stone and it rolls over and is quiet, or if it
continues to roll it is because of new tensions that come into
play with the onward movement of time-space.   The stone cannot refer back to the kick in such manner that the kick continues with it through time.   But that is just what a rabbit
does.   When you kick it, it runs for several hundred yards
and then starts up again to run, all because of the kick.   The
kick, though past, is still something to which the rabbit can
refer as an object and which, therefore, can still operate
through the rabbit.

What is the device by which the living and thinking organism can designate objects that are past in time and remote
in space?   It is the symbol.   It may scarcely be proper to
say that unconscious organic processes use symbols, but it is
certainly true that these organic activities interact with objects
past and future and have something akin to the symbol.   Even
the lowest forms of vegetable life do this.   But in the mind
we find the use of symbols definitely developed.   The word
"orange" is a symbol which signifies a physical object.   But

how can such marks on paper or sound in the air symbolize
any object so remote in character and, it may be, so remote in time and space, as a physical orange? Only because the mind has this unique feature of interacting with objects that are past. Does that mean that the physical orange
is carried in some disembodied form in the mind and out of
time and space? By no means. Our whole point is precisely that the physical orange is still physical and occupies that
time and space which is physically proper to it. But while
still thus remote in time and space it can be an object that
acts through the organism on objects that are present or future.

III. THE CONCEPT

A concept is a symbol which serves to designate an
object by reason of an associated system of habits. For instance, the word "snake," when ejaculated in a certain situation, is a concept because the sound, in that situation, is
associated with a system of habits and this system gives the
sound a significance, i.e., renders the sound a signifier of
something. If, in uttering the sound, one makes a certain
quick movement, starts to one side, looks and points, the
system of habits which give designative value to the sound
are most pronounced. Of course, the habits which make the
sound a designator of some form of experience may be purely verbal habits. The concept cannot attain any high degree
of refinement, accuracy, and scope of application until the
habits are largely verbal. But it is the system of habits associated with the sound, the gesture, the mark or other sign,
which makes it a pointer, designating some object. A concept, then, is a pointer indicating something not itself in the
world of nature.

But what we have just described is not the only kind
of concept nor the only use of the concept. Concepts are
not only used to point out objects in nature; they are also
used to designate other concepts. The system of habits associated with a word or sentence may not only serve to make
it designative of some form of experience, but may also
make it a pointer to other words or sentences which are also
pointers. And these again may point on to still others.
Thus one pointer (for every concept is a pointer) may indicate another, and this a third, and so we may pass from
concept without referring to nature. And this game may become so interesting, in fact is so interesting for many, that

most of their time is devoted to marshalling battalions of
concepts in serried ranks, devising new concepts and constructing ever more intricate combinations of concepts. They
may do this until they forget there is a world of nature. In
fact, thinkers of this type have become so absorbed in the
game of concepts that they have actually asserted, and established a massive philosophic tradition to the effect, that
the world of sense was less real (whatever that may mean)
than the concepts; that sensory experience, and even space
and time, are a transitory flux that pass like a dream,
while only the concepts were sure and permanent, eternal in
the heavens; or that the world of sense in space and time
was derived from the concepts, or strives toward the concepts as an ideal; that the world of experience was a fleet-
ing phantom while the concepts were the steel girders of reality.

There are, then, two uses of concepts: (1) to designate natural objects and (2) to designate other concepts. But
number (2) may be sub-divided again, for there are two ways
in which concepts may be used to designate and organize other concepts. One is called "mere imagination"; the other is
called thinking. Imagination becomes thinking only when the
transition from concept to concept is controlled. But controlled how? Here we stand face to face with logic and scientific method. We must give some consideration to both,
first taking up logic in the strict and narrow sense as distinguished from methodology.

The logical categories do not enter into the structure
of the world of nature. They are not categories of experience. They are simply the necessary rules which must be
observed in the use of symbols. They are the constitutive
principles, not of the world of nature, but of symbolism and
the use of symbols. They have to do with the nature and
uses of the concept, but have nothing to do with the natural
world except indirectly as concepts are used to designate objects of that world and as symbols themselves are of nature.
Just as we have laws or principles which enter into the constitution of language and its use, so we have principles
which enter into the nature and use of any symbols whatsoever, whether they be language symbols or other kinds. Just
as grammar is the study of the structure and requirements
of that special kind of symbols called language, so logic, as
a study, is the study of those more general and pervasive
requirements to which all symbols whatsoever must conform
if they are to be symbols at all. For instance, if x is used

to symbolize a and the next moment b and then again c, and in each case the significance of x is changed arbitrarily at the caprice of the individual, x loses its symbolic value. It ceases to be intelligible. The one significance it has contradicts the other. Such arbitrary symbolism destroys itself. It is not only impossible to use such a symbol for communication, but also impossible to think with it. Such symbolism would be only the wildest kind of dreaming. Logical requirements, then, are the requirements of all symbols that enter into thinking. And since it is impossible to think without symbols, logical requirements are the requirements of all thinking.

IV. THREE KINDS OF TRUTH

What, then, is truth? Or what do we mean by a true concept? There are three senses in which we may use the word "truth."

First, there is the truth of the designating concept. A concept is true when the system of habits associated with a symbol are adapted to the object which it is used to designate. For instance, a certain sensory experience befalls me and I say: There is a cow. The system of habits associated with the word "cow," when uttered in that situation, come into operation and I advance to milk the object. But I find the habits are not adapted to it. The object cannot be milked. It is, after all, a bush in the twilight. But suppose my habits had been adapted to it and it was truly a cow. As an object, then, what is it? It is all that experience which ensues when the system of habits are carried to fulfillment. That is the object truly designated by the concept "cow." The concept is always a pointer, and the associated habits give point to the symbol.

If another organism, say a fly, were reacting to the cow, the experience constituting the cow would be different. Of course, it is probable that the fly never does react to that time-space structure of experience which we call cow, but to something very different. For instance, when resting on the cow's back or dodging the cow's tail, it probably is not reacting to the cow at all, any more than we would be if we were dodging the pebbles kicked down a cliff by an invisible cow. But supposing the fly did react to the cow. Its experience would be entirely different from mine. Which experience is the object called cow? Our answer is: Both.

The cow in any given situation, with respect to any organism that may react to it, is the experience of a certain time-space structure.

If one may risk absurdity and speak of an absolute cow one might say that the cow is all that experience of a time-space structure (Alexander would say space-time plan) which any organism ever has had or ever will have when reacting to it. But the object designated by our ordinary concept, cow, is no such absolute or infinite system of experience as that. It is rather that order of experience undergone by the human type of organism in the conventional situations. Knowledge by acquaintaince requires that we have some of that experience which constitutes the object; but the experience without the concept is not knowledge; and it is not necessary that we have the same experience in order to know the same object.

We have been considering truth in one sense. It might be called truth in the sense of true knowledge of natural objects. But there is another sense in which the word "truth" may be used. It is the truth of the logical category. Its truth does not lie in adaptation of a system of habits to an object of experience, because it does not apply directly to experience. A logical category is true if it is necessary to the constitution of symbols and to the preservation of the significance of a symbol through all the combinations and transitions of symbols which elaborate thought requires. This is a very different kind of truth from that which consists in the correct designation of an object in nature. It has to do with the constitution of symbols as such, regardless of whether they are being used to designate some natural object or not. In other words, logic only sees to it that the symbol is fit to designate something; but the actual process of designating lies outside the field of logic in this strict and narrow sense. Logic must keep the tools sharp and bright, but it makes no use of the tools itself.

Methodology has to do with the use of the tools. And this brings us to the third sense which may be given to truth. First, we had truth in the sense of true knowledge, meaning the correct designation of an object in nature. Second, there was truth in the sense of the logical constitution and organization of symbols. Now, third, we have truth as a method or process of reaching true knowledge by using the tools prescribed by logic. There is truth in the sense of knowledge; there is truth in the sense of logically constituted symbolism; and there is truth in the sense of scientific inference as a process.

The difference between strict logic and scientific method might be illustrated by the case of the so-called law of thought that A cannot be both A and not-A. As a law of strict logic it means that a symbol destroys its symbolic value if it designates both A and not-A. As a law of scientific method it means that one space-time is not another. *

V.   SCIENTIFIC METHOD

Putting it roughly, we may say that scientific method is a device by which we disencumber ourselves of the great mass of experience in order to pick our way through the intricate space-time structure of all experience. The quickest, easiest, and surest way to pass from one object to another in thinking, especially when one is dealing with a great number and variety of objects, is to ignore everything about the objects save their space-time structure and to consider only certain distinctive features of that. Now, of course, all the sense qualities of experience cannot be ignored. We cannot pick our way through the intricate structure of experience unless we have at least a few sense data to guide us. But science endeavors to reduce these data to the very minimum, or, at least, to those particular data which serve to guide us in making our inference, but which may not give us any of the sensuous flavor and fullness of the experienced object. Science sifts out the great massive flood of experience, winnows it, and breaks it up until it discovers those rare and scattered bits of data which serve to guide inference through the maze of the time-space structure. These bits of experience called data which are thus selected by microscope and spectroscope, by mortar and acid and many other devices, these data are made to shine like jeweled lights at strategic points and critical turns of the space-time structure. But the world thus plotted and planned by science presents a wholly different aspect from that which is known by way of ordinary experience. The total concrete object, which can be known with some degree of accuracy as illustrated in the case of the cow, is not the object which engages the attention of the scientist. He has not time to deal with such a cumbersome mass of experience.

---

*See S. Alexander, <u>Space, Time and Deity</u>, p. 197.

Let us illustrate. Science has a concept which designates not the experience of heat, but that motion called energy, or the space covered by the mercury in a thermometer. There is no particular resemblance between the rising and falling mercury and the experience of heat and cold. Science does not designate the experience of a falling body, but the ratio of motion which is the distinguishing feature of the space-time structure. It designates not light as experienced but the vibrations, which again is space-time structure. It designates not the experience of sound, but the vibrations of the air, etc., etc. So it is that science develops a technique for dispensing with the massive bulk of experience, dealing only with certain carefully selected data, the ultimate precipitate of analysis. All else is cast aside as irrelevant.

What we have said of science in general is just as true of psychology and sociology as it is of physics and chemistry. It is not so manifest in them partly because they are more complex, partly because they have not yet developed an adequate technique, and partly because they are so young that they are not yet thoroughly scientific in their thinking. We do not mean that all science must be reduced to the term of physics and chemistry. On the contrary, we are very sure that each science must develop its own viewpoint, its own method and technique; and each must interpret the world in its own categories. But since all experience has the form of time and space, all science that studies experience (and science can study nothing else) must work out the complex time-space interrelations of those data of experience which it has selected as its own peculiar subject-matter.

Scientific method transforms the character of our experience because it transforms our habits of response. The stimuli that once aroused us no longer stir us in so far as we assume the scientific attitude, for the scientific attitude means to be responsive to certain rarified and selected data at certain loci in space-time. The massive bulk of experience is ignored. In so far as we are scientific the concrete object with all its savor and rich sensuous fullness and emotional stir is gone. It has disappeared like a bubble. Compare the world as known and felt by the modern scientific man with the world of the primitive man as revealed in his folk lore. To be sure this latter world is full of fancy, illusion, error. But all this efflorescence of illusion and emotion springs from a rich concrete sensuous mass of experience which he has not learned to ignore. The child has it; the poet has it; the great originative scientist has it who breaks with the scientific tradition of his day and, like Darwin or Galileo, blazes new paths through the jungle of experience. But the established scientific technique does not have it and cannot have it, because of its very nature.

Now the question we want to raise is this. Can any such vast and elaborate scientific technique, as we see developing in the civilized world of today as never before in history, exist in our midst without greatly transforming our appreciations, our habits of response, our capacity for growth, for joy, for fullness of life? Certainly a technique rapidly accumulating from generation to generation, and becoming ever more pervasive in shaping our habits, appreciations, and outlooks, cannot be without effect. What effect will it have? The answer to that question has already been given. The effect it must have is revealed in the very nature of scientific methodology or technique. It impoverishes the world of experience. It destroys the capacity to appreciate the "surplusage" of experience. What does that mean? This surplusage of experience means all those data, and all that unanalyzed datum, which is irrelevant to our established scientific theories, but is indispensable to the development of more complex problems that are bound to arise with an evolving civilization. It means, furthermore, all that concrete, scientifically meaningless experience which makes seven-eighths of the joy of living--a lover's kiss, the colors of the sunset, a child's soft little hands, the heart of a rose.

Yes, but, you answer, our scientific technique has not destroyed in us the capacity to enjoy the bits of concrete experience just mentioned. Of course not. We could not illustrate our point with experiences we had ceased to appreciate. The only point is this: Does scientific technique have any effect upon human life? And, if so, what effect? It seems there can be but one answer. It vastly magnifies our efficiency in procuring anything we want and have the capacity to enjoy; but it greatly diminishes our capacity to enjoy. It gives us wonderful instruments of achievement, but narrows and distorts our vision of what is to be achieved.

But there is art and religion to correct this one-sided development of science. Exactly. The more science advances, the more elaborate, constraining, and pervasive its technique becomes, the more we require art, religion, and the personal intercourse of love to save our souls. But while science has advanced with leaps and bounds since the Middle Ages, since the days of Greece and Rome, since the

days of Thor and Brunhilde, have art and religion kept pace
with it?   Are art and religion more or less pervasive
throughout our life in comparison with those days?   Is scientific technique more or less pervasive?

Are we asserting our case is hopeless?   Not at all.
We are simply pointing to what we believe is a manifest fact
which must not be ignored and can be corrected if we face
it.   We must turn to the cultivation of art and, above all,
religion for salvation.   But how does religion correct the
fatal distortion of life brought about through scientific method?   That we must treat at some other time.

PART 2:
STRUCTURE/PROCESS--QUALITY--VALUE/GOD

INTRODUCTION

These three essays contain sustained elaborations of
Wieman's theory of value and how it entails the conception of
God and the renewal of human life. Wieman was convinced
during this period, 1931-1936, that if the religious world settled for a conception of an "unknowable God," which it did,
very little progress would be made in bringing the necessary
interdependence of religious inquiry, science, and philosophy
to bear on the world's problems. Both the establishment of
the doctrine of the "unknowable God" and its demise have
played roles in the recent turmoils of religious inquiry.
Wieman's conception of God as naturalistically experienceable
and empirically knowable must be seen in light of the interdependence of religious inquiry, science, and philosophy that he
deems necessary for the survival of the quality of life and the
conditions that must be present for the transforming work of
creativity.

Wieman's "Religion in John Dewey's Philosophy" is one
of his several attempts to expound his religious philosophy
with regard to Dewey's influence. An earlier essay, "Religion in John Dewey's Experience and Nature," Journal of Religion, V (Sept. 1925), pp. 519-542, was reprinted as Chapter XII, "Religion and Reflective Thinking," in Religious Experience and Scientific Method. Wieman also included several pages of analysis of Dewey's thought in The Issues of Life.
The crucial point in the relationship between the thought of
Wieman and Dewey came in Wieman's "John Dewey's Common Faith," a glowing review of Dewey's A Common Faith,
in the Christian Century, LI (November 14, 1934), pp. 1450-
52, and the aftermath in "Is John Dewey A Theist?" by Ed-
win Ewart Aubrey, Wieman, and Dewey, in The Christian
Century, LI (December 5, 1934), pp. 1550-53. Since that
time Wieman has qualified how Dewey influenced him and how
their philosophies differ. Wieman's later assessments of

of Dewey can be found in The Source of Human Good, Intellectual Foundation of Faith, and "Intellectual Autobiography," in Bretall. Nevertheless, Wieman admits to a deep and abiding influence of Dewey on the formative stages of his own religious philosophy.

    "God and Value" and "Values: Primary Data for Religious Inquiry" illustrate how Wieman's conceptions of God were being formulated at mid-career. What later came to be called creative event and creative interchange were being conceptualized in these two essays as structure of integration, process of progressive integration, and unlimited growth of connections of value.

    Wieman stressed that both religion and science were committed to the "unknown" but that "the unknown does not mean the unknowable." ("God and Value.") And he stressed that if the conception of God were to make any difference to the quality of life and the renewal of life it had to be shown that "God is both the most beneficent actuality and the supreme ideal." ("God and Value.") During a time when the dominant voices of theology and religious philosophy were saying that there were no values possible for the human situation except those from beyond nature imposed upon the human scene, Wieman's analysis of "appreciable activities" led him to conclude that the unlimited growth of connections of value in human life is God. ("Values: Primary Data for Religious Inquiry.")

    These essays should be read against the background of Wieman's The Wrestle of Religion with Truth, 1927; Methods of Private Religious Living, 1929; The Issues of Life, 1930; Is There a God? (with D. C. Macintosh and Max Otto), 1932; Normative Psychology of Religion (with Regina Westcott Wieman), 1935; and American Philosophies of Religion (with Bernard E. Meland), 1936.

RELIGION IN JOHN DEWEY'S PHILOSOPHY*

Instrumentalism as a term of reproach has been applied to the philosophy of Mr. Dewey. We believe, on the contrary, that in whatsoever sense instrumentalism is an evil it is something in our lives which Mr. Dewey has most persistently been striving to correct.

To recognize the fact that men devise instruments and use them to attain desired ends, and must do so in order to live in the human way, cannot be called "instrumentalism" in any individuous sense. That fact is so manifest that every one recognizes it. Instrumentalism as an evil can only be an undue glorification of instruments, giving them an exalted place which is more than their due, or asserting that certain realities are instrumental when they are not. In case of Mr. Dewey his insistence that philosophies, and concepts generally, find their chief importance in serving as instruments is probably chiefly responsible for setting his philosophy before the world as instrumentalism.

Instrumentalism in a bad sense, we have said, is giving undue importance to instruments or attributing instrumentality to matters that are not instruments. But these are just the common evils of life which Mr. Dewey has been most earnestly trying to overcome. Consider some cases of instrumentalism which are seriously pernicious. For example, we find that fire is useful to cook food and keep us warm, and we use it in that way. But in the course of time this instrumental function of fire so focuses our attention upon fire and deepens our interest in it that we place it upon an altar, worship it, and sacrifice human beings by the hundred to express our reverence for it. That is a case of perverting our interest in the fire and our use of it in such a way as to constitute a great evil which might well be called "instrumentalism." It is a perversion of the instrumental function of fire. It is quite probable that the lyric fancy of man, rather than his practical interest in instruments, led him thus

---

*Reprinted from The Journal of Religion, Vol. XI:1, January, 1931, pp. 1-19.

to glorify fire.   But his fancy would not have fastened on
fire if the instrumental function of fire in his life had not
drawn his attention to it.

But let us take another case of perverted instrumentalism which is much nearer home.   Our economic and industrial system is a gigantic instrument for producing goods
to satisfy the wants of men.   Our machines, our laboratories
and techniques, our finance, our executive organizations,
should serve this end.   But we are rapidly coming to treat
this titanic instrument in very much the same way the primitive man treated fire.   Instead of using the economic and industrial system to provide goods for the wants of man, we
are using the wants of men to provide consumption so that
the machines can be kept going and the system working.
Thus we pervert the instrument by glorifying it out of all
proportion to its due, and sacrifice men to it in far greater
number than the primitive sacrificed his fellows to fire.
This is another case of instrumentalism in the evil sense.

But underneath all other perversions of the instrument is the most fundamental perversion of all.   This basic
evil, which lies at the root of all the others, is what Mr.
Dewey persistently attacks.   It may be described in a general way after some such fashion as this.   There are certain
fascinating, not to say blissful, experiences which come to
men as they fulfil the functions of life and devise and use instruments by which the distinctively human way of life is conducted.   When the delight to be found in these experiences is
clearly recognized, men tend to cultivate the experience for
the sake of the enjoyment it yields and in disregard of the
bearing it has on the rest of life.   They treat it as an end
in itself.   They wrench it out of its rightful function and
make it serve other ends that may be pernicious, or no ends
at all.

In other ages, and to a large degree still, men justified this procedure by a kind of rationalization.   They construct a myth which makes it appear that this experience has
great importance in some other realm beyond the world of
observable consequences and physical operations.   Since they
seek and cherish it as an end in itself, that is, without regard to observable consequences and without regard to anything that can be achieved by physical operations, they feel
it necessary to justify this perversion and make it seem not
a perversion, by holding that this experience gives them access to a supernatural, or noumenal, or otherwise trans-

cendent, realm. In highly sophisticated ages, however, such
as ours is coming to be, these myths and rationalizations
are sloughed off and men brazenly, without feeling the need
of any justification, seek enjoyments without paying any attention to their instrumental function, that is to say, the contribution which such ways of enjoyment may have for the other interests of human living. This brings on epicureanism,
decadence, and the disintegration of that organized system of
mutually sustaining activities which is indispensable to the
maintenance and furtherance of life. Instrumentalism in the
good sense is the cure and prevention of this evil.

In philosophy the delightful experience which is thus
wrenched from its rightful function in the conduct of life is
the enjoyment found in constructing and contemplating systems of propositions which are perfectly consistent and coherent, so that you can start at the beginning and think
through the end of the system with the superb clarity and un-
deviating accuracy of pure reason. Such systems are wonderful playthings. They stir the lyric fancy of philosophic
minds much as fire stirred the fancy of primitive minds.
They arouse the ardent enthusiasm of philosophers much as
our splendid system of economic production inflames the imagination of engineer, financiers, and executives. Consequently in the past, in more naive times than ours, philosophers revered such a system of propositions as being God
himself or as revealing God or in some way constituting values which were the supreme ends of life--ends in themselves.
It was the old adoration of the fire upon the altar. It is the
same impulse which leads communistic Russia to revere economic production as God. Some modern philosophers are too
sophisticated for this, but they are guilty of the same perversion. They attribute to these systems of propositions a
value similar to the value which the roue attributes to sex.

In certain circles of present-day religion the function
of life thus perverted is not fire nor economic production nor
a system of propositions, but a kind of experience called
"religious experience" or "inner experience." This experience is held to be God, or the unique manifestation of God,
or somehow the presentation or representation of those values which should be sovereign over all the rest of life. Now
there is a kind of experience (which is the experience sometimes meant by the religious, although not always), in which
the individual is most blissfully sensitized to the qualitative
richness of the world about him. This experience certainly
has an important function to fulfil in the conduct of life. But

to set it apart as somehow being God or representing God or
giving access to God or constituting value as the rest of life
cannot, the rest of life being subordinated as mere means to
this, while this is means to nothing else, to set it on an altar as the primitive man set fire, the business man sets
money, or the engineer sets economic production, or the
philosopher a system of propositions, is to be guilty again
of the old perversion which gives rise to most of the evils
in life which might be avoided. This is the evil which Mr.
Dewey opposes in all his work, but especially in his The
Quest for Certainty.

The kind of certainty which is condemned is that which
philosophers have sought by developing a system of propositions by logical and mathematical principles from certain
original axioms which are held to be incontrovertible. Mr.
Dewey has no objection to such systems, mathematical and
logical, provided they are used rightly. Such systems of
propositions we must have in order to analyze situations, to
observe the conditions and consequences of physical operations, to make inferences from what we have observed, to
devise new and better operations. In short, we must have
such systems of propositions before we can have anything to
investigate or any way of investigating it or any intelligent
striving after higher values. Therefore, as long as a deductive system is properly used, it is indispensable for the
intelligent conduct of life.

But Mr. Dewey objects when such a deductive system
is believed to constitute, or to make known to us, a realm
of supreme importance where the highest values can be
sought and found by contemplation or ratiocination or intuition or any other method than that of observation and physical operations. The highest values that ever are to be
achieved must be achieved by physical operations. The mathematical and logical systems are indispensable tools in this
supreme enterprise of human life. But when these systems
are set up as objects of supreme devotion in themselves, or
as revealers of a realm where greatest values must be
sought and found by another method than the only one by
which highest values can be attained, then we make the old
disastrous blunder that human life is always making.

The deductive system of ideas in which the philosophers have sought their certainty may give aesthetic satisfaction. The completeness, symmetry, and consistency of a
system of ideas logically developed from accepted premises

may well give exquisite aesthetic delight to men of certain intellectual bent. But to think the aesthetic experience we derive from such propositions is an experience of transcendent beauty shining forth from the realm of ultimate reality is error, he declares. Furthermore, such a system in itself, apart from its instrumental application to the practical problems presented by the physical world, does not solve any problems, although we may use it to give us the feeling that all our problems are solved. Also, such a system does not give us an object which is worthy of any man's devotion, except as an instrument to be used in making observations, physical operations, and inferences. When such a system is revered as an object of greatest value, we have again the old betrayal of the great venture of human living.

Mr. Dewey's instrumentalism, if you want to call it that, consists in the claim that everything should be both instrumental and consummatory. Nothing should be regarded as an end in itself if by that you mean that it should be sought, revered, or enjoyed without regard to what it contributes to the rest of life. On the contrary, everything should be valued in the light of what it contributes to the rest of life. If we enjoy anything, do anything, revere anything, without regard to its effect upon other concerns, we are sure, sooner or later, to interfere with the increase of the good. For anything enjoyed, done, or revered in such a reckless, abandoned manner as that will mess the program by which life can be improved.

Thus far we have considered the negative side of Mr. Dewey's teaching. Let us now turn to the positive side. We are chiefly interested in the kind of religion which Mr. Dewey advocates. For Mr. Dewey does advocate a religion, contrary to the opinion of some, and does so very explicitly and very earnestly. Indeed, we believe his entire philosophy, rightly understood, is an exposition of a religious way of living. In the book of his which we are now chiefly considering, The Quest for Certainty, his most explicit statements about this religious way of living are to be found in the last chapter, on pages 303 to the end of the book.

This religion which Mr. Dewey advocates consists in giving supreme devotion to the highest possibilities of value which the existing world can yield without knowing specifically what these possibilities are. We do not know them because we do not know, except in a very partial and tentative manner, what is the nature of this existing world which car-

ries the possibilities. All further knowledge must be left to
the labor of scientific investigation; and any claim to have
knowledge by any other method is an illusion. But religion
is passionate devotion to the best there is, even while still it
is unknown. Religion must make use of the best knowledge
we have. But if it is to retain its rightful function and power it must not identify itself with any form of knowledge, for
all knowledge is more or less tentative and subject to constant reconstruction. The essence of religion is immediate
realization that there is this unknown best, and passionate devotion to it, regardless of the fallibility of all our knowledge.
Religion becomes "invincible" when it (1) lays aside all claim
to knowledge other than can be attained by scientific method
and (2) gives supreme allegiance of life to the possible best
even while it is still unknown. Such a religion does not depend for its vitality and power upon the truth of any specific
belief or upon the success of any projected program of action, but forever stings to passionate quest because of its
mystic devotion to the best there is or ever can be. We say
"mystic devotion" because it is realization without specific
knowledge. This driving propulsion of religion should be intelligently directed by scientific method, but the drive will not
depend upon the correctness of scientific specifications or upon the success of the scientific program. Thus the function
of religion in life is to provide the invincible striving and un-
quenchable zest; the function of science is to provide the specifications for the guidance of this striving. The function of
philosophy is to formulate a theory to guide this total enterprise of human living.

Let us try to develop the fuller meaning of this way of
religion, following up implications which, so far as we know,
Mr. Dewey has not developed, and reaching conclusions which
he might or might not support.

The "possibilities of existence" is a vague expression.
We cannot concern ourselves with the totality of existence for
several reasons. For one thing, it is altogether too vast and
complex. Furthermore, a great part of it is apparently too
trivial, negligible or neutral in its bearing upon any interests
we may entertain to be of any concern to us. Also, Mr.
Dewey would say, it is too pluralistic, multiform, chaotic,
and conflicting to be considered a practicable object with which
to work for anything.

So the first thing we must do is to isolate or distinguish that particular form or aspect of existence which bears

these possibilities for which we want to work. Doubtless the process or processes which carry these possibilities must be brought to light by the method through which anything else is learned about existence, namely, by observing the conditions and consequences of physical operations. But the human race throughout its history has been making such observations and operations in a more or less desultory manner. Above all the several sciences have been doing it; and physics, most successfully. Out of all this we ought to be able to form some idea of what process or processes going on in existence are the most promising and hence the ones in which we must make our observations and operations in search of greatest values. We say "in which" we are to operate, for any process which carries highest possibilities for us must be one in which we play some part; otherwise we can have no part in the values it may bring forth.

First let us ask, Do these processes in which we must work to seek and to achieve the highest possibilities of value constitute any kind of unity, or are they essentially discrete and plural? Let us first assume that they are discrete and plural, and let us consider several of them.

Most people would admit that human intelligence is at least one process going on in existence which must play some part in bringing forth whatever highest values existence may have to offer. Certainly human intelligence is the factor about which Mr. Dewey seems to have most to say. But to say that human intelligence always functions in such a way as to bring forth the highest values is to make a statement so flagrantly false as to be absurd. Of course one can arbitrarily define intelligence as that which does bring forth highest values; and then, by definition, the question is settled. But intelligence, as that word is ordinarily understood, is often exercised by scoundrels to tear down and destroy what is most precious. Unquestionably intelligence is one factor in that which brings forth the highest values, but it is intelligence only when intelligence interacts in the right way with innumerable other factors. Therefore what is really important is not so much intelligence as it is this required kind of interaction between intelligence and other elements.

Still again, most people would say that biological evolution is a necessary factor in bringing forth higher values. But to say that biological evolution always, simply because it is evolution, brings forth ever higher values is to make a statement as absurd as was the like claim for intelligence.

It is not biological evolution taken by itself as discrete and separate, but only biological evolution interacting in a certain way with many other factors, one of which must be intelligence. Or, if intelligence has not yet come into existence, it can be biological evolution only as it issues in intelligence.

Still again, the biological functioning of the organism with its cells, viscera, and adaptive reaction to the environment, including other organisms, is a factor which all would admit must enter into the process which brings forth highest values. But here again it plainly is not biological organic functioning as such. Just because an organism is functioning does not mean that values are being sustained or promoted. It is only when the functioning of the organism rightly interacts with many other factors, including biological evolution and intelligence, that there is anything of value.

Another indispensable factor in the process promoting value is the smooth working of social institutions. But these do not promote values, no matter how smoothly they work, if this working does not interact in the right way with the other factors we have mentioned and with many we have not mentioned.

Still again, the social heritage as it is accumulated generation after generation is a necessary factor. But the mere accumulation of a social heritage does not inevitably bring forth any increase of value. It may, on the contrary, diminish or destroy values so that, as a consequence of this accumulating heritage, values become less and less. Values are promoted by the social heritage only as this accumulating heritage rightly interacts with intelligence, biological evolution, organic functioning, the smooth working of institutions, and much else.

The same is true of science with all its techniques for research and achievement. Science, no matter how rapidly it may develop and powerful it may become, does not increase values unless it interacts in the right way with the other forms of intelligence which cannot be called science, as well as with the other factors mentioned above.

The same is true of earth and sun and air and food and shelter and health and everything else which may be mentioned as indispensable factors in the process of existence yielding value and the increase of value. None of these fac-

tors constitute, sustain, or promote value when they are
taken all together unless they interact on one another in the
right way. In fact, it is not these several discrete and separate factors at all which sustain and promote value, but it
is a kind of interaction between them all.

What, then, is that process of existence which sustains and promotes values to the maximum? It is one very
distinctive sort of interaction going on between intelligence,
organic evolution, functioning of the organism, social heritage, social institutions, climate, soil, etc. It is not the
total interaction going on between these factors, but only one
kind of interaction. Thus we reach the conclusion that if we
are to find what it is in existence which sustains and promotes values, and hence what it is in which and with which
we must work if we would achieve values to the utmost, we
must search for it not as plural, not as consisting of various different things taken separately, but we must search for
one single kind of process, a process of interaction between
many different factors.

The several different factors that enter into this process of interaction, such as earth, air, social heritage, institutions, the sciences, organic functioning, and so on, have
their important function; and we must deal with them. But
if we do so in such a way as to promote values, we must always do it with a view to promoting a certain kind of interaction between them. Hence it is this interaction which is
the object of our supreme concern. To this process of interaction we must adjust our lives. In it we must play our
part, and to it we must give our devotion.

But what is the nature of this interaction to which we
have constantly referred? To answer that question we must
have some idea of what constitutes value. When we find out
what value is, we shall be able to say, in a general way,
what is the nature of this distinctive kind of interaction which
sustains and promotes value, for this is the process of existence to which we must conform and to which we must give
our lives if ever we are to attain the fullest measure of value which existence can yield.

In stating what constitutes value in the view of Mr.
Dewey, we shall not follow closely any statement he has
made. He has written many scattered articles upon the subject, not always holding exactly the same view. We shall
state a theory of the nature of value without trying to say

what Mr. Dewey would say or trying to agree with him, but
stating a doctrine which we believe is not essentially different from his view.

The raw material out of which value is made consists
of enjoyments. But mere enjoyments, taken as so many experiences, do not constitute values. One may derive enjoyment from committing a murder, torturing another human
person, singing a song, or writing a poem. But the mere
fact that enjoyment is experienced does not mean that there
is value. Value is only that particular kind of enjoyment
which is derived from my judgment that what I am doing is
a sustaining and promoting function with a whole system of
mutually sustaining and mutually enhancing enjoyments. In order that an experience constitute genuine value, two things
must be true of it: (1) It must be causally efficacious in promoting the most inclusive system of interdependent and mutually enhancing enjoyments. (2) I must have knowledge of
this fact and derive my enjoyment of the experience from this
knowledge of its function in sustaining or promoting the system.

Thus my enjoyment must be derived from the meaning
of what I do, if it is to be a case of value. Value is enjoyment derived from this particular kind of meaning, or, otherwise stated, from this particular kind of judgment. In order
that there can be value, the conditions and consequences of
enjoyments, both my own diverse enjoyments and the enjoyments of others must interact on one another in such a way
as to determine one another. The more pervasive, potent,
and complicated is this mutually determining interaction, the
greater is the value we can experience providing we search
out the ways and means (1) of so adjusting our enjoyments as
to make them mutually sustaining and mutually enhancing and
(2) of making each individual cognizant of his functional participation in the system as a whole. The latter is a problem
of the right kind of education, not to say religious education.

Thus the individual, by shaping his own enjoyment in
such a way as to promote and generate a whole system of
mutually sustaining and mutually enhancing enjoyment, finds
in his own enjoyment not only an immediate experience but a
meaning which enables him to participate in the system as a
whole. He cannot have all these other enjoyments which enter into the system, as immediate experiences of his own;
but he can have the value of them in the sense that he knows
they are causally connected with his own immediate experi-

ence and hence constitute the meaning of his present experience.

It should be noted that when we have such a system
we may find enjoyment in experiences which, without the system, would not be enjoyable at all. These experiences become enjoyable when we experience them as sustaining and
promoting a system of enjoyments. They become enjoyable
by virtue of their function in this system. Enjoyments do
not constitute value when they merely happen to an individual in such a way that he does not recognize any interaction
between them and other enjoyments of such sort that they
mutually sustain and mutually enhance one another. It is only when we judge that our present experience does enter into such a process of interaction, and when our enjoyment of
it is colored by that judgment, that we can be said to experience "value." Thus judgment "enstates value" to use one of
Mr. Dewey's own phrases.

As a test case, let us take the feeling of having committed one's self completely to the most important concern
that can possibly engage the life of man. This is one of the
most satisfying, not to say blissful, experiences which an individual can undergo. It is pre-eminently the religious experience, to use a much abused and misinterpreted word; for
religion is precisely reacting to something as though it were
worthy of the supreme devotion of all human living. Now
this feeling of commitment is a very common experience
among the insane. A "sense of mission" is one of the fre-
quent characteristics of insanity. Such an experience may be
wholly without value, according to Mr. Dewey, no matter how
ecstatic it may be. It becomes a value only when the ecstasy takes on that added quality which arises when the individual sees how the conditions and consequences of what he
is doing are causally related to other enjoyments in such a
way as to constitute a most inclusive system of mutual support and mutual enhancement. Without intelligent judgment
of this sort there is no value, no matter how much ephemer-
al ecstasy there may be. The same is true of love, friendship, tasty food, and all the rest.

If you wish to call any enjoyment taken as an immediate experience, and without regard to such judgment, a "value," of course you can, says Mr. Dewey. But if by "value"
you mean something that can be sought intelligently, something that can be increased indefinitely, something that can
be cultivated, controlled, measured, and compared, then you

cannot identify value with casual experiences of enjoyment
without regard to judgment concerning their conditions and
consequences, for without mutual adjustment of the conditions
and consequences of our enjoyments there is no way to seek
value intelligently, no way to control or cultivate it, no way
intentionally to increase it or to judge between enjoyments as
to which is better or worse.

Value, then, is any enjoyment which sustains and promotes a system most inclusive of other enjoyments and has
that quality of enjoyment which comes from the judgment that
it sustains this relationship to other enjoyments. The value
of existence is increased by increasing this system of mutual interdependence and support among all enjoyments actual
and possible.

The highest possibilities of value which existence can
be made to yield are achieved just in so far as five requirements are met.

The first of these five is to modify the physical,
physiological, psychological, and social conditions under which
we experience our enjoyments in such way that each enjoyment is more causally effective in promoting other enjoyments. In other words, our enjoyments must be bound together so that they enhance one another in ever more subtle,
potent, and pervasive ways.

The second requirement is that the system be so designed that wide reaches of experience which would otherwise
be dreary or trivial or painful become positively enjoyable
because of the knowledge of the important function which they
fill in this most inclusive system of mutual enhancement and
mutual support.

The third requirement is to make the system inclusive
of a greater number of enjoyments, ideally of all enjoyments.
The value of existence is increased in proportion as the system becomes inclusive of all enjoyments, past, present, and
future. That, of course, would require the exclusion from
existence of all enjoyments which cannot be made to fit into
any sort of inclusive system of mutual support and mutual enhancement.

If my present experience is enjoyed because of its
causal efficacy in promoting other enjoyments, then those other enjoyments are mine to that degree and in that form. The

meal another man eats can never give me the gusatory pleasure it gives him.   But the immediate gustatory pleasure
does not constitute value, as Mr. Dewey is considering it.
The value of the meal is experienced by the man only when
his enjoyment takes on that modification which ensues from
his judgment that it fills a function in a whole system of mutually sustaining and mutally enhancing enjoyments.

Now this kind of value is something which I can share
with the man who eats the meal. With this understanding of
the nature of value, the distinction between my value and the
other man's value breaks down. If my value consists in the
experience of doing something to sustain and promote the total system of enjoyments, and if the other man's value also
consists in doing something to sustain and promote that same
total system, then the distinction between his value and my
value ceases to be important.

Therefore, when we say that the third requirement for
increasing the value of existence is to multiply the enjoyments which enter into the system we do not have to consider the distinction between his enjoyments and mine.

The fourth requirement for increasing the value of existence is to expand this system of mutual support and mutual enhancement of enjoyments throughout space and time.
Time is much more important than space, for it offers
greater possibilities for expansion. How much of the past
and how much of the future do I take into consideration in
judging and so in appreciating the value of my present experience?   This scope of time is a fourth element entering in to
what we have called the "expansion" of the system.

Last of all, the individual must be so educated and
otherwise so equipped and conditioned that he can use the
best methods for ascertaining the causal efficacy of what he
does when he does anything to sustain and promote the system which constitutes the value. If the individual cannot
judge the efficacy of his act in sustaining and promoting the
system that constitutes value, then he does not have any experience of value at all, no matter how blissful may be his
experience. For value consists precisely in the enjoyment
we get not merely from the immediate experience but from
our judgment of the part which our experience plays in the
system as a whole.

Now it is plain that if the individual is to be so

equipped as to share thus intelligently in the system of mutual support and mutual enhancement of enjoyments, he must
have a certain amount of food, shelter, culture, social advantages, etc.   Here is where the question must be settled
concerning distribution of food, shelter, leisure, academic
opportunities, and the like. It is not a matter of one person
giving up in order that another person may have more, but
ideally it is a problem of so distributing these advantages
that each individual can contribute the maximum to the development of a system of mutual support and mutual enhancement which each individual can experience in its totality as
a system.   Thus the value which each individual finds in life
will not be measured by the comforts and pleasures he experiences but by the magnitude of the system of mutual support and mutual enhancement which he is able to experience
by contributing something to its maintenance and promotion,
even though the immediate enjoyments in the form of pleasures and comforts which fall to his lot be only a minute part
of the whole.

If this be the nature of value and the way it is increased, we are able to see what must be the nature of that
process of interaction going on in existence which carries
the highest possibilities of value and hence the one to which
we must give our full allegiance if we are to realize to the
utmost the possibilities of value which existence can yield.

This process is that which gives rise to communication by way of symbols; and, after communication is
achieved, it is the process of increasing mutual understanding by way of communication. For only in such a process
can we develop and magnify the kind of system which we
have said constitutes value. This process which gives rise
to communication goes far back into cosmic time. It is not
merely evolution in general, for many lines of evolution do
not issue in communication. But it is that particular process of interaction between earth, air, sun, physiological organism, biological evolution, which issues in communication;
and it is then that further interaction between all these together with social heritage, institutions, psychological conditions, scientific techniques, etc., which issues in even deeper and more comprehensive community or mutual understanding between all communicating individuals, or individuals who
are capable of communicating.

When we speak of "increase" in communication, we
do not mean merely increase in radios, newspapers, and the

like, except as these extend and deepen mutual understanding. For it is mutual understanding which magnifies the kind of system which we have said constitutes value. The process which carries highest possibility of value is that interaction between many factors which generates and promotes to the maximum communication and community.

What name shall we give to this process? Shall we call it the "process of progressive integration"? Or shall we give it the name which religion has most frequently given to the object of supreme concern? The name we give it is not very important. But it itself is supremely important if it be the bearer and mediator of the greatest possibilities of value which may ever be brought forth in the world of exist-ence. It is that upon which we are dependent and to which we must commit ourselves completely if the greatest possible values of existence are ever to be realized. There is nothing else equal to it in importance so far as we can discover by the method of observation of, and inference from, the condi-tions and consequences of physical operations, which is the only legitimate method by which knowledge is ever attained.

Here we have something going on in the world which is observable; upon which and in which we can operate with our bodies, our techniques, our machines; and to which all the resources of science and the whole of human life can be dedicated for the sake of the possibilities of value which it offers. Such dedication of human life is the kind of religion which is implied in Mr. Dewey's philosophy, as we under-stand it.

But religion does not stand or fall with the correct-ness of the view just presented concerning the nature of the process which carries highest possibilities of value. Reli-gion must not commit itself, as Mr. Dewey rightly insists, to any belief as though it were final and infallible. To make loyalty to a belief a religious matter is to put a knife to the throat of religion. Religion can be supreme devotion to the highest possibilities and to the process which carries such possibilities, even when our beliefs about them are highly fallible. Beliefs may come and beliefs may go, but the per-ennial aspiration of human life must go on forever. To lim-it aspiration to those processes and possibilities which we can clearly specify and surely predict (supposing there are any such) would be to destroy scientific investigation and every other exploration of the unknown, to eliminate artistic activity, to throttle creative group discussion and romantic love, and to set up in the place of religion the social conventions of Main Street. Our religion must be a search and striving to actualize the highest possibilities of value even when these possibilities extend beyond the scope of our knowledge and imagination, and even when the process which carries these possibilities is but dimly or incorrectly discerned by us. To deny that this can be done is to deny the most characteristic fact which distinguishes the human way of living from that of the lower animals.

GOD AND VALUE*

Love uses glowing words; but accurate thinking demands cold, abstract terms. Our present effort must be a striving for the latter. So we shall discuss God in terms of structure and process. Everything intelligible is a structure. What is purely ideal and does not exist, is structure only. What exists is some process having a structure, unless it be chaos. If God in terms of structure and process awakens no response in the loving heart, we can only plead that there is a time for love and a time for clear thinking. Both are important and each can promote the other, but words appropriate to one are not appropriate to the other. We fear religion has suffered much from failure to make this distinction between the verbal needs of these two interests.

God is that structure which sustains, promotes and constitutes supreme value. It may be infinite. This structure characterizes the process of existence to some degree, otherwise it could not enter into our experience at all; and we can discuss only such structures as enter into our experience. In so far as this structure of supreme value enters into existence, we can speak of God as a process. But it extends far beyond existence, into the realm of possibility. And the whole of existence is by no means conformant to this structure of God. The terrible magnitude of evil makes this plain. In so far as this structure is bare possibility, it cannot exercise control over existence. But in so far as it is a process, it does exercise control. For nothing is causally efficacious save a process of some sort.

What must be the nature of this structure of supreme value? Some things about it we can discover by making an analysis of value. However we may define value in its elementary form, it would seem that supreme value must be some system or structure which brings lesser values into re-

*Reprinted with permission of Macmillan Publishing Co., Inc. from Religious Realism, edited by D. C. Macintosh (Chapter VI, pp. 155-176). Copyright 1931 by Macmillan Publishing Co., Inc.

lations of maximum mutual support and mutual enhancement.
It might be claimed that such a system would have only instrumental or extrinsic value. Such a claim, we believe, is
not valid. A system which brought lesser values into such
relation, that each derived maximum value from all the others, would be one in which each served and promoted all the
others. Then the value of each would be its meaning for the
system as a whole, i.e. its functional activity in sustaining
and improving the total system. Thus the system as a
whole would endow each activity with maximum meaning and
value, and each activity would give value to the whole.
Hence it would be only a matter of viewpoint which was
called means, and which end. From one standpoint the system would be means, and the subordinate activity end; from
another viewpoint the reverse would be true.

Such a system of maximum value is achieved in so
far as all intelligent, self-conscious, goal-seeking activities
of men, and as much of the rest of nature as possible, are
brought into a single structure in which each sustains, lib-
erates and magnifies every other to the highest degree. This
mutual support and enhancement must be not only between
contemporaries but also between successive generations,
ages, and cultures. Such a structure we call the structure
of integration; and the process by which it is achieved we
call the process of progressive integration.

This structure as bare possibility is not causally efficacious. But to the degree that it is the structure of actual existence, that is to say, to the degree that it is a process, it does promote its own fuller embodiment in nature.
To claim that all of nature is dominated by such a structure
and process, is to fly in the face of all observable evidence.
But to deny that there is any manifestation of this process
anywhere in nature, is equally to run counter to what can be
observed. To say that there is a process in the world which
operates to increase the structure of value, and to that degree is the embodiment of this structure, does not necessarily imply that the process is teleological in the ordinary
human sense of that word. Of course, so far as human beings recognize the value of this structure and strive for it,
we have that much human teleology operative. But over and
above human effort and intelligence, a certain degree of
structure in society, human mentality and elsewhere, would
seem to increase the probability of further increase of such
structure. The mere fact that it exists and so operates in
the form of a process, does not make its increase inevit-

able, but it does increase the probability that it will increase. The dice of contingency are loaded in its favor by
the mere fact that it exists in the form of process.

IS GOD PROCESS OR POSSIBILITY?

We have said that God must be a process, not merely a principle, and have indicated the reason. We have also
asserted that that to which all human life should be dedicated by reason of its supreme value is not merely some
possibility or system of possibilities but is rather the process which carries these possibilities. We must show reason
why we make this claim for many hold the opposite view.
Many claim that the most important reality which can concern human life is not anything that exists but rather some
non-existent possibility. Not what is but what ought to be,
is the matter of supreme concern, they say. Not what is
but the best that ever can be, should command our highest
allegiance. Therefore, if we are going to use the word God
at all we should apply it to these possibilities which are more
precious than anything that exists.

This is an issue of the first importance: Should we
give our supreme devotion to some process of existence because it carries the highest possibilities of value? Or
should we focus our attention upon these possibilities as being
more important than the process which makes them to be
possibilities? We believe there can be only one right answer to this question and that is that the process cannot be
considered of any less importance or of any less value, than
the highest possibilities which it carries.

When we cut off the possibility from the process which
makes it a possibility, and prize the possibility as more important than the process that carries it, we are assuming a
self-defeating and self-contradictory attitude. The possibility
of highest value is not a possibility except by virtue of the
process which makes it such. To say that the process is
mere means and therefore of less value than the possibility
which is the end, is to set up a wholly vicious dichotomy between means and end. The highest possibilities of value can
never be attained except by way of the process which leads
to them. Until we can find in the process the identical value of the highest possibilities which it carries, we cannot
ever find the highest possibilities of value, for the greatest
value requires precisely this integration of means and end.

Therefore, the object of supreme devotion, since it should
be the greatest value, must be not only the highest possibilities but also the process which carries these possibilities.

Still another objection should be considered which is
sometimes raised against this identification of process and
possibility as being the rightful object of supreme devotion.
Some hold that the best is not a possibility at all, but an impossibility. Therefore, if we are to be faithful to the best,
we must not supinely yield to the vulgarity of existence, either actual or possible, but must give our highest devotion
to that non-existent impossibility that never can be. R. B.
Perry, Bertrand Russell, Herman Randall, Joseph Wood
Krutch, George Santayana, many an aesthete and lover of art,
and others, have been eloquent on this point.

But he who adores the impossible, implies that his
adoring of it is of great value. Indeed he exhorts, and insists, that the most important thing in human life is to give
our adoration to this impossibility or these impossibilities.
But this adoring is itself a process of existence because he
who adores is an existing personality. Therefore the most
important thing in human life for him and for all mankind is
to attain and to maintain that state of existence in which due
esteem and appreciation can be given to this impossible best.
Thus here also some process of existence is inextricably involved in the highest value and one cannot be faithful to the
one, nor highly appreciate the one, without like faithfulness
and appreciation of the other. That process of existence
which lifts us to the level where we can appreciate this impossible best is, along with the impossibility itself, the most
important reality which can enter into human life.

Here, then, are the two reasons why God cannot be
identified with value apart from some process of existence.
First, if the value be a value because it is a possibility of
existence, it cannot be a possibility and hence cannot be a
value apart from some process. Second, if the value be a
value even when impossible of existence, then that process of
existence which enables us to value it as such, cannot be ignored or excluded from the high esteem we give to the impossibility itself. Thus in any case some process of existence must be combined with some possibility (or impossibility) to make up the object of our supreme devotion. Since
God is the name we give to such an object, God must be
identified with that process of existence which carries the
possibilities of greatest value, or which lifts us to the level

where we can appreciate and adore the impossible best, which impossible best then becomes the characterizing value of the process which is God.

Henceforth when we speak of the process of greatest value we shall correlate it with the highest possibilities but shall not introduce the further complication of impossibilities. We shall do this partly to avoid a very confusing complexity in statement, and partly because we believe that when the so-called impossibility becomes appreciated and adored by existing persons, it thereby becomes involved in existence and, as a value, is no longer an impossibility. But we shall not further pursue the subtleties of the problem involved in value when it is conceived as a non-existent impossibility.

IS THE BEST ONE OR MANY?

When we inquire concerning what is the most important thing in all the universe, to which we have given the name of God without regard to what further specifications may accrue to it, we are faced with a further misunderstanding. It appears in the guise of an objection which assumes some such form as this: You cannot exalt any one process as supremely important. What is most important for one person at one time is not most important for the same person at another time and much less so for some other persons. What is most important in one situation is not so in another. What is most important for one age, race or civilization, cannot be most important for every other. Hence the most important, meaning that which carries highest value, is not one but many. Indeed it is an unknown and unpredictable multiplicity.

Unquestionably there are many different values, whether by value one means a state of consciousness or an existing thing or an indefinable quality or a kind of relation between certain existent things or however one may define value. But when there are several different values it would seem obvious that an organization of them, into a system of such sort that they sustain and promote one another, is better than those same values disorganized in such a way that they obstruct, exclude and destroy one another. This would seem to be so manifest that it scarcely requires an argument. It applies not only to the values which an individual may experience from time to time but also the values experienced by different individuals. For example, a certain kind

of music heard by an untutored ear gives me ecstasy but
palls upon me the more I hear it. Furthermore, others do
not enjoy it and so my own enjoyment cannot be deepened
and my sensitivity quickened by that inevitable modification
produced by social interaction. Also, it is not the kind of
music which can be cherished by successive generations and
thus acquire a tradition by which the individual can be
trained and sensitized to fuller enjoyment of it. Contrast
such music with the opposite kind which does not pall but
leads me to deeper enjoyment the more I hear it; which is
enjoyed by others and so through social interaction the enjoyment of each is magnified and his powers of appreciation
increased; which is enjoyed by successive generations and
thus acquires a traditional sentiment and shapes the customs
of a people so that the individual can be cultivated and re-
fined by the culture of that people to find the greater enjoyment of this music. Certainly the second kind of music has
greater value than the first.

What has been said about music can be said about all
values. Some experienced values can be organized into a
system wherein they mutally support and mutually enhance
one another. The satisfactions found in truthfulness can be
organized into such a system along with many other enjoyments, while the satisfactions found in lying cannot be so organized or at any rate, not into such an inclusive system of
mutual support and mutual enhancement. The enjoyment we
get from rejoicing in the good fortune of other people lends
itself to a most inclusive system of mutual support of enjoyments, while the satisfaction derived from vindictively over-
throwing the fortune of others out of malice and envy cannot
be so organized. So likewise there are gustatory delights,
erotic delights, the enjoyment of power and all sorts of enjoyments which can be distinguished by reason of the fact
that some of them lend themselves to the kind of organization of which we have spoken and others do not. Some can
be progressively magnified by entering into such a system
and some cannot. Plainly it would seem that they which do
lend themselves to such increase and stability are better than
they which do not.

What, then, might conceivably be called the greatest
possible value? Would it not be some system which includes
the greatest number and diversity of enjoyments but adjusts
them to one another in such a way that they (1) support one
another and so make each more secure, (2) magnify one another by reason of the increasing sensitivity which the sys-

tem produces in the individuals who participate in it, (3) enable each individual to find in his experiences not only immediate satisfaction but also the satisfaction, which is often much greater, of fulfilling a function in sustaining and promoting the system as a whole which may be carried down through history indefinitely, (4) a system which is not static but creative inasmuch as it enables one individual to integrate his enjoyment, idea, insight, technique with that of others and out of this integration to bring forth new and different enjoyments, ideas, insights, techniques to further enrich the system.

Now the sort of system we have described does actually occur more or less in human history. Indeed such a system is what constitutes a culture in the noblest sense of that word. Such systems of culture grow and then decline. But however much such a system may undergo transformation it never wholly passes out of existence unless the race which carries it, together with every record of that race and all other races which have had any contact with it, also pass out of existence. Even when such total extinction does occur, supposing it ever does, there is always the likelihood that the record of that perished culture will be unearthed and thus the system again become a living contribution to the historic enrichment of the experience of the race. Indeed we might say that this rediscovery and conservation of the cultural riches of the past is one of the very important functions of that process by which values may be increased.

We have tried to indicate what might constitute the highest possibility of value. It would be a system in which enjoyments are organized, not statically, but creatively inasmuch as the organization would bring into existence many enjoyments which could not otherwise occur and would make many experiences enjoyable which would not otherwise be enjoyable at all. Ideally it would make all experience enjoyable even when painful because of the recognized function which such painful experience might have in sustaining a total system of value. How nearly such an ideal system can be approximated we do not know, but that systems do occur which approximate such an ideal, however remotely, would seem to be apparent.

If the highest possibility of value be of the sort we have indicated, what is the process which sustains and promotes such possibility? It would be that process by which values are organized in the way mentioned. This process

might be called progressive integration. However, it would
be a great mistake to think that any sort of increasing organization produces the kind of system we have described as
constituting greatest value. On the contrary it would seem
that only that kind of organized interaction between individuals can yield greatest value which elicits the most complete
self-expression on the part of each individual member and
promotes greatest mutual understanding. Such a process cannot be called the social process because social process
means every sort of interaction between individuals and
groups, and the greater part of such interaction is not of
this sort at all. In fact, we do not think the adjective "social" has any merit at all for, while the process of organizing satisfactions which we here have in mind certainly includes interaction between human individuals and groups, it
is by no means identical with all such interactions; and it includes, furthermore, interaction between human individuals
and their non-human physical enironment as well as interaction between these non-human factors.

But we cannot pause here to describe any more fully
what we believe to be the nature of this process which carries highest possibilities of value. We do not know much
about it; perhaps no one does. But certain features of it
would seem to be rather obvious. However, our chief purpose in this section has been to refute the objection that the
highest possibility of value is different for each individual,
and for different ages of culture. We claim, on the contrary, that the highest possibility of value is the attainment
of a kind of unity, namely a system in which all these values experienced by different individuals and in different times
are organized so far as possible in such a way as mutually
to sustain, enhance and creatively interact on one another;
while all satisfactions which cannot be so organized must be
pronounced disvalue if they are obstructive to this organization, and if not obstructive they are relatively very trivial.
Thus, the very nature of highest value shows that it must be
unitary since it requires the unification of otherwise separate
values.

GOD AND THE UNKNOWN

There is another objection which we must consider.
It is the claim that we are very ignorant, that we are en-
compassed with mystery, and therefore it is only naive presumption which can claim to know or even attempt to inquire

concerning what process in all the universe carries highest possibilities of value.

Our ignorance we would admit, and furthermore, would strongly emphasize. Whatever increase in knowledge has been achieved by the advancing sciences has only enabled us to discern more clearly how vast and dark is the mystery that enshrouds us. Just a little section here and a little region there and a portion yonder have been brought within the wavering light of a partial knowledge; but of all the rest we are quite ignorant.

Immediately after this acknowledgment is made, certain philistines raise a protest that runs like this: How can we give our supreme devotion to a process and possibilities of existence about which we know so little? Or if we can do it psychologically, what is the use of it? Isn't religion far better if it gives its attention to matters about which we have most specific and reliable knowledge? If religion insists on giving attention to what is so little known, then let us discard religion. Why concern ourselves with matters which lie beyond the reach of assured knowledge and efficient control?

We shall endeavor to show that the supreme importance of religion lies precisely in the fact that it does give highest allegiance to matters about which we have very little knowledge and no great control. This is true not because it is desirable that we should have little knowledge about the most important matters. It would doubtless be far better if we had the most complete and accurate knowledge about them. But the hard fact is that we do not have such knowledge. It is precisely the most important things in life about which our knowledge is least complete and least accurate. Yet men have often claimed to have accurate and full knowledge of these matters of greatest importance. They have been led to make this wild assumption and dogmatically insist upon it, because their need of such knowledge has been so dire. When we most urgently need anything, we frequently resort to the device of making ourselves think we already have it. It has been the folly of many religionists--and many non-religionists--to claim they had more knowledge about God, that is, about the process and possibilities of highest value, than they really had.

But the fact that our knowledge about such matters is very limited does not make them any the less important. To ignore them for the sake of lesser matters about which we

have most specific knowledge and efficient control, is folly
just as great as to claim a knowledge we do not have.

DEVOTION TO THE UNKNOWN

We submit that the most distinctive characteristic of
the human, that which has enabled him to become more than
a beast, is precisely the fact that he is able to, and actually does, focus his interest and efforts upon the unknown.
The unknown does not mean the unknowable. Pure science,
for example, is almost exclusively devoted to searching out
the unknown, the unattained and even the unimagined processes and possibilities of existence. As soon as anything becomes known, that is, as soon as a clearly formulated and
well-articulated concept has been achieved and tested concerning any matter, pure science has no use for it except to use
this concept as a means to explore still further regions of
existence and possibility which are not yet known or attained
and, in great part, not even imagined.

Some will say that the unknown which science ex-
plores is always imagined at least in the sense of having an
hypothesis concerning it. But that is only half the truth.
While there must always be a hypothesis for use in investigating a specific problem, the specific problem is not likely
to be investigated unless it is believed that it will lead on to
still other problems and these to still others which are as
yet not even imagined. As soon as the scientific investiga-
tor begins to suspect that his specific problem is a blind al-
ley, that is, that it does not thus open out into regions as
yet unknown and in great part unimagined, he is not likely to
have much interest in it. Therefore, we say, this devotion
to the unknown, the unattained and the unimagined, is the
very breath of life to science.

But this interest is not only the breath of life to science. We have mentioned science first not because it illus-
trates the matter any better than many other branches of human life, but because it happens to be the assumed bulwark
and standing ground of those who object to this interest in
the unknown and unpredictable. Pure science is interested
in trying to extend the accuracy and scope of our powers of
prediction. That means that it is almost exclusively interested in those regions where we have not yet learned to predict with accuracy or with scope or at all. The supreme
lure of pure science is the unknown and the unpredictable be-

cause its whole reason for existence is to transform the unknown into the known and the unpredictable into the predictable.

But this dominating concern with the unknown (or, if
one wishes to express it, the little known) and with the unpredictable, is not limited to science. It is, we claim, the
source of all that is distinctively human as over against the
subhuman. Take the simple matter of conversation and discussion. The zest and joy of discussion lies in the fact that
they who enter into it may hope to find emerging out of the
discussion new insights and new perspectives that were wholly unpredictable, unimaginable and unattainable to the individuals before they engaged in such intercourse.

Of course, conversation does not always issue in any
such high fulfillment. Most commonly it does not. Perhaps
most commonly it is just a kind of gabble, a kind of automatic response which individuals make to one another when
they meet, not unlike the sniffs, squawks, and cries which
the lower animals display toward one another. But when conversation becomes distinctively and peculiarly human, as
over against the subhuman, it does show creative character.
Doubtless there are some people who never engage in a conversation without a preconceived notion of just how it should
proceed and who refuse to follow it when it begins to open
up unexpected and unimagined vistas.

Science and discussion are not the only ways in which
this distinctively human interest shows itself. All fine art
is of this sort. He who attempts to produce a work of art
in the form of music or prose or poetry or any other form,
by simply reproducing some established and well-known pattern without bringing forth anything which was previously unknown and unimagined, is not an artist at all. The same is
true of human love. The glamour and romance of love lies
in the anticipation of unknown and unpredictable experiences
arising out of the intimate and profound communication of
two personalities. And this is precisely what occurs in genuine love. He who would try to make all the communal experiences of love conform to a rigid preëstablished pattern,
would stifle love and make it a routine way of adapting two
personalities to one another with least fuss and with minimum
attention given to one another. Still again social reconstruction and innovation is a further way of seeking for higher values than any thus far achieved in our established institutions.
So also is the gathering up and conserving of the social her-

itage from the past and adding to it our own experiences and
out of this assimilation of the old and the new achieving new
insights and bringing further possibilities of value to light.
This might be called creative education.

But these unknown, unimaginable and unpredictable
possibilities of value which are explored and actualized by
way of science, discussion, art, love, social reconstruction,
education and conservation of social heritage, are not six
separate realms of possibility. They are six different ways
of exploring and actualizing the unknown possibilities of value which lure men on and make the human way of living
worthwhile.

THE FUNCTION OF RELIGION

To be religious after the manner we here propose is
to be sensitized to the process and possibilities of highest
value while these are still very obscurely known, and to be
sensitized to them not merely as possibilities to be explored
by some one special art or science, but as that total system of highest value, sometimes called the Kingdom of God,
to which all the arts and sciences and the whole of human
life should be dedicated. Such dedication is religion of the
sort we wish to advocate.

Always the chief function of a worthy religion is to
quicken to the maximum this interest in the process and possibilities of greatest value which necessarily, in great part,
exceed the reach of our present knowledge and control. If
they are infinite, as they may well be, they will always not
only exceed, but infinitely exceed, the scope of our knowledge and control. The reason why it is supremely important to have this interest quickened to the maximum has already been made plain. Without it there can be no science,
no art, no love, no creative education, no progressive increase of a social heritage which brings forth ever new possibilities of value, no progressive reorganization of society
to achieve further values, in a word, no life that is distinctively human. For the distinctively human life is the life of
aspiration.

But, it may be asked, if man already has interest in
unknown possibilities by way of the special arts and sciences,
what is the use of religion? Before these specialized activities arose, religion may have served a useful function in

that it represented man's interest in unexplored possibilities
of value. But now that we have these efficient techniques
and specialized interests, each of which opens out into its
own reach of possibility, what is the use of religion?

The answer to this is threefold. In the first place,
any interest which is pursued in disregard of other interests
interdependently connected with it, becomes an evil in respect to these others, because it interferes with them. But
all the different arts and sciences are more or less interdependent. Hence the unreligious pursuit of any art or science, meaning the prosecution of it without regard to the total system of good to which it belongs, becomes an evil. In
the second place, the supreme good, as we have seen, is an
inclusive system in which each constituent interest takes on
maximum value by virtue of its function in sustaining and promoting the whole system. Therefore, if the several arts and
sciences are cultivated without religion, that is, without regard to the contribution they can make to the total system in
which they all achieve greatest mutual enhancement, we cannot hope to serve the supreme good. In the third place, the
conscious and social existence of man requires a very complex and delicately balanced system of innumerable compo-
nents in order to endure at all. The more highly developed
and specialized become the various arts and sciences without
religion, religion being devotion to this most inclusive system upon which we depend for all experience of value, is a
dangerous evil. It threatens the very existence of man as
a conscious and social individual.

This structure upon which we are dependent for all experience of value and all increase of value is not the universe
as a whole, but it is a certain structure in the universe.
This structure we call God because it alone is worthy of the
supreme devotion of all men in all ages. No single art or
science is sufficient to explore it or adjust man to it. That
is the task which requires the cooperation and conjunction of
all the arts and sciences. Hence the increasing specializa-
tion of the arts and sciences, instead of making religion less
needful, makes it more and more important for human living.
It becomes increasingly urgent that we do not allow any lesser loyalty to usurp the place of this supreme loyalty, which
is to God.

He who prosecutes any art or science should do so
religiously, which means that he should pursue it not for its
own sake alone, but for the sake of the important contribu-

tion it may make to unveiling, or adjusting man to, that total structure of value which is God.   It is not true that religion can ever be superseded by the arts and sciences.   Rather religion becomes increasingly important and ever more
urgently needed as the arts and sciences become more specialized.

It is always necessary to distinguish between religion
and philosophy in respect to the function just mentioned.
Philosophy attempts to formulate a theory concerning that
structure of existence and possibility which constitutes value.
Religion, on the other hand, is devotion to it, devotion meaning practical effort and emotional appreciation, as well as intellectual inquiry concerning it.   Religion means to take this
structure of existence and possibility which constitutes value
and make it the sovereign allegiance of our lives.   Furthermore, a religion which is worthy does not take the philosophical theory as object of devotion.   Of course, an intelligent
religion will use the philosophical theory.   But as soon as
any theory or belief is set up as the ultimate object of supreme devotion it becomes a great evil, for our theories are
never completely and adequately true.   Therefore, a worthy
religion will recognize the fallibility of every philosophic theory, indeed it will recognize that such theories are even
more infected with error than most products of the human
mind, and therefore will give its devotion not to the theory
but to the structure of process and possibility at which the
theory is aimed.

EVIL RELIGION

Religion cannot achieve knowledge or do any practical
work except by way of quickening human interest in the process and possibilities of highest value to such a pitch that
men will strive more earnestly and zealously in the various
arts and sciences to achieve fuller knowledge and to further
actualize these values.   Therefore, since religion, apart from
the arts and sciences, has no way of gaining knowledge or
doing work, it is very easy for it to cultivate enthusiasm for
the unknown and unattained values without directing this enthusiasm into any practical endeavor or intellectual search.
Then we have what we call fatuous mysticism.   Then the enthusiasm exhausts itself in gloating over the fact that there
is something of supreme importance, but doing nothing more
about it beyond going into convulsions of ecstasy and adoration.   To keep the gaze of men lifted up toward values which

lie beyond the controlled and predictable possibilities of life, is the supreme function of religion. Nothing could be more important. But if men merely gaze and gloat without striving to increase the knowledge and actualization of these possibilities by the best methods available, religion may become a liability instead of an asset.

But a greater evil frequently befalls religion. It consists in turning away from these unknown and unattained possibilities of value, ceasing to quicken human interest in them, and giving attention only to the attainment of goods that are already known and specified objects of human desire, such as more food to eat, better clothes to wear, more herds, more productive land, more money to spend. Of course, food, clothes, herds, land, money are indispensable tools to use in seeking further possibilities of value. We cannot seek unknown goods except by using known goods. Any religion which quickens interest in unknown possibilities of value in such a way as to make men disregard the known goods, is falling into the fatuous mysticism just mentioned. But we are now speaking of another and opposite evil which sometimes arises out of revulsion against fatuous mysticism. It is that of turning away from search after the highest good, because we know so little about it, and giving attention exclusively to known goods and particular specific problems. But when religion ceases to lift the aspiration of men toward the highest, however unknown this highest may be, it ceases to serve its own proper function and becomes merely a superfluous competitor with the arts and sciences, trying to divert the energies of men from these to itself. We must give our attention to particular, specific problems and known goods. But that is the work of the special sciences and the practical arts. If making religion "scientific" means to make it try to do this work which is properly the work of the special arts and sciences, religion becomes a blundering anachronism, always thrusting its inefficient efforts into the work of specialized interests to interfere and mess things generally and making an intolerable nuisance of itself. The aspiration which religion represents must always find expression in the efficient techniques and in the pursuit of known and controllable goods, but it must always treat these as tools and instruments and trails leading on. There is a function of life which is more important than any efficient techniques of life because it is the source from which the arts and sciences spring and the constant inspiration of their existence. It is the function of keeping the flare of human aspiration blazing high. A religion which does not do this

becomes a pest. Religion must fire men with the realization of God, that is, with the sense of the process which
carries highest possibilities, but with full recognition that we
have much yet to learn about it.

But suppose, an objector might say, suppose this process is something we already know, something as familiar to
us as our children's faces. And suppose the highest possibilities of value that ever can be attained are already attained and there is nothing higher that can ever be reached.
What then becomes of all this talk about devotion to the unknown and unattained? Our answer is that if this speculative suggestion should be true, it still holds that we do not
know with certainty that the process as familiar as our children's faces carries highest possibilities, and we do not
know that this which we already have is the best that ever
can be. Therefore, we cannot give our unmeasured love and
loyalty to it. Therefore it still holds good that, if we are
to be intelligent, we must give supreme allegiance to what
is not fully and certainly known. We know with certainty
that the supreme good is. But what it is, we do not know,
even though it should turn out to be something very close at
hand and fully in the light of consciousness.

Religion must not be scientific if by that one means
to identify it with the techniques, conclusions and theories of
the sciences at any stage of their development. Religion
must not be social if by that one means to identify it with
the hopes, strivings and ideals for a better social order
which may happen to prevail at any given time in our history.
Religion can and should serve the sciences and the social
strivings of men but it can do so not by identifying itself
with them and so losing its own unique indentity. It can
serve them only by fulfilling its own unique and indispensable
function, which is to renew the courage and striving of man
by quickening him with a sense of the best that is and ever
can be, even when he cannot claim to know with certainty or
completeness what it is. He can know that God is, without
knowing specifically what God is. And he can know that there
are highest possibilities without knowing specifically what they
are. He can know this for much the same reason that he
can know that what he does now will have some bearing on
what happens to-morrow, even though he does not know just
what will happen to-morrow and does not know just what doing of to-day will have the most important bearing upon it.

Religion that functions in this way has enormous saving power if by "saving" one means enabling a man to rise up out of any sort of disaster or disillusionment and go his way with unabated zest and hope. Indeed, the hour of most bitter disappointment and overwhelming defeat is just the time when his sense of God, that is, his sense of the unspecified process and possibilities of highest value, becomes most vivid, because a man has at that time no cherished ideas and projects to give him the illusion of having attained or conceptually grasped the highest good. We are so constituted that whenever we are moving successfully toward some specific and highly prized objective we constantly fall into the illusion that this particular goal is the most important thing in the world. But these special ends of endeavor never do constitute the greatest value, however important they may be as constituent elements in the total structure of greatest value, and often they are not even constituents. Therefore, the hour of disillusionment, of failure, disappointment or other disaster, which sends the man without this kind of religion to despair, cynicism, suicide or insanity, is just the time in which the man with this kind of religion experiences a marvelous rejuvenation because of his revivified sense of the structure of supreme value.

If in the hour of such bafflement a man projects some specific picture of this supreme good and identifies his picture with the reality, he is displaying that compensatory functioning of the mind with which the psychiatrists have made us familiar. But if he does not do this, if he fully acknowledges his ignorance, but recovers with acute vividness and power the apprehension of the unquestionable fact that there is this supreme good and dedicates himself to it, not knowing specifically what it is, nor claiming to know, nor even cherishing the conviction that he himself must be delivered from his troubles, but finding his release and exuberance in seeking to serve and find the good, then he is doing nothing that is pathological but is living in the most intelligent manner.

Imaginative representations of God may well occur if they are used simply as symbols. We must have symbols to think at all. Intelligence is impossible without symbols because thinking is impossible without them. But to treat the symbol only as a symbol, and to remember our ignorance, is to save ourselves from that subjectivism which is a persistent curse.

Professor Montague has rather wistfully expressed

the hope that what we cherish most should not be dependent
on what we cherish least. We believe this is a wrong approach. If highest value is to be found in meaning--and we
do not know where else to seek it--then whatever sustains,
promotes and leads to what is dearest, has this dearest as
its meaning, and therefore has in itself all the value of the
dearest. Hence it is our fault, not the fault of the nature of
things, if what we cherish most is dependent on what we
cherish least. We must learn to cherish the latter as much
as the former. If we do not, it is because we are unregen-
erate. We must learn to appreciate the kind of value which
consists in meaning. God is not necessarily what we cherish most, but is rather what we must learn to cherish most.
The natural bent of the human heart is by no means a reliable guide to the supreme good. One does not love God until he is converted. To be converted, in this context, means
to be so changed that one prizes most highly that upon which
we are dependent for the greatest values. That is God.

God is not merely an abstract order that does nothing. Neither is he the process of nature that does everything regardless of value. But he is the structure of supreme value viewed as possibility of existence, and also that
kind of process in nature which most nearly approximates
this order of supreme value and promotes further approximation to it. Thus God is both the most beneficent actuality
and the supreme ideal.

Some may jump to the conclusion that human life is
that in the universe which meets the two requirements which
we have said are the essential characteristics of God. But
that is a great mistake. Most of human life does nothing of
the sort. Some few rare activities of man do conform to
these requirements. But some of the activities of every
man, and most of the activities of all men taken collectively,
are about as far removed from the kind of process which
sustains, promotes and constitutes greatest value as anything
you can imagine. The deification of humanity is the most
pitiable absurdity man has ever perpetrated. But individuals
and groups can participate more or less in that ordered
process which is God; and to participate in it is the one high
calling of man.

VALUES: PRIMARY DATA FOR RELIGIOUS INQUIRY*

In order to know a street car or anything else we must have before us the right data.   Then we must connect these data together in the right way.   In the case of the street car the data are a loud noise of a certain quality, a blurred mass moving in a straight line, and much else.   But connecting the data in the right way is just as important as getting the right data.   The loud noise must be connected with the blurred mass, and the straight movement of this mass must be connected with the steel rails.   This right way of connecting the data we shall call the pattern.   The philosophical word for it is concept.

So we see that knowledge of any reality consists of two parts: getting the right data and connecting them in the right way.   No reality of any importance that we come to know ever gets wholly into consciousness all at once.   All we ever experience of it at any one time are some of the data.   The data are always certain bits of experience that have to be put together into a pattern.   Habitual or other automatic physiological behavior helps us to form these patterns.   When we experience enough of these data to know the pattern, we are able to recognize the reality we are experiencing.   We know it is a street car, if that is what it is.   Or we know it is the United States and not France.   Or we know it is God and not something of less importance.   We never experience the whole of it in knowing, but only enough data to get the pattern.   Then we swiftly fill out the pattern in imagination or by habitual reactions so that we can have the further experience of it that we are seeking.   We are always liable to error in doing this.

Religious inquiry has its own distinctive kind of data just as any other field of search must have.   The pattern by which these data should be connected is equally important.   But the problem of the pattern is another matter to be considered later.   Just now it is the elementary bits of experience which concern us, and these we call the data.

*Reprinted from The Journal of Religion, Vol. XVI, No. 4 (October, 1936), pp. 379-405.

We are proposing that the bits of experience which should concern religious inquiry are values. Values are the primary data which must be found in the right connection or pattern in order to yield the experience which is sought in the religious quest. The highest object of religious concern is attained by finding that pattern of values which is the distinguishing mark of the reality having greater worth than all else.

The ground on which we base this claim--that the primary data for religious inquiry are values--is the fact that religion is loyalty to what is held to be sovereign over human life. The only reality which can rightfully hold such a place of sovereignty is what has most value. Hence values are the data in which and through which we must find this most worthful reality.

THE RAW MATERIALS OF VALUE

We have not space to make a survey of all the theories of value which have been presented to the world in the past and present. The usefulness of such procedure is questionable in any case. Running through so much theory is likely to divorce one from the raw facts of life out of which the theories are made and to which they must apply. Our task will be, first, to ascertain what are these raw materials out of which to develop a theory. Then on the basis of these we shall formulate our guiding principle in the realm of value.

It took men a long time to discover the kind of facts with which one must deal to formulate useful principles about light and heat. The mere feeling of hot and cold did not provide the needed data. Men had to find something that would uniformly expand and contract, like mercury. In the case of light they had to find a certain kind of wave. So also in the case of values many false starts have been made. The materials that have been investigated for the purpose of developing a guiding theory of value have generally been elements entering into value right enough; but they were like the feeling of hot and cold. They were not of such a sort that an objective principle about value could be developed out of them. Let us glance at some of these various kinds of data that have been set forth as the raw materials out of which to formulate a principle of value but have been mistakenly so treated according to our view. We do not wish to deny that these elements we are about to consider enter into every experience of value. Most if not all of them may be genuine constituents of anything that can be called a case of value. We are saying only that these are not the constituents which can most profitably be used for forming a theory of value that can helpfully guide conduct, direct the appreciative consciousness, and provide cues for solving problems.

1. Emotion, or that more general term, feeling, has been selected by some as giving us the essence of value. Emotions and feelings are certainly involved in all experiences of value. But no amount of observation and analysis and interrelating of feelings, cut off from the personalities having them and from the situations calling them forth, can be made to yield a rational structure or principle in solving the important practical problems of life. Strenuous efforts to derive a theory of value from a study of emotions have produced nothing of great importance except the demonstration that this is the wrong way to go about constructing a theory of value.

Specific emotions, like love, have been set forth as the true nature of value. Love is certainly one kind of value, but one could scarcely bring all values into this category. Also love is a very vague term. It must be analysed into forms or relations that can give us some guidance and light.

Others have taken certain general characteristics of emotional experience as the guiding thread, such as satisfaction, liking, pleasure, happiness. Satisfaction of desire, or liking, does enter into any direct and appreciative experience of value. But it is precisely when we mistrust our own likings and satisfactions that we need and want a guiding theory. Any principle which does not go beyond these cannot be of any great importance. To tell any man to follow his own satisfactions in order to reach great value is like telling him to follow his nose to get to town. The nose must be pointed in the right direction. The same is true with our likings and satisfactions.

Happiness has in it all the ambiguity of liking and satisfaction. Also it is the most vague of all concepts. What is happiness? What yields happiness? These queries are fundamental to the problem of value, but they are not answered by simply saying happiness.

2.   Intelligence has sometimes been honored as the
substance of all value. Does that mean that intelligence can
never be evil? Apparently that is meant, and yet there seem
to be flagrant cases of evil intelligence. If one says evil is
negative value, then what is the criterion which distinguishes
the positive from the negative value of intelligence?

That feature of intelligence called knowledge has been
held to be the important factor. Even if we accepted Socrates' dictum that no one ever chooses the evil knowingly, still
knowledge would not be the only good but rather the condition
required for choosing the better. Usually some such confusion lies behind the claim that value can be summed up in
knowledge.

The same ambiguity lies in putting the essence of value in understanding or wisdom. If wisdom means always
choosing the better, we still must ask what distinguishes the
better from the worse. One must have wisdom in order to
be able to choose rightly, but what is it that distinguishes
the right from the wrong choice? The ability to choose the
good may be wisdom, but what is the criterion which distinguishes the good from the bad?

Consciousness has sometimes been taken as the standard of value. It is true that we can have no experience of
anything, including value, without consciousness. But that
does not tell us what is better and worse or high and low in
the way of value. Consciousness is a required condition for
all experience, but it does not determine the nature of the
experience.

3.   Biological patterns have been said to be the determining mark of value, such as survival or adjustment or
life. But it is easy to find instances of evil that have survived and good that has perished; hence survival cannot be
the invariable mark of value. It is certainly better that the
good survive and the evil perish, but it is not survival that
makes the good. Rather it is the good that makes survival
of value. The same general principle applies to adjustment
and life. There is good adjustment and bad, and good life
and bad. Hence these terms give us no guidance at all.
Life is a term most addicted to pernicious use. One can use
it with an unction which gives it a glow by which all distinctions and problems are obscured. All the evil we ever experience is due to life, quite as much as the good. Nothing
can be so good as life and nothing so bad. But merely to

say Life with a capital L helps us not at all.

4. Personality has been glorified in the same way and with the same pernicious confusion. Personalities are good and bad to all extremes. Hence it is not mere personality, but something about personality which is the value.

Sometimes integration of personality has been thought to be the gauge of all value. It is true that integration is one value but certainly not all. Personality may be integrated in the interest of evil as well as in the interest of good. The devil must be a highly integrated personality.

Growth of personality is another alleged standard. But the nature of the growth must be specified. Growth of what? Growth of personality. Growth of evil or of good personality? Of good. Then what is it that distinguishes the good from the evil? Obviously it is not growth unless one specifies more clearly what this growth is.

5. Certain phases of society have been identified with the principle of value, such as love, communication, and co-operation. If one started with these and carried his analysis far enough, he might find the essence of value. But the rudiments of value lie far deeper than these vague, general, and comprehensive terms. Also it is obvious that value cannot be set up as social in contradistinction from individual, or vice versa.

6. Patterns in the physical world, such as order and purpose, have been selected as criteria of value. Doubtless value implies order of a kind, but what kind of order is better and what kind worse? More order is not necessarily more value unless it is the right kind of order. The same is true of purpose. The universe might have a purpose and still not be good, for purposes are both good and evil. I could not think of a more horrible universe than one which had a fiendish purpose to torture and impoverish, lifting life only just high enough to inflict the worst possible experience of evil and then dragging it down to destruction again, only to repeat the process. Purposive evil seems to be worse than non-purposive. At any rate, purpose of itself does not give us a clear distinction between better and worse.

7. Value has been identified with a kind of tertiary quality which cannot be described or distinguished by any principle. When you experience it, you simply have it.

Like the color blue you may distinguish it by comparing it
with other things, but the pure qualitative experience of a col-
or is ineffable and indescribable. So, it has been said, is
the nature of value. You know values by intuition and by no
other way. You can test your own judgment only by appealing to the intuitive sense of others. If you disagree or are
uncertain, there is nothing more to be done about it. But
that means that this approach gives you nothing at all to help
you when you are perplexed.

It may be that values have their ineffable qualities
that cannot be described or distinguished or specified in any
way save by immediate intuition. But obviously you cannot
form a guiding theory out of that ingredient of value. A
great many other kinds of reality besides that of value yield
up ineffable qualities to consciousness when we experience
them. It may be said that every existing thing, when immediately experienced, gives to consciousness ineffable qualities. But it is not these ineffable qualities which guide our
conduct or enable us to distinguish the things experienced.
Rather we must discover structures of thought by which to
distinguish such things and guide our conduct in respect to
them. So it is with value. Values have their ineffable qualities, but these are not the materials out of which we can
form a guiding theory.

8.   Abstract principles have been identified with value. It is certainly true that any theory of value must be an
abstract theory, just like any other theory whatsoever. But
if the theory is to have any application to this existing world,
or to the qualities of experience, it must apply to something
beyond itself.

The various elements which we have discussed under
eight heads are not alien to value. One reason for considering them is that they do, for the most part, enter into any
experience of value. We accept them but deny that one can
get a helpful theory of value out of them. For such a theory one must go on to something else.

We believe the factor in value which lends itself most
readily to a guiding pattern or principle by which to discover,
appraise, and appreciate values is appreciable activity. Activity is objective. It can be observed, computed, foreseen.
It can be controlled, redirected, elaborated. Activities can
be connected in meaningful and supporting ways. Through
activity all practical problems are solved. Above all, ac-

tivity turns us outward. What we experience through activity is the nature of objective reality.

But the activity must be appreciable. Otherwise it is
not the datum in which value can be found. Activity may be
a mechanical routine or a spasmodic impulse or a dizzy
whirl. None of these carries value except in so far as it is
capable of yielding rich qualities of emotional experience.
An activity is appreciable when it yields enjoyment as soon
as one learns to appreciate what is involved in it.

To be appreciable does not mean necessarily to be appreciated. One may engage in an activity without finding the
value in it because he is not able to appreciate it. When
one does appreciate an activity which carries value, he has
an emotional experience. But this emotional experience is
not the value. Rather it is part of the experience we have
when we appreciate the value. It is in this sense that we
say appreciable activity is the best place to start in our
search to find the nature of value.

There are a number of reasons why we cannot identify value with those states of consciousness called enjoyment
and suffering. What we enjoy, when we have the state of
consciousness, is not the state of consciousness itself. This
can be easily demonstrated by a simple experiment. Let
one focus his attention upon his own state of consciousness
and turn his attention away from the landscape or the friend
or the conversation or the delicious food or the organic processes of his own organism or the music or whatever may be
the object of enjoyment. Immediately, or very swiftly, the
state of consciousness called enjoyment begins to grow weak
and thin and fade away. Or let one try the experiment on
the conscious state of suffering. If one is able to turn his
attention quite completely away from the objective cause of
the suffering (sometimes this is not possible), the state of
suffering loses its intensity and may quite disappear.

When we enjoy or suffer, it is not a state of consciousness that we are enjoying or suffering but something
else. If we can find this something else, we shall be on the
trail of value.

While we cannot, for the reason mentioned, identify
value with the subjective states of enjoyment and suffering,
these states are essential parts of the experience of values.
That does not mean that every enjoyment is a positive value

and every suffering a negative or disvalue.   But it does mean
that value must register itself in human consciousness in the
form of suffering or enjoyment.   We would have no interest
in the question of value were it not for deep experiences of
enjoyment that we want to recover; were it not for bitter sufferings which we want to avoid or understand or extract some
meaning from; were it not for experiences of anticipation, un-
fulfilled, frustration, disillusionment, or imaginings of enjoyment more rich or deep or noble or otherwise better than
what we have thus far experienced.

        For these reasons we must seek the nature of value
by some critique of enjoyable and sufferable activities.   What
enjoyments and sufferings indicate the presence of value and
which show we are experiencing disvalue or negative value?
Which indicate the greater value and which the lesser?

ACTIVITY AND MEANING

        Since these two, activity and meaning, are of first
importance in our interpretation of value, we must try to
make plain the idea we wish to express by each.   An activity is, first of all, a change.   But it is not every change.
A change is an activity when it is so related to other changes
that they mutually modify one another to the end of meeting
the requirements of a system to which they belong.   For example, gravitational changes mutually modify one another in
such a way as to meet the requirements of the gravitational
system.   Hence they are activities in respect to this system.   Or, again, many of the changes that transpire in a
cell are so related to many other changes in the physiological organism that they all mutually modify one another to
the end of meeting the requirements of the living system.
Still, again, many changes in the environment are so related
to certain changes in the living organism that they modify
one another to the end of meeting the requirements of a system of life which includes the organism and its sustaining
environment.   It is plain that almost any change can be di-
vided into smaller units of change.   Thus every activity is
made up of sub-activities so connected as to form the activity in question.

        We have shown that gravitational changes are activi-
ties with respect to the gravitational system.   But they are
not activities, necessarily, with respect to the system of a
living organism or with respect to that system of life which

includes the organism and much of its environment. However, some gravitational changes do enter into the system of life and thus become activities with respect to it. For example, the gravitational changes by which a living organism maintains its equilibrium are activities with respect to the system of its life. The flow of the air into the lungs is a gravitational change, since it is the weight of the air that makes it fill a partial vacuum. It is obvious that such a change is an activity of first importance in respect to the living organism. Chemical changes that occur in the soil may play an important part in nourishing plants which in turn nourish men. In such cases the chemical changes are activities in respect to the human system of life.

It is plain that a change may be an activity with respect to one system and not in relation to another. Indeed, one of the great problems of life and value is to make changes which are sustaining activities in one system to be likewise sustaining activities in other systems. The world is so deficient in value because such is not the case in great part. Changes which sustain one system are often destructive of others.

Not all activities are values. An activity is a value only when it is appreciable. To be appreciable means that some living consciousness sometime, somewhere, some way, may be affected by it with joy or suffering. This does not require that the consciousness have any knowledge of this activity. Many changes enter as sustaining activities into the system which we enjoy without our being conscious of them specifically. They qualify consciousness without being objects of consciousness. Oxidation of the blood in my lungs qualifies my consciousness when I am not at all conscious of what is going on. These changes pertain to value, however, if their removal or cessation would destroy the system which yields the experience of value.

An activity, as we are using the term, is not purposive necessarily, although some activities are. However, this depends on what one means by purpose. If one says every change is purposive when it is so related to other changes that they mutually modify one another to the end of meeting the requirements of a system, then, of course, all activity is purposive. But this is not what is ordinarily meant by purpose.

When we say that an activity is a change which enters

into mutual modification with other changes to maintain a
system, we do not mean that they do this irresistibly.
Something outside the system may prevent these correlated
changes from functioning together as the system requires
and so impair or destroy the system.   Thus a piercing bul-
let may disrupt that coordination of changes which a living
organism requires to keep alive.   So also may a great
drought and many other things.

   With this understanding of activity let us now turn to
the interpretation of meaning.   Activity and meaning are
closely related but not identical.   One change means another
change when the first represents the second to an actual or
possible experiencing mind.   One change can mean another
most effectively if the two changes are so connected that,
when certain modifications occur in the one, certain other
correlative modifications occur in the other.   Thus, when a
mind experiences the first series of modifications, these can
serve to represent the second series which is not being immediately experienced but which the mind can know to be oc-
curing if the connection between the two is understood.

   So we see that the connection between changes which
makes them to be activities within a system is a connection
which is best fitted to make them carriers of meaning by virtue of the fact that they can represent one another to a mind
that understands the connection between them.   A throbbing
pulse means the presence of life to a mind that is able to
understand the connection between these throbs and that system of coordinated changes in the organism which makes it
a living thing.   Rising smoke in the distance means the presence of fire to a mind that understands the connection between smoky changes in the atmosphere and correlative
changes called combustion, which may be at the time quite
beyond the reach of immediate experience.   The intelligent
mind is always seeking for these correlations between series
of changes, because this is the only way in which it can deal
with its world effectively and appreciatively.   It is always
seeking for changes that mutually modify one another within
a system and are therefore activities with respect to that
system because the discovery of such systems fills the world
with meaning.

   Some changes are artifically set up by men for the
distinct purpose of carrying meanings.   Such changes are
generally rather trivial in themselves but are artificially
made to correlate with important changes so that men can

get the meaning of these important changes without undergoing the hardship and danger of actually experiencing them immediately.   Thus red lights are set up to mean danger.
Words are spoken to mean any number of things.   The speaking of the word is in itself a trivial change but is so correlated with other trivial changes (words) and all these with actual and possible changes of vital importance that the words
enable us to get the meaning of these important changes.
The meaning of the important changes is that connection between them by virtue of which certain modifications in one
involves further modifications of a specific sort in the others.
A certain sound on the roof means falling drops of rain and
driving wind, these mean swishing trees and soaking mois-
ture in the earth, the reviving of crops, the rising of rivers,
dangerous roads, delayed transport, a change in the stock
market, more prosperity, the re-election of a candidate to
office, etc.

Meaning is that connection between the here-and-now
and the far-away which enables a mind that understands the
connection to experience the far-away through the mediation
of the here-and-now.   This ability to transmit the far-away
to the experience of a mind by way of representation is what
we call meaning.   This ability depends on two things: (1)
the right connections and (2) the mind's understanding of
these connections.

Words are necessary to analyze, explicate, and communicate any great complexity and scope of meaningful connections.   But the most rich, vivid, and urgently practical
meanings reside in the connections between activities which
are much more intrinsically important than words.   When I
experience the touch of flames or the cries of rage or the
sob of a friend or the tremor in a human body or the leer
on a face, and thereby know that I am caught in the grip of
a total system of mutually controlling activities which operate to destroy or to fulfil with abundance, then it is that I
have the most vivid and rich and compelling experience of
meaning.   This tongue of flame, this cry, this sob, this
tremor, this leer, means not merely a system of interconnected verbal activities.   It means that some vitally important part of the actual world is moving on to disaster or to
blessedness, and will go one way or the other according as
I choose between alternative courses of action.   Then it is
that the here-and-now, by virtue of representing what is not
here-and-now, becomes rich, potent, stirring, overwhelming,
or exalting with meaning.   This is the kind of meaning which

opens the gateway into the most abundant values. Through
growth of this kind of meaning there may be unlimited increase of value.

Meaning, as set forth here, is not subjective. The
experience of the meaning is subjective if you equate experience with subjectivity. But the meaning which is experienced, namely, the connection of mutual control or correlation between changes, is no more subjective than a mountain
or a city. The understanding of the connection is subjective,
if you equate subjectivity and understanding. But what is understood is not. That system of mutually modifying changes
is out there in the physical and social world and will destroy
or enrich according as you deal with it one way or another.
That system is a system of meaning in relation to any actual
or possible mind that is able to understand and appreciate the
connections. It is not meaning in relation to a mind that is
not able to understand and appreciate these. Meaning is dependent on understanding and appreciation, but that which is
understood and appreciated is not subjective.

VALUE AS A KIND OF CONNECTION

What is enjoyable for one person is not for another.
We can never hope to have everyone enjoy the same kind of
things, and it would not be desirable for them to do so. The
interest of life would greatly diminish. Also we note that
what one person enjoys at one time is sometimes loathsome
to him under other conditions. Therefore, value cannot be
identified with specific things such as doughnuts or ocean voy-
ages or the Mr. Jones who is such an enjoyable friend to
Mr. Smith or with the United States or the poems of Tenny-
son.

But no matter how diverse may be the enjoyments of
different people, or of the same person at different times in
his development, one thing seems to be plain. These enjoyable activities, utterly different though they may be, can be
had only when they are so connected that they do not destroy
one another. I may enjoy Mr. Smith while you like Mr.
Samuel; perhaps you cannot bear Mr. Smith. But if my way
of associating with Mr. Smith is of such a sort that it destroys your fellowship with Mr. Samuel, and if your attempts
to keep company with Mr. Samuel continuously disturb my
visits with Mr. Smith, it is plain that values are being destroyed or nullified.

Appreciable activities may be very different, but they can be so connected as to support and enhance one another, or else to impair and destroy one another. Perhaps many enjoyable activities have no effect upon one another at all for either good or ill. Yet it is impossible to have any appreciable experience which is not made enjoyable or sufferable by reason of the way many activities are connected with one another. The millions of cells of the organism must function together in the right way else you cannot have any enjoyment whatsoever. You cannot be conscious or living. The activities of your organism must be rightly connected with many activities going on in your operative environment in order to enable you to understand and appreciate the thought and feeling of Mr. Smith or even to know he is present. The same is true of any other appreciable activity you might want to mention.

Every enjoyment is an experience of some combination of activities even though they be subtle vibrations of organic adjustments which the ordinary powers of observation cannot detect, along with vibrations of light waves, and the like. Therefore, when we have any enjoyment, what we are actually experiencing is a great system of activities all connected in such way as to yield that sort of enjoyment.

Thus far, we have been considering very simple enjoyments as though they were solitary isolated experiences. But experiences never are wholly isolated. Certainly every appreciable activity has in it the reverberations of past experiences and anticipations of future; and those past and future experiences consisted, and will consist, of activities organized according to some system of interconnections. In the great enjoyments these connections reach very far and very deep and may include many, many people besides our own solitary selves.

If value is what makes an experience enjoyable, then our analysis would seem to indicate that value consists of the way activities are connected with one another. They may be connected in such a way as to make them enjoyable or the opposite. Every enjoyment is the enjoyment of connected activities, even though we may not be conscious of the several individual activities and their connections which make them enjoyable.

Another striking fact about the experience of enjoyment must be noted. Many causes of interconnected activi-

ties which are enjoyable when taken by themselves cease to
be so when their wider connections are experienced. Also,
many connections which are not appreciable in themselves become so when the wider relations are discerned. However,
that does not mean that we are blind and helpless about the
value of the wider connections prior to our experience of
them. Certain kinds of connections are of such a sort that,
when one understands them, he can know with a high degree
of probability that they will lead on to still further connections that make them even more appreciable.

All this points to the conclusion that value is not enjoyment, but it is that connection between activities which
makes them enjoyable. When we experience enjoyment, it is
not merely our enjoyment that we enjoy; what we enjoy is a
certain connection between activities even though we may not
be conscious of that fact. And these connections can be extended indefinitely to render stable and progressive the order
which we enjoy. Value, then, is that connection between appreciable activities which makes them mutually enhancing,
mutually diversifying, and mutually meaningful.

We prefer the term appreciable rather than appreciated. In many cases an activity by itself cannot be enjoyed,
but, when taken in its connections with other activities, it
yields the richest and most vivid qualities of emotional experience to him who has capacity to appreciate the significance of these connections. These connections are values
even when not appreciated. They are there to be appreciated
and so are appreciable. He who does not appreciate them
does not thereby nullify their value. It is his high vocation
as a human being to learn to appreciate them.

There is a further reason for speaking of appreciable
rather than of enjoyed or even enjoyable connections. We
shall sometimes use the term enjoyable as distinguished from
enjoyed, and we think it valid if certain misunderstandings
are avoided. Appreciable is a more precise term because
with it these misunderstandings are not quite so likely to
arise. Such terms as enjoyed, enjoyment, and enjoyable may
blind us to the fact that there are high austere values which
can be experienced at times only through great pain and suffering. They are genuine values because they make life more
abundant in two ways: (1) in the richness of emotional quality and (2) in the meaningful connections which enter awareness when we appreciate them. Some may be confused by
saying that suffering is enjoyable. Still others may think that

such a statement means a morbid or sadistic enjoyment of suffering. This is not meant at all. But it is true that in great suffering one may be appreciative of noble values. So, while we shall often speak of enjoyable connections, it may be less confusing for some to think of appreciable.

We find that some enjoyments involve activities which support other enjoyable activities. Thus eating wholesome food is an activity which supports many other appreciable activities, while eating unwholesome food is an activity which does not. Wholesome food is of more value than unwholesome because it enters into a more inclusive system of mutually sustaining activities which are enjoyable. The same is true of honesty as over against dishonesty, good music as over against bad, stable government as over against gangs of robbers, good government as over against bad. One economic system is better than another on the same basis.

But appreciable activities not only support others; in many cases they actually enhance them. Thus wholesome food not only supports other enjoyable activities, but it makes those others more appreciable. I enjoy my work or my friend or a trip to town or almost anything somewhat more if I have had a good dinner. Honesty not only supports but may enhance the value of many other activities. The same is true of good music, a stable government, and a just economic system.

A third principle of value may be noted. Activities must be connected in such a way as to permit increase in their diversification and number without permanently destroying their mutual support. It is quite possible to have a system of mutual support which is achieved and maintained by excluding all other activities and fixating the system. In political order this is dictatorship as contrasted with democracy. Connections of value must provide for increasing diversification on the part of the activities which are connected. Some activities should be extremely different from others in order to fulfil diverse functions within the total system. When a system becomes fixated, regimented, or otherwise organized in such a way as to prevent the emergence of new and more diverse and more numerous activities within the system, it loses one of the cardinal principles of value. A system of value should be tolerant of conflict, provided the conflict is constructive and not destructive. Constructive conflict, going on within a system of interrelated activities, is the process by which the system is reordered in such a way

as to include a richer diversification of unique activities.
Hence mutual diversification is a third characteristic of that
connection between activities which makes them appreciable
and gives them value. He who is able to appreciate the
greatest number and diversity of unique activities rightly connected will have the richest meanings and the most abundant
qualitative richness of emotional experience. The right connection, we shall see, is fivefold.

A fourth feature of that connection which we identify
with value is meaning. We have seen that meaning is the
connection of mutual modification or correlation between actual and possible changes when this connection is used and
appreciated by men. We must repeat that meaning is not
subjective even though a connection is not a meaning except
in relation to a mind that understands and appreciates the
connection. The swaying trees mean the wind is blowing.
They do not have this meaning for a mind that is unable to
appreciate this connection between trees and wind; but the
connection between swaying trees and blowing wind is an objective fact. So with all meanings that are genuine and true.
Of course, there are many false meanings.

Through meaning we can gather a world of value into
a little space of time. Through meaning sorrow and pain can
make us aware of great values. Dull routine can be meta-
morphosed into fascinating work or play. Meaning makes
possible the unlimited growth of value. It can transform the
world with wealth and glory.

When once we have experienced this added enjoyment
which an activity can take on by reason of the meaning it
carries, we have passed through the door that opens into the
greatest values life can bring. For the enjoyment found in
meanings opens out toward infinity. There is no known limit to the increase of satisfaction that is gotten by way of
meanings, whereas every other way of getting satisfaction has
very narrow limits.

But there is still a fifth characteristic of this connection between enjoyable activities which makes them mutually
sustaining and mutually enhancing. An activity which is not
enjoyable in itself may become extremely enjoyable when we
see its connection with a great system of other activities
which gives to it wide, rich meaning. An activity may even
be exceedingly painful, and yet be enjoyable by virtue of the
meaning it carries. That sounds paradoxical, but it is not.

We choose this painful but meaningful activity because of the enjoyableness of its meaning, not because of the enjoyableness of its pain. This enjoyableness of its meaning is not merely our anticipation of future pleasure or relief from pain. That may be the reason for submitting one's self to the dentist's chair. But when one has discovered the depths of enjoyment found in meaning, he will often experience far more satisfaction in this meaning of it without anticipating future pleasures than any pleasurable experience could ever give to him without such scope of meaning. Thus the functional connection between activities which gives them meaning can take experiences which are painful, or otherwise intensely disagreeable, and make them highly enjoyable. In suffering of childbirth there may be joy that a child is born into the world.

After this survey we can look back and see what is the unit of value. The unit of value is not an enjoyed activity, but it is that connection between activities which makes them enjoyable or, better, appreciable. The difference between enjoyed activity and enjoyable, or appreciable, is very important. If we take any enjoyed activity as the unit of value, then increase of value would have to be the mere increase or additive sum of enjoyed activities. But an appreciable activity need not be an enjoyed activity at all. An appreciable activity is one that would be enjoyed if one experienced it in that connection with other activities wherein they all supported and enhanced one another in consciousness. At the higher levels of intelligence this connection may be that of meaning. At the lower levels the connection between the activities may simply serve to vivify, clarify, and make more controllable and anticipatory the qualitative richness of conscious experience, with very little meaning. In either case we have value.

When an activity is not experienced in those connections which make it contribute either to the qualities of consciousness or to the meanings, it is not enjoyed. But if it has these connections in actuality and possibility, even though no consciousness has yet come into the system sufficiently to experience them, it is enjoyable, but not enjoyed. Many activities are appreciable by virtue of their connections with other activities although certain individuals may not be able to appreciate these connections. They are appreciable but not appreciated. Values are appreciable connections when not appreciated.

We can now summarize the fivefold principle by which

to distinguish activities which are better from those which
are worse. It is the principle of mutual support, mutual enhancement, mutual diversification, mutual meaning, and
transformation of suffering into an experience which is positively appreciated. This fivefold principle is the principle of
value. It sets forth the essential nature of value. One activity is better than another not merely because we enjoy it
more. The immediate subjective feeling of enjoyment is no
criterion of value. But one activity is better when it is
more appreciable by virtue of its connection with other activities. This connection is that of support, enhancement,
diversification, meaning, and transmutation.

TESTING THE PRINCIPLE OF VALUE

Let us apply this principle of value to the most difficult field and thus subject it to the most severe test. This
most difficult area is that of fine art and, perhaps, most especially music. What music is better as fine art than other
music? A piece of music is great music, it is high art or
most excellent, not because I happen to enjoy it most the
first time I hear it. But there are at least six tests I can
apply to it.

1. Does it grow on me? If it is great music, I
ought to like it better after I have heard it many, many
times. If it is music of low grade, it will in time pall. If
it is great music, one hearing of it will sustain and enhance
the enjoyment of other hearings. If the several hearings are
rightly connected, they should mutually sustain and mutually
enhance one another.

2. Does it interconnect many different experiences,
besides those of hearing the music itself, so that they sustain and enhance the enjoyableness of one another? Santayana,
quoted by John Dewey, has said that any scene of nature,
odor, combination of colors, social contact, owes the deep
aesthetic enjoyment which it yields to the "hushed reverberations" of other experiences. From early infancy we have
seen colors and landscapes, experienced odors and social contacts which are so related to this present experience that
they are subconsciously revived or lifted to the borders of
consciousness, adding a deep richness, vividness, and emotional tone to what is now being experienced. Great music
will have this connection with many diverse experiences of
life, so that they add to the music a deep rich resonance.

The music will help to organize and interconnect many different activities of life so that in our feeling they become mutually sustaining and enhancing as they were not before. Not only will this occur in the form of a "hushed reverberation" at the time of hearing the music, but also we shall engage in many activities with a new sense of their interconnection and underlying unity that we did not have and could not have had without having experienced the music. Such is the case if the music is truly great.

3. Does it enable us to share with others some of the deeper experiences of life, such as joy, sorrow, love, hope? When grief is expressed in music, we can share it together as we cannot when it is not artistically presented. When joy, triumph, love, fun, any experienced event that yields the emotional qualities of life, is expressed in the form of music or other great art, it draws us into a community of shared experience. We become mutually sustaining and mutually enhancing participants in a shared body of experience. Our appreciation of the experience is vastly enhanced this way. What would otherwise be nothing but misery becomes transfigured with a kind of glory.

4. Does it unify history? Does it help us to share the experiences of the dead, the living, and the unborn over many generations? Great art does just that. It opens the gate into the great community of the ages. It taps that deep stream of rich experience which flows through history and gives mankind one of the most precious forms of its oneness. In great art we can know how man felt many, many ages ago, and as they will feel ages hence, if this art has been appreciated throughout all these times.

5. Does it integrate the individual personality? Great music helps to resolve inner conflicts. It relieves tensions, fears, worries. It helps to make the many diverse activities which go to make up the individual personality more mutually sustaining and enhancing.

6. Does it have tragic value? Great tragic art flings about human misery, failure, despair, a world of meaningful connections. Art selects, sifts, clarifies, so that we can see the important connections between one experience and many others. In actual life these connections are often lost in the midst of innumerable details that are irrelevant to the major issues and meanings. Above all, tragic art rears above the bitter event a great doom of pos-

sibilities. We sense something of the high calling, something of what ought to have been and might have been, in
contrast to what actually did occur. This gives to the occurrence, otherwise mean and miserable, a glory. The actual
event artistically portrayed had a function, although that function was frustrated. These possibilities rising high above the
actual event, and made visible by art, give a greatness to it.
The clear vision of these possibilities and of this meaning
gives tragic value in the midst of bitter experiences. Only
in art and with the help of art can this vision reach its greatest clarity because art leaves out the irrelevant.

Music or any other art is great by these six tests.
There may be others, but these help illustrate our principles
of value and show how it applies to art. The same principle
of better and worse could be demonstrated in any other kind
of value, such as that of physiological well-being or health,
pleasure, workmanship or skill, friendship and all the values
of primary association, economic and political value, moral,
aesthetic, cognitive, and religious values. These all have
their characteristic differentia by which they are distinct
kinds of value. But they all consist of connections of mutual
support, enhancement, and meaning between appreciable activities. The connections of mutual support may be of such
a sort as to promote health or pleasure or skill or friendship or economic value or political order or moral goodness
or beauty or truth or religious loyalty.

VALUE AND POSSIBILITY

Any such system of connected activities making a value always includes some which are possibilities. Indeed, any
portion of the system may be in the realm of possibility.
Take the situation in which one enjoys the beauty of a rose.
Many interconnected activities are required for this, including the many physiological activities involved, the support of
the earth, the light of the sun, the right distance of the ob-
server from the rose, and many more.

Certainly the whole universe is not brought into the experience. Many things may happen in the world without affecting in the least the enjoyment of the rose. Whales may
spout in the open sea, people may die around the corner,
famine may stalk the land of China, and another revolution
may break out in Russia without affecting in any way the connections which make up the value experienced in that situation.

But while it falls far short of the whole universe, it is, nevertheless, a very complicated system of connections. In any case the total system always extends beyond existence into possibility. Wherever there is any enjoyment, there is always a prospective reference. There is always some anticipation. Whenever anyone enjoying anything thinks that in the next second it will all be blotted out, the enjoyment is affected. This outreach and anticipation, although it be no more than anticipation of a continuance of the present experience, shows that every system of connections that is at all enjoyable must include some possibilities on beyond the actual existing state of affairs.

Any part of the interconnected elements may be a possibility only. The rose itself may be a possibility. I enjoy the present situation because I anticipate the rose. Or the rose may be present but the consciousness to enjoy the rose may be only a possibility. It is not at all necessary that a conscious subject be present in order to have value, provided a conscious subject is included in the total system in the form of a possibility. Thus there was value on this planet long before any living thing existed here if there was a growing system of connected activities which would finally bring forth a living conscious mind. In any situation of value the conscious subject that is to do the enjoying may be one of the possibilities and only a possibility. A conscious appreciative mind was only a possibility relative to the earth's existence prior to the appearance of living organisms. But that possibility gave to the earth's existence a value.

Does God have a conscious appreciative mind analogous to that of physiological organisms? That is a speculation which may be true. But man's sense of value, his highest loyalty, and religious devotion must have more solid foundation than such a speculation can provide.

GOD AND VALUE

With this understanding of the generic nature of value religious inquiry will ask: What reality is of greatest value and on that account the rightful object of man's supreme devotion? In terms of the theory of value here set forth, the most important reality which can command the loyalties of men is the unlimited growth of the connections of value. Unlimited growth does not mean progress necessarily. It means a growth which carries infinite possibilities, however obstructed and beaten back it may be.

Every specific system of activities having value is
definitely limited, whether it be a living organism with its
sustaining environment, or a society of organisms, or a
community of minds with all their meanings and with a historic development and institutional structure called a culture.
Each of these must perish. Each has a certain form of existence with limited possibilities, making it incapable of
carrying the growth of connections of value beyond a certain
bound. Therefore, God cannot be identified with any of
these. If values and meanings are to grow indefinitely, each
of these limited systems of value must pass away in time
and give place to some other order of existence and value.
Therefore, while none of these is God, God works through
them. God is the growth which goes on through the succes-
sion of these limited systems of value. God is the growth
which exfoliates in all manner of different forms of value.
In all these different forms he works to achieve maximum
mutual support, enhancement, and diversification between
them; and at the human level he adds to all this the growth
of meaning and transmutation of suffering. God is the growth
which springs anew when old forms perish. When one organism dies, others spring up. When one society perishes, others arise. When one epoch of culture declines, others in
time come forth. This unlimited growth of connections of
value is God.

> Thou turnest man to destruction;
> And sayest, Return, ye children of men.
> For a thousand years in thy sight
> Are but as yesterday when it is past
> And a watch in the night.
> Thou carriest them away as with a flood;
> They are as a sleep:
> In the morning they are like grass which groweth up.
> In the morning it flourisheth and groweth up;
> In the evening it is cut down and withereth.

But the growth of connections of value goes on through all
generations.

It may be that sometime the universe will resolve itself into chaos, and there will be no growth of mutually sustaining activities. That such will ever come to pass is a
speculation only. But just supposing it did. Still the growth
of connections of mutual support and meaning seems to be
infinite in its possibilities. Infinite possibilities do not mean
that all possibilities will be realized or that growth must nec-

essarily go on forever, although it is quite conceivable that it might. It means only that this growth of connections carries unlimited possibilities which may be more or less completely actualized and which spring up in new forms when old forms are destroyed.

If the theory of value here presented is moving in the right direction, it is this growth which intelligent religious inquiry must seek to understand ever better. Religious endeavor must seek to align human activities with it and commit human living ever more completely to its sustaining, guiding, and quickening power if this interpretation of value have any truth in it.

In summary: The most important fact about the universe for the religious man is the unlimited growth of those connections between activities by which they become sustaining, mutually enhancing, mutually meaningful, mutually diversified, and mutually transform one another into enjoyable experiences when in themselves they are not enjoyable. How completely the total cosmos may be transformed by this growth no one can say. But this growth with its infinite possibilities is the reality of greatest value. This is true no matter how incompletely these possibilities may be actualized.

PART 3:
RELIGIOUS INQUIRY

INTRODUCTION

In these four essays one finds Wieman writing directly about the problem of "religious inquiry." But as one
reads Wieman's attempts, through the empirical analyses of
his religious inquiry, to get at that process that operates in
human life to transform it, save it, and lead it from evil,
one becomes conscious of the fact that his religious inquiry
is not done in isolation from the demands of the power of
scientific technology and of philosophical integrity.

Wieman's religious inquiry confronts the problems of
rapid social change, science and technology, cultural complexities, ethical relativism, and interpersonal relationships
in a world grown small by virtue of the threat of destruction
and the quest for interdependence. While religious inquiry is
given to the task of describing the structure and process of
creativity that transforms and saves human life, science and
its technological power must search out and provide those
conditions that must be present for creativity to prevail, and
philosophy and its tools of rationality, coherence, and integrity must be used to formulate a theory of a ruling commitment to this creativity so that in every time of the practice
and application of religious commitment the total self of the
person will be given over to the actual sustenance and guidance of creativity itself and not just to ideas and concepts of
it.

The theme of worship in "Commitment for Theological Inquiry" should be read in light of what Wieman has written about worship in other places, especially in The Wrestle
of Religion with Truth, Methods of Private Religious Living,
Man's Ultimate Commitment, and Religious Inquiry: Some
Explorations.

113

THE NEED OF PHILOSOPHY OF RELIGION*

In an age when the traditional religion is fairly satisfactory and needs only to be clarified and systematized, the intellectual work in religion is properly called "theology." It is very important and very useful. It gives power and depth and scope to religion. It greatly increases its effectiveness as a vital function.

But in an age when the traditional form of religion is not satisfactory, when its basic structure must be re-examined and the abstract essentials distinguished from the passing forms of concrete life, philosophy of religion comes to the front. In such a time the thologians are likely to say that there is no real difference between theology and philosophy of religion. What they mean is that in such a time the work they have to do is really that of philosophy of religion. In this they are right, although there is a difference between theology and philosophy of religion.

The theologian endeavors to present the object of religious devotion in a form that is intellectually acceptable to the people of his time and group. That means he must organize beliefs about the supremely worthful in such a way that they do not contradict one another and are not contradicted by other propositions held to be true. Thus theology gives intellectual expression to religious devotion.

But philosophy criticizes the assumptions of that devotion. It seeks to lay bare the essential characteristics which make this reality worthy of such devotion, if it has such characteristics. Philosophy of religion wants to know if the essentials are there; theology wants to make sure that the form of presentation is acceptable to the mental needs of the people of that time and place.

This distinction between theology and philosophy of religion may be made clearer if we compare religion to eating. If religion is like eating, then the reality which inter-

*Reprinted from Journal of Religion, XIV:4, October 1934, pp. 379-395.

ests the religious person is analogous to food. In that case
the theologian is the one who puts this food into such form
that it is palatable and can be most readily eaten. The theologian is a good cook. But the philosopher is a dietitian.
He does not prepare the food for eating. He does not present God in a form that is digestible to the ordinary religious person. That is not his business. He does not talk
about jelly and fried chicken and cake. He talks about vitamins and proteins. Now, no one ever hungered for vitamins
and proteins. Of course, what he really needed were these,
but he could not take them in the abstract form of vitamins
and proteins, although these were truly the essentials. He
had to have them in the form of jelly and fried chicken and
the like. The theologian talks about beefsteak and lettuce.
The philosopher talks about starches and calories. Consequently, simple souls are likely to think that the philosopher
is discussing something that has no connection with their
yearnings. In this they are mistaken, but their mistake is
very understandable.

We have come to a time in the history of the world
when the religious diet must be changed. This diet has always been changing throughout history, not in respect to the
essentials, not in respect to vitamins and proteins, not in
respect to the reality of God, but in respect to the concrete
form in which these essentials are taken. At one time they
may have been taken in the form of roots and berries and
slugs and insects, later in the form of raw fish or bear and
deer. So also, in religion, you can trace the many forms
in which men have sought and found the reality of God. That
does not mean that everything that men have ever worshiped
was truly God any more than everything people have ever
eaten truly had in it the essentials of nutrition. There has
been a great deal of religious malnutrition as well as physiological.

It is a dangerous thing to change the diet without the
services of a dietitian, especially if the new food is of a sort
that was never before eaten by men. Does it have the essential elements of nutrition? It must be palatable, but that is
not enough. We must have the services of the dietitian as
well as the cook. We must operate with those concepts
which enable us to detect the essential reality in the new
foods, whether that essential reality be proteins or deity.

Is the religious anemia of the modern man due to the
fact that he has not been able to find in the new "isms" and

religions of our time the ancient nourishment which gives to life its vitality and power?   Is the ancient deity found in these new religions?

Also, there is another peculiar problem.   How to keep the zest of life through a keen sense of the supremely worthful for all human living and at the same time be keenly self-conscious and critical, that is the problem.   It can be solved only by a religion which has attained some sense of the supremely worthful for all human living by way of the critical understanding.   But that also requires the services of philosophy.

A swift survey of the outstanding characteristics of our time will help to reveal the peculiar need for philosophy of religion in such an age as this.   These outstanding characteristics come under the heads of social change, sophistication, and cultural problems.

SOCIAL CHANGE

Social change is always going on, but it has rarely been so swift and radical as it is today.   In recent times the intellectual and institutional structure of life has not been able to keep up with the rapid transformation of the actual processes of living.

The process has run away from the forms, standards, ideals, affections, loyalties, objectives.   Undoubtedly this maladjustment between the process and the ideology of life has occurred in the past, but perhaps never in the same degree and not in the same way.

Swift and radical change in the past has generally been due to one or more of three causes--conquest, internal disintegration, and natural catastrophe.   In case of conquest, two cultures were brought together so that either they merged or one dominated the other, or both.   But in such case the problem was not to rear a new moral and religious structure. It was to merge or otherwise adjust two structures already in existence.   Such a task might well call for the services of philosophy, but it plainly did not so urgently demand a clarification of the basic principles on which any culture must be reared as does the present state of affairs, where the problem is not so much to merge two old cultures as to rear a new one to fit the requirements of a new way of living.

When extreme social change was due to internal disintegration or natural catastrophe, the need of philosophy was
even less imperative. Such a change meant a lapse to some
more simple, more primitive, way of living. In the purlieus
of society can always be found some forms that can be used
and developed to meet the needs of life when it thus declines.

But the cause of social change in our day is none of
these we have mentioned. It is science and machinery. It
is a change that has made life not more simple, but more
complex. It has not diminished our powers of achievement
but has increased them. It has not reduced our economic
wealth but has vastly increased it. It has not made us less
dependent on one another, but more so. It has not decreased
the materials and opportunities for enjoyment but has brought
them to a bewildering confusion. We do not mean that this
change brought about by science and machinery has thus far
made life necessarily more joyous or satisfying or meaningful, but only that it has increased the complexity, the power
to do things, the interdependence, and the materials. Hence
the social change we have undergone in the recent past is not
only different from other historic changes in being more
swift and deep, but is also different in kind.

The sovereign loyalties which dominated the life of the
past cannot dominate ours. The affections which mellowed
and sweetened past lives cannot be ours in just the same
form. The objectives which lured them on cannot command
our powers. The appreciations which warmed their hearts
must reach us in different forms. All this means that we
must give religion a new form fitted to the new way of living.

But there has been too much unintelligent tampering
with religion. There has been too much changing of the form
of religion without regard to the basic reality which any form
must hold if it is to meet the requirements of living. There
are too many new forms of religion being foisted upon an un-
suspecting world. It is not enough to change the form of religion. We must first clarify those principles which essentially underlie any noble religion, and with these to guide us,
and only with these, can we undertake the reformulation of
religion. We must be sure the vitamins and proteins are in
the new forms. This is the reason that modern social change
requires philosophy of religion.

Another characteristic of change today points to the
same conclusion. The difference between successive genera-

tions has become so great that the transmission of affections, loyalties and appreciations from one to the other has become exceedingly difficult. We have long passed the time when this transmission could occur automatically and unconsciously. It has become a highly technical and self-conscious process called "education." But we are rapidly coming to the place where it is impossible, or at any rate unprofitable, to do it even by professional education.

Experts in the field of education are coming to see that what we must do is no longer to attempt to transmit our loyalties, affections and appreciations, but rather give to the rising generation those methods and principles by which they may be able to develop their own objectives and ruling interests. But educators have not come to see so clearly, as yet, that this is possible only if we have brought to light the underlying principles by which any noble way of living can be shaped. It is not merely a matter of skills and techniques. It is quite as truly, and even more imperatively, a matter of having those abstract, guiding principles which must determine good life, whatever form it may assume. Until we have grasped these with a fair degree of clarity and have learned how to hand them on from generation to generation, we cannot bridge the widening chasm that separates the mature from the immature. But this chasm must be bridged, else culture will decline toward barbarism.

Still another feature of our social change should be noted. It has become so great that the individual is clearly conscious of a shift in the major objectives of life as he passes from the cradle to the grave. Thus, if he develops a satisfactory way of living in his young manhood, and clings to it, he is likely to find himself in an alien world when he becomes old, like Sir Bedivere when King Arthur's court was dissolved in ruin. Sir Bedivere, however, could lapse into a simpler way of living in a simpler world. But the man of today cannot. Rather, he must live in a more complex world. What is a man to do when the morality and religion of his youth is unworkable in his later years? Three things he might do. He might hold fast to the ways that were worthy in his youth and endure the maladjustment which such ways involve in the new and different world. Or he might cast off the old ways and shop around in the various new religions and moralities that are on display, finding nothing satisfying in any of them. Or, in the third place, if he has the basic guiding principles which an adequate philosophy of religion can provide, he can progressively modify and devel-

op his religion and morality along with the changing world.
Some few have been able to do this. They alone can live
wisely.

SOPHISTICATION

There has been sophistication in every age of high
civilization, but it is probable that sophistication today has
gone more widely and sunk more deeply than in other times.
At any rate, there is a great deal of it, chiefly because of
our present means of communication and transportation.

By "sophistication" we mean that state of mind in
which it is impossible for a person to accept uncritically
any way of life. A sophisticated person can accept a way of
life after having critically examined it. He might even
adopt some very ancient system of religion and morality.
Some sophisticated people have done just that. But a sophisticated person cannot do what most men through human history have done. He cannot grow up into a system of values
with its loyalties, affections, standards, never asking whether it is good or bad, but simply living it as the way of life
for any human. If he accepts any way of life, he must do
it self-consciously and critically. That is what we mean by
sophistication.

There are a number of causes for this widespread
sophistication. In examining them, we shall be thinking especially of sophistication in religion. We have mentioned
modern communication and transportation, but these are not
real causes. They are only the means by which the real
causes are rendered pervasive and potent.

One of the causes of sophistication is modern psychology. People have become very sensitive about "compensatory illusions," "escape mechanisms" and "wishful thinking." They have been taught that much of morality and religion is a disguised form of these, and so they are on their
guard. They examine critically any way of life that may be
presented to see if it be not an example of one of these.
They have become skeptical, skittish, uncertain, lest they be
caught in wishful thinking.

Another cause of sophistication is the obvious maladjustment of traditional religion to the modern world. This
maladjustment makes traditional religion unrealistic. In its

time this body of tradition may very well have been the way
in which men came to grips with reality. In a very different cultural context these old words and forms had a very
different meaning from what they now have. But today they
often generate illusions rather than adjust to reality. Realization of this makes people critical and sophisticated toward
all religion.

Again, the scientific spirit has developed in men a demand for intellectual integrity. This does not mean that
people in any appreciable numbers understand science or are
scientific. It only means that they have heard and felt
enough about science to be more critical, more cautious,
more insistent on evidence, less ready to accept a belief
merely because it is handed down, or because it makes one
happy, or because it is upheld by a revered person or institution, or because it is respectable so to believe, or because
it gives one the zeal to do right or to resist temptation or
for any other personal or social advantage, or to satisfy a
subjective need. Not to be bribed into holding a belief by
personal or social advantage or by subjective need, is what
is meant by "intellectual integrity." While there is precious
little of it in the world now as always, there is probably
more of it than in most times. It is a virtue but it also
makes for critical-mindedness and sophistication. It takes
away the naiveté of life.

Knowledge of other religions besides one's own, with
consequent comparison and criticism leading to discernment
of faults in all, and possibly to dreaming of a religion better
than any, is a further cause of sophistication. It also makes
impossible the naive acceptance of any religion. It is likely
to make one feel that no religion is satisfactory and so cause
one to stand aloof from all.

Finally, the widespread discussion of religion is both
cause and effect of religious sophistication. The religious
discussion so rife today is not like that of other times, which
was the discussion of the objects of religious interest. A
healthy religion, like a healthy hungry man, is not interested
in its own digestive processes. It is interested in the objective reality. In case of religion this is God or salvation or
sin. Only the sick or the sophisticated talk about religion
rather than the objects of religious interest, and the digestive
process rather than the food which satisfies hunger. The discussion of religion today is of this sophisticated sort, and it
greatly magnifies the sophistication.

The sophisticated person can be genuinely religious in only one way, and that is to search out and test, and so be intellectually satisfied that he has to do with the reality that is supremely worthful for all human living. Only so can he give that wholehearted devotion which is religion. But to do this requires the implements of philosophy. If he is not equipped to use these implements, he may hold on halfheartedly or desperately to some form of religion, the while he practices unconsciously some crude uncriticized form of religion, or he may restlessly try one kind of "ism" after another without finding anything that satisfies. Only with the tools of philosophy can he achieve a vital, personal religion which can make life noble, zestful and intelligent. By the "tools of philosophy" we mean the tools of criticism.

OUR CULTURAL PROBLEMS

Our age has certain cultural problems that are peculiar to it and which distinguish it from other ages. An analysis of these problems will further reveal our need of philosophy of religion.

The first of these peculiar problems is a great increase in economic goods, but produced under the control of social customs which make it impossible for the great majority of people to have abundant access to them. Our storehouses are bursting with actual and potential wealth. By potential wealth we mean that even when the actual goods are not there, we have the power to produce them in great quantities. But while these economic goods are accumulating and wasting unused, millions of people who have helped to produce them are in dire need. While we suffer bitter want, the goods, actual and potential, pile ever higher; but we block one another when we try to get at them. We reach out after them while they rot and rust and waste away, but we live under such a code that each gets in the other man's way whenever he tries to get access to these rich supplies.

This is one of the most bizarre, one of the most unbelievable situations that has ever arisen in human history. It is so anomalous and so foolish that it cannot last long. Either we shall cease to produce in such quantity and lose the power to produce, or else we shall find some way of getting at these great stores of economic wealth and using them for the common good.

What prevents us from enjoying this great wealth we are able to produce is the system of loyalties and ideals under which we live. These might be briefly described as free competition, individualism, and domination of life by the profit motive. But any ruling system of loyalties and ideals constitutes a morality and a religion. Thus the cause of our economic depression, poverty and misery is not economic scarcity or inability to produce, or lack of mechanisms for distributing these great quantities of goods we can produce, but it is the intellectual and institutional structure of our dominant loyalties. These must be reconstructed before we can hope to gain access to the economic abundance that is rightfully ours. The mastering loyalties which make us act the way we do, stupidly frustrating one another when we try to get at the goods we have produced or can produce, must be changed.

Some may ridicule the thought that philosophy can reshape our loyalties in such a way that our powers can be released to distribute and enjoy the wealth that is ours. It is true that philosophy could not do this by itself alone. But mighty pent forces are storming and pressing to break through this tangle of frustrating ideals and habits. Hence philosophy does not have to do the work alone. It only needs to show how this tangle may be straightened out in certain respects and then the great urges of life will break through to develop a new way. It can set forth certain basic guiding principles which help to release us from the tangle of outgrown habits and ideals and give some sense of an outline of the new way of life that must be developed by the processes of actual living.

The second great cultural problem which distinguishes our time might be stated thus: Great increase in power of achievement but no cause sufficiently dominant to draw all this power into its service. When we speak of today's marvelous increase in human power, we think first of the machines that have been invented and are now being perfected. They are a large part of it, but not all. We also have the techniques of social control, the social mechanisms, the fact-finding devices, propaganda, methods of organizing individuals into corporate bodies, executive and administrative agencies, and so forth. We can mobilize vast masses of men, not only in war but also in other enterprises, and not only their bodies but also their minds, their inventiveness, and other resources of personality.

All this power we have, actual or potential, but we
do not know what to do with it. So we waste our time and
energy in a dizzy whirl of trivial matters. Or we throw ourselves into dissipation to escape the ennui, or we exploit and
destroy and yearn for great destructive conflicts like war in
order to give us a chance to use our power.

Here, again, the cause of the difficulty is that we have
outgrown our old loyalties. The great causes of life as they
are handed down to us from the past are not formulated in
such a way as to absorb our energies and awaken our supreme
devotion. Our machines, our social devices of achievement,
our methods of procedure, our mechanisms of power, simply
cannot gear into these causes because of the form in which
they come to us. These forms were suited to activities of
another age, not to ours.

We need to formulate the supreme objectives of life in
a new way, in a way suited to make use of our present powers of achievement and our uttermost loyalties. It is not so
much that we need new objectives in any ultimate sense, but
we need to see these supreme objectives in new perspectives
and with wider horizons and in relation to other activities.
We need to get at those underlying principles which reveal
the scope and diversity of these supreme causes.

The third peculiar cultural problem of our time is an
increase in the materials and opportunities for happiness without standards adequate to guide us in our choices and appreciations. The humblest today has access to the cultural achievements of the greatest. Shakespeare, Dante, Homer, and innumerable lesser works can be gotten in paperbound books
for ten cents. The greatest singers, speakers and thinkers
can be heard over the radio in the humblest home. Science
and its inventions are being put into popular journals so that
the high school boy can read and understand. Even history
of philosophy is being written in such a way that the common
man can get some sense of what it is all about.

Some may say that this popularization of truth, beauty
and goodness degrades them and leaves only the sham forms
of them, not the reality. The reply is that if anyone thinks
he has the insight and acumen and taste to appreciate the
highest and best, he can today, as never before, gain access
to the original works of the greatest in history and find them
more readily than ever.

However, it is true that all this abundance of culture
seems to be a hodgepodge heaped up round about us but which
no one is able to enjoy.   And the cause would seem to be
rather obvious.   One must have standards by which one is
reared from infancy in order to appreciate the cultural riches
of life.   Furthermore, great achievements of truth, beauty
and goodness can be fully such only in the context of some
great body of culture to which they are native.   A heteroge-
neous assemblage of such works cannot give abundant richness
to life.   They cannot be appreciatively assimilated in that
way.

Nevertheless, the fact still stands that we have the
materials and the opportunities, the leisure and the means,
for developing a richness of life such as was never before
possible.   What we lack, what modern civilization lacks, is
a set of standards fitted to its genius, by which to develop
capacity for appreciation, and ability to participate in the
creation of an organic unity of culture wherein each work and
act would help to illuminate and enhance the value of all others.   Such standards again call for that grasp of fundamental
principles which it is the work of philosophy to uncover.

Such work of philosophy is not so much needed in an
age in which a ripe tradition has gradually arisen which
guides the individual in his development from infancy so that
the interactions of society enlarge his capacity for appreciation and his powers of creative participation to the utmost of
his ability.   But our age has all the powers, materials, opportunities and means for the flowering of a magnificent culture, lacking only the standards.   When tradition does not
supply these, philosophy must serve as a midwife to help
bring them to birth.   Philosophy cannot create them, but it
can help to bring them to consciousness.

A fourth distinctive cultural problem of our time is a
great increase of interdependence but without integrating loyalties, habits and sentiments which would enable us to live
together cooperatively and in creative community.

Our interdependence is obvious.   No longer does a
man go to the well in his back yard to get a drink.   He gets
it out of a faucet, which means that in drinking he is caught
in bonds of interdependence with a vast network of finance,
industrial workers, experts, machines.   When he goes to
town, he no longer hitches the horse to the buggy and drives,
but he gets on a streetcar; and again he is enmeshed in

bonds of interdependence.   He gets his ideas from a newspaper which covers the planet with a network of news-gathering and idea-formulating activities.   His fears, hopes, likes and dislikes are likewise shaped by doings and sayings of others spread far and wide.   When the man in Corning, Kansas, sells his goods or services, the price is ruinously lowered or lucratively increased by what is happening in Russia, China, Japan and France.

But the ideals and habits which shape our conduct and our feelings are not fitted to such a close network of interdependence.   They are fitted to a much more loosely integrated system of living.   For example, the traditional ideal of national sovereignty was fitted to a time when the nations were relatively independent.   But they are no longer independent.   Hence the way of living which is shaped by this ideal causes hideous disasters in our modern world.   Or, again, the ideal of laissez faire, free competition and private initiative in making the most money you can for yourself, was an ideal which was fairly well fitted for pioneer conditions in which each man was loosely bound to the activities of others.   But in our modern world, with its compact and intricate connection of each with all, such an ideal and such living spread havoc.

We need to develop loyalties, sentiments, ideals, which will enable us to reap the rare and precious values which can come out of these close bonds of interdependence if we use them to unite our forces in co-operation and creative interaction.

A fifth problem of our time is the drift toward collectivism with the danger of diminishing seriously our personal freedom.   Collectivism is inevitable in our modern world and is all to the good, providing it does not destroy personal freedom.   By "personal freedom" we here mean that the stimulus and the opportunity to exercise individual initiative, to think for one's self, to experiment, criticize, invent, not necessarily machines but ways and devices for living.   There can be no high culture without such freedom. There can be no richness of life unless each can develop his own unique individuality, think the thoughts, make the criticisms, and perform the acts that no one else but he could bring forth.   But such freedom and uniqueness of individuality will destroy culture, especially in our modern world, with its delicate and intricate interdependence, unless each individual so functions as to stimulate the individuality of

others and contribute the expression of his own individuality
to the enrichment of the life of all. The life of all can be
variegated and full only when it is constantly enriched by con-
tributions of highly developed and unique individualities.

The danger is not in collectivism understood in the
sense just described, but it is in that kind of collectivism
which imposes uniformity, which regiments and suppresses
freedom and uniqueness of thinking, acting and appreciating.

Since the end of the Middle Ages there has been a
struggle, and a winning struggle, to achieve personal freedom and development of the individuality of persons and
groups. But in recent years there has been a turning back
toward the establishment of control, order, system, regimentation. We see it in Russia, in Germany, in Italy, in the
United States, even in England and France, as well as in
other countries. We see it not only in business and industry
and politics. In art, also, there is a turn toward classicism
and systematizing. We have the drama of O'Neill and the
novels of Romain Rolland setting forth philosophies of life.
In science there is a turning away from the theory and practice that science consisted chiefly in the use of specialized
techniques and the accumulation of facts, toward the opposite
view and practice that science strives to discover or achieve
a rational order in the universe. Philosophy also is return-
ing to rearing of cosmologies and world-enfolding systems.

This turn of history is inevitable. It is forced upon
us. Civilization, with its delicate balance and finespun interdependence, could not survive if the old individualism were
allowed to run rampant. Therefore it is being suppressed
and will be more and more, ruthlessly if need be, in order
that our whole civilization may not perish. But must we suffer also the decline of liberalism? Must we suffer the loss
of that freedom to think, to criticize, to experiment, which
is essential to every vital culture? Yes, we must, unless
one great need is supplied.

When interdependence increases more rapidly than the
cohesive tissue of society, conflict, destruction and collapse
are inevitable unless coercive control and regimentation are
supplied sufficiently to make up for the lack of cohesive tissue. By cohesive tissue we mean those integrating loyalties,
affections, sentiments and habits which keep people working
in harmony and creative community. There can be spontaneity, originality, freedom and liberalism in a closely woven

system of interdependence only if this cohesive tissue has
been developed sufficiently to keep the creative activities
harmonious and co-operative. If not, then regimentation
must be imposed.

Perhaps this is the most serious problem we face at
this turning-point in history when the old individualism is being driven out by necessity. Can a new individualism be developed, an individualism in which the needed harmony and
community is sustained by integrating loyalties and sentiments so that there need be no permanent suppression of individuality by regimentation?

At present we do not have this cohesive tissue.
Therefore regimentation is necessary. But need it be permanent? May we not develop cohesive tissue, integrating
loyalties, and unifying sentiments, sufficient to hold us into
a co-operative and mutually sustaining community without the
need of regimentation with its suppression of individual criticism and creativity? Certainly philosophy cannot do it.
Nothing can do it except a great religion adequate to our
time. Philosophy is a necessary guide and help in the growth
of such a religion.

When we speak of the need of philosophy of religion,
we do not mean the work of professionals who make philosophy of religion their chief business. We need such men, of
course--more of them than ever before. But that is not the
primary need. The primary need is for a widespread interest among great numbers of people in this problem of finding
what is essential and fundamental in the passing forms of religion and holding fast to that when new forms are developing. Great numbers of people must become inquirers in religion and not merely passive believers.

In this sense philosophy of religion must become a
great co-operative enterprise engaging the thought of thousands of people who make no pretense at being professional
philosophers. If philosophy is to assist in the development
of the religion we sorely need, a great many people must
take some creative part in this endeavor to grasp the basic
reality which must be found anew in the development of any
great religion. We believe such widespread interest and endeavor is occurring today.

Whatever one may think of the ideas of C. G. Jung--
and certainly many of them are seriously questionable--his

vocation and contacts put him in a strategic position for discerning the modern temper and religious needs of the modern man. We quote him:

> During the past thirty years, people from all the civilized countries of the earth have consulted me. I have treated many hundreds of patients, the larger number being Protestants, a smaller number Jews, and not more than five or six believing Catholics. Among all my patients in the second half of life--that is to say, over thirty-five--there has not been one whose problem in the last resort was not that of finding a religious outlook on life. It is safe to say that every one of them fell ill because he had lost that which the living religions of every age have given to their followers, and none of them has been really healed who did not regain his religious outlook.... It seems that side by side with the decline of religious life, the neuroses grow noticeably more frequent... everywhere the mental state of European man shows an alarming lack of balance. We are living undeniably in a period of the greatest restlessness, nervous tension, confusion and disorientation of outlook.... Every one of them has the feeling that our religious truths have somehow or other grown empty. [C. G. Jung, Modern Man in Search of a Soul, pp. 264, 266, 268.]

These facts would seem to make plain that we must have a religion adequate to our time, else we cannot go on. No philosophy can be a substitute for such a religion. Neither can philosophy construct such a religion. But philosophy of religion is an indispensable aid in bringing such a religion to birth and to maturity.

COMMITMENT FOR THEOLOGICAL INQUIRY*

Worship is the practice of commitment. But commitment to what? Everything depends on the right answer to that question. It is not answered by uttering the word "God." The theologies of our time attach the most diverse interpretations to the name of deity. For Edward Carnell, God is a supernatural person. For Brightman and Bertocci, God is a cosmic person. For Tillich, God is being itself, having no distinguishable character whatsoever. For Billy Graham, God is something else again. These are only a few of the many meanings attached to this word. Therefore to say that worship is commitment to God without further explanation is to conceal the problem. Not only does it conceal, it is pernicious because, when the problem is concealed, each person worships whatever kind of being he chooses to call God. This is vicious when it is not silly.

This wild diversity in what people call God would be much more dangerous than it is if most cases of worship were genuine. Fortunately, perhaps, considering this diversity, most cases of worship are not genuine. Genuine worship is commitment of the total self to the kind of being one worships. When the kind of being worshiped is the source of evil, mistakenly thought to be the source of good, commitment to the source of evil produces the monsters of iniquity.

If this diversity should continue in what is worshiped and if worship should be genuine and effective, our lives would be torn apart with conflicting faiths. If genuine worship should cease, life would lose its zest and power. To escape these disasters, theological inquiry must show the way. This will require a commitment of faith, removing barriers to inquiry and driving to deeper levels of search.

Worship of the sort here under consideration is the way a man disciplines, organizes, and channels his total being, so far as possible, into the service and into the keeping

*Reprinted from Journal of Religion, Vol. XLII (July, 1962) No. 3, pp. 171-184.

of what he believes makes for the greatest good for all mankind throughout the course of history. It is the way one
brings into action the resources of the conscious, the unconscious, and the preconscious levels of existence. This requires the daily, constant practice of some ritual of commitment. Even when this ritual lapses into a dead form, it is
still effective if done sincerely and intelligently because the
unconscious levels of the total self are being organized and
directed; and these unconscious levels brought into action
yield maximum power.

Yet the human mind in worship, as elsewhere, is highly fallible, and it is never more fallible than when it arro-
gates itself the high honor of being chosen of God to receive
divine revelation and divine grace. This fallibility, combined
with this arrogance, renders worship one of the major
sources of evil in the world. Of course, when worship is
merely a social convention or a soothing pacifier or an aesthetic indulgence, it is relatively harmless. But that is not
what is here discussed under the head of worship. Worship
as here understood determines the good and evil of human
life more than anything else when it is the practice of an ultimate commitment channeling the resources of a lifetime into one supreme devotion. This need not reduce life to a narrow focus; it can be broadening beyond anything else if it is
directed to what widens the compass of human concern. But
worship does, whether for good or evil, depend on what is
worshiped.

Worship rightly conducted renders us open to what
creates and recreates, saves and transforms, from the evil
to the good. But what does all that? What distinguishes the
good from the evil ultimately, absolutely, universally? Nothing less than ultimate good can rightly command the commitment of faith by way of worship.

Worship becomes passionate and powerful, either for
good or evil, when people think they know, or think they can
discover by way of worship, what distinguishes the good from
the evil to the uttermost limit and for all men everywhere.
Yet it is quite possible to commit one's self in worship in
such a way as to lead to the torturing and killing of thousands
of helpless individuals because they are witches and the Bible
says, "Suffer not a witch to live." Worshiping parents have
been known to rear their children to fear the Lord, the Lord
being incarnate in the parents themselves, with the consequence that the children become rebels or criminals or

crushed nonentities.   Heretics have been tortured by the
zeal engendered by worship.   Worship is a dangerous practice when it brings the whole self into action.   But bringing
the whole self into action is exactly what worship should do.

The individual tends to think that his own makes him
a better man; but his worship may be blinding him to the
greater good and driving him to the greater evil.   Using the
words "Jesus Christ" and saying that it is "God in Christ"
that we worship provides no certainty that our worship is
rightly directed.   These words are religious symbols, to be
sure, but where they lead must be determined by some understanding of what they designate.   For this reason religious symbols which convey no descriptive knowledge are
dangerous.

Worship involves an inescapable problem, and the
greatest evil is to conceal this problem by covering it over
with traditional Christian doctrines and words as though
Christianity itself was identical with God.   To identify Christianity with God is idolatry with all the evil consequences of
misdirected worship.

Since worship is such a hazardous undertaking when
serious, and a waste of time when not serious, many in our
society have decided, either deliberately or by default, not
to worship.   But this does not solve the problem.   He who
does not worship suffers a fate as serious as one who mis-
directs his worship.   Let us keep in mind that we are using
the word "worship" to refer to commitment of the whole self
at all levels--conscious, preconscious, and unconscious--to
what one believes is the source of greatest good for all men.
In this sense one may practice worship without giving it the
name of worship.   The name is not important; the practice
is of utmost importance in determining the conduct of human
life and the course of human history.   Worship may not be
public--it may be entirely private.   Indeed it must be private as well as public if it is to be most effective.   It must
be private as well as public because worship is commitment
of the total self, and this total self can never be made public in all the depth and fulness of its being.

Let us now look at the fate of him who does not worship.   Modern life is diversified, disorganized, and preoccupied with trivialities.   Consequently, one is pushed about in
all directions unless there is an undercurrent of commitment in his life that brings the deeper drives of personality

into action continuously. To keep this undercurrent strong
and continuous, the daily practice of commitment is required
whether done consciously or unconsciously. Individuals who
do not practice this kind of commitment are herded and driv-
en this way and that without knowing what is done to them.
They are helplessly subject to the driving power of those who
do have a ruling commitment. They are herded like sheep
by any one who comes along with a faith strong enough to
bring the total self into action and hold it steadfast to a way
of life that resists the passing fads and countercurrents and
is able to drive on through ignominy, contempt, and defeat.
In this respect the story of Hitler and the effect he had upon
the German nation is instructive. If Hitler's worship had
been rightly directed, the world today would be ringing with
praise of him. If he had been victorious, perhaps the world
would be ringing with praise of him anyway.

Such are the fateful consequences of worship, on the
one hand, and of not worshiping, on the other. They who do
not commit themselves fully to anything--they have lost control of their lives. Their existence becomes trivial and
petty. They float on the surface of life, driven by transitory
movements. History has no meaning for them. By commitment to what one believes ultimately distinguishes the good
from the evil; one identifies himself with something that runs
continuously through history. In this way the brief span of
his little life is merged with an undercurrent that gives a
purpose to the whole of human existence from its first beginning to its end, so he believes. This meaning of history may
be an illusion; but worship, of the kind here under consideration, endows history with meaning, whether illusory or not.
Without commitment of this sort, history can have no meaning for the individual. History takes on meaning for a whole
people when they worship what they together believe is the ultimate determiner of the good of life.

Here are the issues at stake. Either we worship or
we do not, understanding that one may worship without doing
it self-consciously and without calling it worship. If we do
not worship, we become the helpless victims of those who
do. If we do worship, either we worship what does in truth
create the greatest good, or we do not. If we do not, we
bring upon ourselves and upon others the great evil of misdirected worship; and no evil can be greater because the ultimate commitment of worship brings all the powers and resources of human life into action.

This is the theological problem of worship. To ignore it by assuming that it has been finally and securely solved by accepting the Christian tradition is to be irresponsible to the point of folly in dealing with the most fateful issue at stake in human existence. To push the problem beyond the reach of rational inquiry and all empirical evidence by saying that the ultimate determiner of human good is beyond history, or otherwise inaccessible to all the natural powers of the human mind, is to close the door against all responsible thinking on the problem.

With regard to this problem there is another kind of irresponsibility that is widely prevalent in our society today. It assumes the form of denying that there is any distinction between good and evil that is absolute, ultimate, and universal. It is very common for people today to say that good and evil are relative--meaning relative to the time and place, relative to the individual and the culture, relative to the period of history and to the unique situation. Such being the case, so these people say, to talk about an absolute and universal source of good is to talk nonsense. If these people are correct in what they say about the relativity of all values, there can be no ultimate commitment and consequently no worship of the sort here defended.

I shall show a little later that the ultimate distinction between good and evil is not relative to time and place and person, or to the standards of the prevailing culture, or to a limited period of history. The ultimate distinction between good and evil underlies all life and all consciousness, all culture, and all history, and in that sense it is universal and absolute. But first of all we must grant the element of truth in what is said about the relativity of values.

Human judgment about good and evil is relative to time and place, person, and culture. Not only is it relative, it is often perverse. It is distorted by jealousy and envy and by fear and hate. Therefore, when people set up an absolute standard for judging good and evil, it is likely to be a device enabling them to reject criticism and correction and build up an arrogant feeling of righteousness over people who differ from them. Christian people have been as much addicted to this as any others, even when they profess to surpass all others with the transcendent virtue of humility.

Here we have the two horns of a dilemma. On the one hand is the relativity of all judgments of value, making nonsense of any ultimate commitment. On the other hand are the consequences of not practicing an ultimate commitment by bringing all resources of the individual and of the culture into action. The consequences are that without such a commitment we become helpless before the overwhelming thrust of power exercised by those who are fully devoted to what they believe creates, sustains, and transforms toward the greatest good.

Is there a way of escape between the horns of this dilemma? There is, but before pointing to it, let us see clearly the difficulty. We cannot escape the fallibility and perversity of the human mind. They who claim to escape these human limitations by way of the Bible, or by way of the revelation of God in Jesus Christ, or by way of divine grace, or by way of the church, or by way of transcendence, or by way of religious symbolism uninterpreted by logical and descriptive knowledge are deceivers. They deceive themselves, and they deceive others. We must honestly acknowledge the fallibility and perversity of the human mind in all matters of religious faith. Its arrogance and presumption in the practice of worship must be recognized. The horrors of history resulting in part from the Christian religion as practiced by Mr. Jones and by Mr. Smith and by me must not be concealed. The devout Christian can see that non-Christian forms of worship are addicted to these evils; he is likely to conceal the wickedness issuing from his own worship by protesting his humility and his faithfulness to the Christian tradition.

These are the dangers and evils of worship standing over against the dangers and evils equally great if we do not worship. Worship can be saved from perversion, and its dangers and evils can be brought under control if three conditions are met. By meeting these three conditions we can commit ourselves ultimately and fully and yet hold ourselves subject to correction and receptive to ever deeper insights that may help to save us from the misdirected devotion of a lifetime. A self ultimately committed and yet subject to correction may sound like a contradiction of terms. And so it is unless the three conditions are met. These three conditions which are required to save worship from perversion will be examined in sequence.

The first of these three required conditions is not in itself sufficient. Indeed, taken by itself alone, it can only aggravate the dangers and evils of worship. But it is one

necessary condition when taken in conjunction with the other
two. It is the requirement that worshipful commitment be
directed to what is accessible to empirical inquiry. What is
accessible to empirical inquiry may be transcendent in several of the meanings of "transcendence." But it cannot be
beyond the reach of what we are able to know by observing
the consequences of our worship. If it is beyond the reach
of any judgment we can make concerning the good and evil
of it, then we shall continue to perpetrate the evils of our
commitment on the ground that what we worship cannot be
judged by any human standard of good and evil. God must
judge us, so it is said; we cannot judge God. The deceptive
trick in that claim is that we put beyond the reach of all
criticism what we judge to be God with all the arrogance and
perversity of our human minds.

On the other hand, it is true that we cannot judge the
good and evil of our worship by observing its consequences
in our behavior unless we already have the ultimate standard
for distinguishing good and evil. This is a vicious circle
from which we cannot escape merely by appealing to empirical evidence. On this account, as was stated in the previous
paragraph, this first required condition is not in itself sufficient. But whatever the ultimate distinction may be between
good and evil, it must be operative and knowable here and
now in our lives if worship is to be saved from perversion.

The grotesque error is prevalent that observation is
limited to sense experience. Of course sense experience enters into observation. But the sense experience is interpreted in context, and this context may involve all the resources of a great tradition. This is true of all scientific
observation. It is also true of all worshipful observation.
When one engages in worship, he observes the ceremony by
sense experience, but the sense experience is given meaning
by the way the individual interprets it. All observation involves sense experience, but it is sense experience combined
with some interpretation. This interpretation may bring into
action the resources gathered by a lifetime devoted to absorbing thousands of years of culture combined with emerging
insights rising out of profound struggles to find the way of
life for humankind. All profound and evaluative observation
of consequences operates in this way. This is what is meant
by empirical inquiry concerning what distinguishes the good
from the evil in human life.

A second condition must be met if worship is to com-

bine ultimate commitment with a mind open to correction and
continuous inquiry. The commitment must be to what creates in me appreciative understanding of the basic values motivating the lives of other people with whom I deal. A kind
of interchange between individuals and peoples does this,
more or less, when required conditions are present. In this
way my own judgment of good and evil is widened, deepened,
and corrected. Consequently, when ultimate commitment is
given to this creative kind of interchange, my mind is open
to new insights, to learning, to correction, and to inquiry
concerning what is ultimately good and evil.

        Ultimate commitment to this kind of interchange, cre-
ating communion between each other to the measure that conditions permit, does not mean that one can have this communion when he seeks it except in some very special relations and situations. Indeed, it should not be sought directly. When it occurs, it will always be spontaneous. But
commitment to this kind of interchange means that one will
always seek to provide those conditions that are most favorable for this relation between individuals and peoples. These
conditions are not only those prevailing in the immediate situation of interpersonal relations. The prevailing conditions
of the entire culture are involved. In some cultures this
kind of interchange may be reduced to a minimum, no matter
how one strives to provide the required conditions. The social situation may produce a state of mind or personal attitude in individuals which reduces the capacity and willingness
to give any consideration to the basic values motivating the
other person or the other people. But commitment to creative interchange means always to strive to correct the conditions inimical to it. It means to work to change political,
economic, educational, international, interracial, and interpersonal conditions in a way to make them more favorable
for this communion between individuals, groups, cultures, and
peoples.

        Creative interchange creates appreciative understand-
ing of the diverse perspectives of individuals and peoples. It
also integrates these perspectives in each individual participant. Thus commitment to creative interchange is not commitment to any given system of values. It is commitment to
what creates ever deeper insight into the values that motivate
human lives. It creates an ever more comprehensive integration of these values so far as this is possible by transforming them in such a way that they can be mutually enhancing
instead of mutually impoverishing and obstructive. This com-

mitment is not to any one perspective on self and the cosmic
whole of things but to an ever more comprehensive and penetrating perspective gained by integrating many perspectives.
This kind of commitment is not to what is objective merely,
or to what is subjective only, but to what unites the subjective and objective by interchange and communion between the
two.   In sum, this kind of commitment keeps the mind open
to new insights concerning the ultimate determinants of good
and evil.

The kind of interchange between individuals and peoples
calling for this kind of commitment with these consequences
is here given the name of creative interchange to distinguish
it from many other kinds that are opposed to it.   It is that
kind of interchange, perhaps better called that kind of communion, that does two things.   First, it creates appreciative
understanding of the perspective of the other person or other
people.   By perspective is meant the way the other person
sees things, feels things, values things--in a word, what life
means to him.   This understanding of the other may be very
imperfect and very limited, and it may be mistaken.   But it
can be more or less correct, profound, and comprehensive.
If this apprehension of the perspective of the other person,
and its integration with my own, did not occur with a high
degree of correctness, no infant could ever acquire the culture into which he is born because this is precisely the way
every individual comes to embody the culture which history
bestows upon him.

This internal integration within each individual which
occurs in creative interchange is essential to the creativity
of it.   Yet this creativity is always in danger of being concealed by the word "interchange."   Interchange provides the
diverse perspectives, but they must be integrated in the personality of the individual if there is to be any creative transformation of his own perspective.   When this integration occurs, it expands the range of what the individual can appreciate as good and distinguish as evil.   This expansion may
continue indefinitely, widening and deepening the sense of values involved in human existence.

This integration of perspectives does not mean, necessarily, that I agree with the other person, although agreement may be attained.   It does mean that I comprehend his
way of valuing, even when I judge to be evil what he calls
good and judge to be good what he calls evil.   This creative
communion with the other party, when in opposition to him,

yields a greater good than agreement. It is the good of
learning from the enemy. It is the good of being corrected
by conflict and deepening my sense of good and evil by comprehending the values of my opponent. In the Christian tradition this is called "loving your enemies." It saves man
from the self-destructive propensity arising out of arrogance,
tyranny, and being unteachable.

This creative communion between individuals and
people, when lifted to a high level of dominance with saving
and transfiguring power, is the revelation of God in Jesus
Christ. Was not the revelation of God the saving and transforming power of the kind of interchange that occurred between Jesus and his disciples? The power lay not in the
man Jesus nor in any of the individuals themselves but in the
kind of interchange that they transmitted from person to person and group to group and age to age. This kind of interchange is sometimes called love, but the prevailing idea of
love is hopelessly inadequate to comprehend the depth and
power of it. The power of God unto salvation is the most
fitting name for it.

This revelation of the saving power of God in the form
of creative interchange has been called the "Word" with a
capital "W." In the beginning was the Word, and the Word
was with God, and the Word was God. It is not called the
Word because written in a book. It is called the Word because it created the human level of existence in the beginning and continues to operate in our midst with saving and
transforming power when required conditions are present.
It is personified because it cannot occur except between persons and in persons. In him (in the Word) was life, and the
life was the light of men. The light shines in the darkness,
and the darkness does not overcome it.

Since this kind of interchange is obstructed and beaten
down by much else going on in human life, "the light shines
in the darkness, and the darkness does not overcome it."
It reaches us in "preaching" when preaching means not pro-
nouncing propositions from a pulpit but creative interchange
in the garage and in the kitchen and sometimes, perhaps, between a man in the pulpit and people sitting in pews. But to
think that it is limited to pulpit and pew is absurd.

The living Word is operating here in our midst, not
beyond history but in history, ready to rise up with saving
and transfiguring power when required conditions are met.

Creative interchange creates the human level of existence, beginning with the newborn infant, if by human level
we understand that level where the individual can expand indefinitely the range and depth of what is appreciated as good
and distinguished as evil. This capacity to expand indefinitely the range of good appreciated and evils distinguished.
Creative interchange created Adam by creating language.
Adam is the language-using animal; and language is that system of signs and symbols capable of meanings that can be
expanded indefinitely in range and depth of different individuals adding some increment of meaning as the meaning is communicated from person to person, from group to group and
from age to age down through history. Thus is language
created, and with it the level of existence is distinguished
by this indefinite expansion in the range of meanings comprehended, contemplated, and used by individuals.

Creative interchange creates the universe when "universe" means what we are able to know and call the universe.
This is so because what we call the universe is the most inclusive perspective created at any one time in the mind of
man by the integration of many diverse perspectives into one
most inclusive perspective. Thus the universe of primitive
man becomes the universe of ancient Egypt. The universe
of ancient Egypt becomes the universe of Aristotle. The universe of Aristotle becomes the universe of Sir Isaac Newton;
the universe of Newton becomes the universe of Einstein.
The universe after Einstein will in time include all that can
be discovered by traveling through space to explore other
planets and by penetrating into the mysteries of the galactic
system by more powerful telescopes and mathematical com-
putations. If we have another world war, the universe known
to man may collapse again into that of primitive man. In
all these cases, however, the universe as known to man is
created by that kind of interchange that creates appreciative
understanding of one another and the integration of our diverse perspectives into a more comprehensive perspective.

If God is understood to be the creator of the universe
known to man, then creative interchange is God.

This kind of interchange creates culture because culture is created by the progressive integration of many diverse individual perspectives into a perspective more or less
common to many people.

This kind of interchange creates history when history

means the transmission of the consequences of past events to the present in such a way as to make us what we are today.

Creative interchange meets the deepest need of each individual because the deepest need of each is to be appreciated and understood for what he truly is and not to be compelled to put on a false front and pretend to be something other than he is in order to win acceptance from others. For the same reason, creative interchange, when sufficiently dominant, saves man from neurosis and psychosis, from crime and delinquency, and from other self-destructive propensities to which he is addicted.

To be sure, creative interchange cannot do all these good things unless required conditions are present so that it is not unduly suppressed and obstructed and its created values misused by all the many opposing interests in human life that run counter to the demands of this divine creativity.

Much more might be said about this divine creativity operating in human life in the form of creative communion. But we must now go on to the third condition that must be met if ultimate commitment of faith is to be combined with a mind open to new insights and continuously inquiring. So far two of these required conditions have been indicated. One is that the commitment be to something that is accessible to empirical inquiry because only in such case can our commitment be corrected by what we experience. The second required condition is that our commitment be to what creates in us the most profound appreciative understanding and integration of the values motivating the lives of others. This is required because only in this way can we learn about good and evil more profoundly and more comprehensively.

Now we come to the third condition required for an ultimate commitment combining the most complete self-giving with a mind open to inquiry and subject to correction.

This third condition is to practice commitment of faith at two levels. These two levels can best be expressed in the form of the prayer by which the individual commits himself in this manner. The prayer might be expressed in words something like the following.

If what I serve with all my life be not the ultimate source of greatest good, may my misdirected efforts come to nothing in such a way as to expose my error and suggest the truth. I offer my life to what does in truth make for the greatest good even though it should be different from what I think it is. If my commitment is mistaken, I give my life and all its work to be destroyed that the good which I have failed to recognize may prevail.

This kind of commitment is not based on uncertainty. It rests upon indubitable certainty precisely because it does not depend on any human judgment concerning what is good and what is evil. The certainty on which it rests is that there is a distinction between good and evil, no matter how mistaken any man's judgment may be concerning what is good and what is evil. One may profess to doubt that there is any such distinction, but his behavior makes plain that there is. The biological organism chooses this and rejects that, even when the mind refuses to choose. The organism may choose wrongly (however you define the wrong); but if the choice is wrong, then there was a right choice that should have been made. If one denies the distinction and on that account lapses into inertia, he has chosen one alternative and it is either better or worse than the opposite choice would have been. Thus one cannot escape the distinction between better and worse and good and evil. They who reject the whole enterprise of human living in despair over what is good and evil have thereby made a choice that is better or worse than its alternative. If one says that the whole of human existence should be wiped off the planet because of its monstrous evil, as Robinson Jeffers declares in his poetry, he is asserting passionately and profoundly that the distinction between good and evil is ontologically prior to human existence.[1] He may be mistaken in the _way_ he distinguishes good and evil, but he has no doubt about the being of this distinction. So it is with every despairing pessimist. The pessimists may be more profoundly aware of a glorious good that has been missed in human life than are the optimists.

The ultimate determiner of good and evil may not be known, whether it is one or many, temporal or eternal, weak or strong. These and like questions are open. But

---

[1] "Ontologically prior to human existence" does not mean that the striving to distinguish better and worse is cosmic. Neither does it mean that it issues from being itself. It only means that the striving is prior to the human level, creates the human level, and will bring human life to the best that man can ever attain.

the distinction between good and evil is beyond question, no
matter how mistaken one may be in his judgments of what is
good and what is evil. If one can be mistaken, there is a
truth that he has missed. This is the certainty sustaining
the two-level commitment, giving it a foundation at the deeper level more secure than any other.

In making the ultimate commitment of faith with this
certainty, one must choose between the ontology of power and
the ontology of good and evil. If one chooses the ontology of
good and evil, he cannot claim that God by definition is almighty. Neither can he claim that God by definition is the
source of all that happens. If one insists that God by definition must be almighty and the source of all that happens, a
question is in order. It is this: "Are you committed to the
good or to the evil?" If the objector answers, "To the good,"
then I ask: "Is the good by definition what inevitably wins in
the end?" If he says "Yes," then he is saying that might
makes right. If he does not say "Yes," he cannot be absolutely sure that the good will win. Also, since there is no
complete harmony and no complete consistency in all that happens, there is no evidence to support the claim that all hap-
penings originate ultimately in what is absolutely good.

In the two-level commitment one is committed to the
good, win or lose. Furthermore, the good stands absolute,
independent of our beliefs and choices even though our choices
are the evidence that there is a distinction to be made between the good and evil. As said repeatedly, what I believe
about the good and evil may be mistaken. But the distinction
is there, and the right choice stands in opposition to every
choice I ever make, supposing that every choice I ever make
has fallen short of being absolutely and precisely the best
choice that would have been made if I had been omniscient
and free of all evil inclination. Obviously, I am not omniscient and not free of all evil inclination.

Since what determines good and evil ultimately stands
independent of our beliefs and choices and beyond our control
and since it does determine in absolute rightness the good and
evil of human existence, the proper name for it is God, no
matter how different it may be from all the traditional and
conventional ideas about God. In the two-level commitment
the word "God" has two meanings, but these two are joined
inseparably. At one level the divine name stands for what I
believe operates in human life to transform and save from
evil. At the ultimate level the divine name stands for what

does in truth transform from the evil to the good, no matter how different this transforming agency may be from what I think it is.

In the two-level commitment we of the West will begin with the beliefs of the Christian religion because that is our inheritance; and we might end with these beliefs after having searched to the uttermost depths of meaning they can carry. But one who practices the two-level commitment will recognize that his understanding of the Christian tradition may be in error and so may the understanding of every other man. No tradition transmitted for centuries through human minds and by a Book subject to diverse interpretations can be free of error. Everything asserted in the Christian religion might be in error. Of course no Christian believes that and should not be required to believe it. But he of the two-level commitment will admit the possibility of it in order to ground his commitment on the bedrock of certainty beyond all question. He will never pray: "I believe, help thou my unbelief." This he will not do because of the dishonesty involved in clinging to a belief when evidence does not seem to uphold it.

The Christian religion can be questioned, but the distinction between good and evil cannot be. Therefore the man of the two-level commitment reaches down to this fundamental that cannot be shaken. This ultimate determiner of good and evil commands his life's devotion. The way he reaches after it takes the form of the Christian religion if he inherits the Christian tradition. If he inherits some other tradition, he will practice this commitment by adopting the forms of that faith. But with the two-level commitment the Christian, the Buddhist, the Muslim, the Hindu, or any other, reaches beyond his beliefs to whatever the ultimate truth may be concerning what is good and what is evil for the human level of existence. If the ultimate truth should be that human existence has abandoned beyond recall the possible good it might have attained and has become so hopelessly evil that the greatest good demands its annihilation, without so much as Noah's ark remaining to perpetuate the race, then so it is. Few of us believe that. It is only mentioned to show in still another way that the distinction between good and evil is ontologically prior to human existence.

In any case, one who practices the two-level commitment, whether in the form of Christianity or in the form of any other faith, will commit himself with all resources of

thought and action to providing the conditions most favorable
for the kind of interchange that creates appreciative understanding of one another and the integration of diverse perspectives gained from one another. This he will do because
this is the only way to learn about good and evil at its deeper levels and farther reaches.

With this understanding of the two-level commitment,
one level is the Christianity which I practice; the deeper level is the true religion opposed to Christianity, if there be
such. The duality is between Jesus Christ, if Christ is not
the revelation of God, and what is in truth the creative source
of greatest good. It was stated above that creative interchange in the fellowship of Jesus was the revelation of God
because in that fellowship creative interchange rose to dominance over the counterprocesses and interests thronging human
existence. But this belief of mine about Jesus Christ might
be mistaken. If you are wiser than I, your belief about Jesus Christ may not be so liable to error, but since even your
mind is not infallible, you might also be mistaken. But if
one practices the two-level commitment, this liability to error does not weaken the power of his commitment and the
wholeness of his self-giving. I can give myself wholly, without reservation, to the power of God unto salvation as found
in Jesus Christ because the ultimate level of my commitment
enables me to admit the fallibility of my judgments.

In this way one brings his total self into action without
reservation, as Jesus did when he said, "Not my will but
thine be done." With this kind of commitment one recognizes
the possibility that he may be fighting the very thing he wants
to serve, namely, what promotes the greatest good. But he
accepts that possibility freely and fully to the last consequence,
even though it should lead him at last to cry, "My God, my
God, why hast thou forsaken me!" This enables one to give
himself completely. He may live tragically but he lives fully,
passionately, free of that life in death that never finds anything to live for wholly. He makes the plunge where one must
either sink or swim, fully aware that he may sink without a
bubble left to show what he tried to do throughout the years
of his life.

While this commitment enables one to go all out for
what he seeks to serve, it does not lead to fanaticism for two
reasons. It is always open to correction, and it is committed to seeking above all else the fullest appreciative understanding of other persons and other ways of life even when

they must be fought as evil by his best standards of judgment. As said before, this is called loving the enemy.

In this commitment a man does not commit himself to his beliefs. His beliefs are the intellectual tools by which he reaches after the actuality operating in human life to create the greatest good. Every actuality is more than, and may be very different from, what the belief about it affirms. At the ultimate level of commitment one commits himself to the actuality, holding his beliefs about it subject to correction because he knows that his knowledge falls short of omniscience.

It is sometimes said that religious belief is existential, involving the individual in the depth and wholeness of his being, and because of this, so it is said, one cannot deal objectively with the problem of truth and error in religious belief. This may be true for those who do not practice the two-level commitment. It is not true for those who do. With the commitment here described the ultimate reach of faith is secure because it does not depend upon the truth of the beliefs by which it is directed. Consequently, one can examine his religious beliefs critically, test them rigorously, and change them to meet the demands of the evidence. When he casts off his old beliefs, the steadfast pull of faith holds firm because it is anchored in <u>whatever actuality</u> makes for the greater good, no matter how different it may be from his beliefs about it. When his beliefs are found to be in error, he can wait in a state of non-belief until some new insight emerges out of which to form a belief he never had before and use it to reach after whatever actuality makes for the greater good. Meanwhile, the drive of his devotion does not falter during the time of no belief. In such a time of waiting, theological inquiry may attain its deepest insight.

Thus faith equipped with a two-level commitment reaches beyond all traditional religious beliefs toward an actuality that operates with a concrete fulness of being that no belief can comprehend. This it can do because, when thus equipped, it recognizes the difference between belief <u>about</u> the actuality making for greater good and what that actuality is in the wholeness of its being.

CONCLUSION

The distinction between better and worse is made by

the physiological organism before consciousness arises.   The distinction made by the organism may not be correctly made, in whatsoever sense correctness may be defined; but they are there prior to consciousness.   Consciousness is created by the striving of the organism to distinguish between better and worse.   This striving develops a focus of attention and thereby creates consciousness.   The organism itself, long before consciousness arises, is able to keep alive only because it chooses one alternative as better than some other.   Thus life itself is created and sustained by making the distinction between better and worse.   If one says that it might have been better if life had never arisen, then he is saying that the distinction between better and worse is ontologically prior to life itself.   Thereby he admits the point here defended.

Distinguishing between better and worse is what creates life and consciousness.   Distinguishing between better and worse is what develops the intellectual life, develops culture, and directs the movements of human history.   All these are developed and sustained moment by moment by choosing alternatives as better and worse.   This is true even when and if the choices are mistaken in the sense of missing the greater good.

This is the bedrock of certainty underlying the ultimate commitment here described.   In this commitment the whole self with the whole tradition of its heritage is given over to be transformed by deeper insights into the sources of good and evil.   The whole Christian tradition is thrown into this commitment to be corrected and transformed, insofar as this tradition is embodied in one's own person and insofar as this embodiment of the tradition falls short of the whole truth about what is good and what is evil.   All is held quick and open and ready for deeper insights.   One is able to hold his religious beliefs subject to question and correction because of an ultimate certainty reaching deeper than these beliefs.   That does not mean that one doubts the beliefs of his tradition.   It only means that he is saved from the blindness, self-deception, and basic dishonesty resulting when one clings to a belief beyond the evidence merely because the whole worth of life seems to depend upon it.   With the two-level commitment one is delivered from this predicament. There is a deeper level where one can find renewal and the courage to live.

With the two-level commitment one can face failure and defeat, death and guilt, rejection and shame, in a word, the "extreme situations," to use the expression of Karl Jaspers. If these come his way he finds in the midst of them an upsurge of life that sustains him beyond belief and beyond his mistaken judgments. He may cry, "My God, my God, why hast thou forsaken me!" But he will also add, "Into thy hands I commend my spirit."

I claim no other kind of inquiry is so likely to go as far in approximating the final truth. It brings into action the total self with all its resources to apprehend the way that man must go to find the greatest good and to be saved from the deadly evils.

EMPIRICISM IN RELIGIOUS PHILOSOPHY*

The religious philosophy of William Ernest Hocking is empirical in the sense that he finds in human experience the reality which calls for worship and religious commitment. This reality is our awareness of a total, unifying whole. In our daily life we strive for ends unattained, we encounter diversities which seem irreconcilable, we engage in futile conflicts, we come to meaningless dead ends. But we could not distinguish these for what they are if we did not experience them against the background of a "whole idea." This awareness of a comprehensive whole is brought to consciousness by reflection and most vividly experienced by the mystic. This comprehensive unity is the goal of all our strivings; and in worship we can apprehend its living presence, revealing the ultimate significance of our lives. In summary Hocking writes: "Religion... is the present attainment in a single experience of those objects which in the course of nature are reached only at the end of infinite progression. Religion is anticipated attainment."[1]

This hasty summary is quite inadequate and only serves as an introduction. The idea here suggested will be discussed more fully in what follows, together with comments indicating how I have developed his teaching in a way to reach conclusions somewhat different from his.

In 1954 Hocking wrote Experiment in Education: What We Can Learn from Teaching Germany. This is a study of American occupation of Germany after the Second World War and the attempt of this occupation to introduce democracy into that country with a view to correcting the continuing influence of Nazism. Hocking was there on the ground and could study first hand what Americans were doing in their attempt at "teaching Germany." His book is a penetrating and constructive criticism of our efforts. The main point of his

---

*Reprinted from Philosophy, Religion, and the Coming World Civilization--Essays in Honor of William Ernest Hocking, Edited by Leroy S. Rouner, The Hague, Netherlands: Martinus Nijhoff, 1966.

criticism is that the American failed to get the viewpoint of the Germans in such a way as to be able to work with them in developing the form of democracy which was incipiently present in the lives and thought of leading Germans and suited to their condition.

My interest in this book is to pick up again the idea developed in <u>The Meaning of God in Human Experience</u> but expressed here in somewhat different form and involved in the study of an actual social situation having important historical consequences. He makes statements about the "empirical route to an absolute goal." This "empirical route" is found in democracy. Democracy is based on the worth of the individual person; but "the worth of the individual derives from a world purpose, within which his own task or function lies."[2] Unless there is a world purpose endowing the individual with worth by reason of his essential participation in it, the claim that the individual has worth is false. Hocking sums up this argument by writing: "No world purpose, no individual worth; no individual worth, no democracy. Ergo: No world purpose, no democracy."[3]

As a student under his teaching I am deeply indebted to Professor Hocking. But the ideas taken over from him have undergone transformation in my own thinking. This difference from him in the direction of my thought was signified by an event occurring in the spring of 1917, at the time I took my oral examination for the degree of Doctor of Philosophy at Harvard. The examination was conduced by Hocking, Ralph Barton Perry and other members of the staff. After the examination was finished I stepped out of the room according to custom, so that the examiners could reach a decision, and was then called back to receive the verdict. As I left the room after receiving the judgment of the examining faculty, Professor Hocking stood at the door as I went out. In his courtly way he extended his hand to me and said, "Some day we'll have a good fight together." Already in the examination I had expressed my disagreement with him on important issues, although in the context of a general agreement.

This deviation from his conclusions has matured through the years but with growing recognition of the profound influence his insights have had in the development of my own thought. In the following essay I shall try to show how my empirical philosophy of religion has developed out of his but has taken a different form.

I shall discuss key statements taken from The Meaning of God in Human Experience because this book has nurtured my religious thinking more than any other book. This work first appeared in 1912. I do not know how much Hocking's own ideas have changed since then, or remained the same, but that is irrelevant to my present purpose. This book is the one I studied more devotedly than any other and I am trying to show how my own thought has developed out of it, beginning with ideas there stated but reaching different conclusions about the metaphysics on which religion should be based.

I

The "Absolute" runs continuously through Hocking's philosophy of religion. I shall defend the claim that human life would be impossible without an absolute, although I shall interpret it somewhat differently from Hocking. I recognize that any reference to an absolute has fallen into much disfavor these days. They who reject this idea seem to associate it with dogmatism, tyranny and the "authoritarian personality." They seem to think that the absolute implies a superimposed, predetermined outcome limiting the necessary diversities in human life, the uniqueness of individual personality, and the unpredictable innovations inevitably arising in the conduct of human living. In this way the conventional thinking of our time sets the "Absolute" in opposition to the creativity which sustains and nourishes human life.

This way of interpreting the meaning of the word "Absolute" is a misunderstanding of what is meant. The Absolute is precisely this very creativity which is necessary to human existence. It is what makes possible the widest range of diversity and the freest, fullest expression of unique individuality, but providing such relations between these diversities that they are mutually sustaining rather than mutually annihilating or frustrating, as they would be without such relations to one another. That is what Hocking means by the "Absolute" and that is what I mean by it, although we interpret the word in different ways.

In response to Hocking's statement that there is an "empirical route to an absolute goal," I shall offer my own interpretation of "absolute goal" found in human experience, even when it is not in full accord with Hocking's view. This I do, not to criticize his thought, but to show how my thinking has developed out of his.

An absolute goal, as I see it, is a goal intrinsic to human existence of such sort that human beings could not exist without it. It is absolute in the sense that the very continuance of human life requires it. Stated in the simplest possible form, this absolute goal is the creation of coherence, the recovery of coherence when it is disrupted, and the extension of coherence by absorbing new insights, when conditions make this possible. This coherence is never perfect and complete. It is always in process of being formed. All development of knowledge is by expanding the range of theories which distinguish and relate events in such a way that inference can be extended more widely from what is now observed to other events and possibilities more or less remote in time and space or otherwise inaccessible to immediate observation. No child could develop a human mind without this widening range of coherence in the form of knowledge.

But knowledge is not the only form of this sustaining coherence. Human association cannot be sustained and extended without the coherence of mutually sustaining activities performed by different individuals and groups. Human beings cannot communicate without the coherence of symbolized meanings carried by language and other symbols. No culture can develop nor be sustained without coherence of values prized and sought by many persons associated with one another. Human history could not occur without coherence of values and knowledge continuing from one generation to the next, when history means the continuity of a culture through a sequence of generations. Language could not exist without logical coherence. The individual person must maintain some degree of coherence (integration) else he becomes mentally deranged.

This continual recovery of coherence together with acceptance of innovations, this widening of coherence in the life of every individual as he matures from infancy to some level of attainment, and this extension of coherence through a sequence of generations when a culture is being created, is what Hocking calls the work of the "whole idea." I call it creativity, or the continuous creation of coherence by way of creative interchange between individuals and peoples. Regardless of how it is interpreted, it is, as said before, an absolute goal in human life in the sense the human existence cannot arise nor be sustained without it. But when I call this an absolute goal in the sense of being necessary to hu-

man existence, I do not mean to assert that this coherence
ever attains, or ever will attain, a final and completed
form.   Neither do I mean that there is any form of it which
eternally comprehends all reality.   At this point Hocking and
I diverge, if I understand him correctly.

Values are conserved and increased by coherence.
"Value" here refers to any liking.   Greater value is attained
by likings undergoing transformation in such a way that they
form a more inclusive system of mutually sustaining likings
in which each liking carries the value of the entire system
to which it contributes, which it helps to sustain, and which
symbolizes in the mind of the person who experiences it.
Thus the little things we value in daily life may take on the
value of a far ranging system which includes the likings of
many other people who have lived, who are living, and who
are yet to be born.   This last is the case when we help to
create, sustain and transmit a system of values to future
generations.   Such a wide-ranging coherence of likings is
created by creative interchange between individuals and between the older generation and the rising generation, whereby the continuity of history is sustained.   The actual empirical reality which we find occurring in human life is creativity operating to create coherence in the forms of language
and logic, in the forms of science and art, in the forms of
love, friendship and community of minds, in the forms of a
coherent culture and the continuity of history.   We can further establish empirically that this creation of coherence operates in human life in the form of a kind of interchange
which I have called creative, and have discussed at length in
other writings. 4

This brings us to the crucial question to be answered
by an empirical philosophy of religion.   To what must our religious commitment be given if the appreciative consciousness
of man is to be created in each individual beginning with infancy; is to be saved from perversion into hate, fear, arrogance and sensuality; and is to be expanded indefinitely in
range and depth when depth means forms of appreciative consciousness like love and justice which underlie and sustain
many other forms of appreciation?   Appreciative consciousness is another way of speaking of an expanded system of
likings in which each liking contributes to, helps to sustain,
and symbolizes the entire system, thereby representing the
value of the entire system to him who experiences this liking with its symbolism.

Is this creation and expanding coherence of appreciative consciousness to be accomplished by commitment to a
Coherence eternally in being and comprehending all reality?
Or is it to be accomplished by commitment to the creativity
actually operating in human life to creat the appreciative consciousness by creative interchange between individuals and
peoples?

It seems to me there can be only one answer to that
question.   The second alternative indicates the kind of religious commitment we must have if the evils of life are to be
overcome in whatsoever measure that is possible.   An objector might reply that the eternal being does operate in human life in the form of the creativity mentioned.   If that is
so, then my contention is granted.   This creativity operating
in human life calls for our religious commitment.   If the objector insists that our ultimate commitment must be given to
the eternal being, because the creativity derives from that
source, I reply: It is impossible for any man to adore, worship or otherwise recognize the eternal being except as the
creativity operating in human life creates in him the appreciative consciousness which is able to worship such a being,
supposing there is any eternal coherence of all reality.
Therefore, no matter how we take it, religious commitment
must be given first of all to the creativity which expands and
deepens the appreciative consciousness of man.

This expansion and deepening of appreciative consciousness is accomplished by the kind of interchange which (1)
creates in me some apprehension of what the other person
values and (2) integrates this newly acquired form of appreciation with my own coherent appreciative consciousness.   The
integration may take the form of recognizing what the other
person values without adopting his likings as my own, but
nevertheless keeping his values in mind so that I can understand him by putting myself more or less in his place.   In
this way the appreciative consciousness of man is expanded
and deepened.

In the Christian religion the name of Christ or Holy
Spirit is given to this creativity which creates and expands
the appreciative consciousness.   It is sometimes called divine grace.   In any case, whatever names are used, it creates love and community and more profound appreciative understanding between individuals and peoples.   By this reference to Christ I do not mean to endorse any of the multiform
Christologies set forth by theologians.   I only mean to say

that "Christ" refers to what is incarnate in human existence, not only once upon a time, but here and now, operating to create, sustain, and save.

Hocking has studied extensively the practice of worship and some of his most valuable insights pertain to it. There is a practice of worship, says Hocking, yielding an experience wherein the striving for unattained goals ceases for the time being as one becomes aware of their final attainment in God. This enables one to return to striving after these goals with a confidence and a courage which cannot be daunted, because the worshipper knows that the ultimate outcome is eternally in being. In worship one rises above the conflicts and unsolved problems because he is aware that they are ultimately solved in the being of God. In worship the alienation between oneself and other persons, also the alienation between oneself and nature, are overcome because in God these seeming oppositions are reconciled. Preeminently the mystic worshipper has this experience.

This is Hocking's account of worship and it is one of the most highly valued parts of his philosophy of religion.

I agree that worship does yield an experience which can be interpreted in the way Hocking interprets it. But I ask: What empirical reality do we actually experience in worship? Is it the eternal coherence of all reality? Or is it the profound awareness that there is a creativity operating to create wider and deeper coherence when we meet the required conditions and when we commit ourselves to it?

The two interpretations of worship might be contrasted as follows: According to one interpretation worship enables us to apprehend the final solution of all our problems. According to the second interpretation, worship puts us more completely into the power and keeping of the creativity which operates to solve our problems by generating insights and deepening appreciative understanding and community between persons and peoples and between human beings and the rest of nature.

According to the one interpretation, worship is an outreach to what comprehends all reality. According to the other interpretation, worship is an inreach to what expands our vision indefinitely, when we meet the required conditions.

According to one interpretation, worship gives us the

anticipation of final attainment. According to the other interpretation, worship yields the experience of being "born
again" into that creativity which, from infancy on through life,
creates the appreciative consciousness in community with
others and in community with nature.

According to one interpretation, worship gives us the
end result of human life. According to the other interpretation, worship gives us the ever renewed creative origins
of human life.

Whereas these two interpretations of worship seem to
stand in radical contrast, I can see how the same experience can be interpreted in either of the two ways. The creativity operating in human life to create coherence in the
form of perception, in the form of inference, in the form of
mutually sustaining activities in society, in the form of interpersonal communion and in the form of integrity in the individual person, does seem to point toward a final outcome.
Thus the worshipful commitment which puts the individual and
the group more completely into the keeping of this creativity might seem to be the experience of this final outcome.
But the question remains: What is the empirical reality actually experienced in worship? To my mind it is the creativity working to create coherence and not the completed coherence of all reality eternally in being.

This brings us to the second part of our discussion
of Hocking's empirical philosophy of religion. We shall now
examine some of the affirmations found in The Meaning of
God in Human Experience which represent central themes running throughout his philosophy.

II

One of his basic teachings is that God is the other
knower of the world. He writes: "Social experience, then,
becomes religious experience only when it is at the same
time experience of Nature power. And nature experience
likewise is religious only when Nature becomes an object of
social experience."[5] He adds: "...the original source of
the knowledge of God is an experience of not being alone in
knowing the world."[6]

I find in these statements a profound truth although I
give my own interpretation to them. As Hocking says, there

are three directions which knowledge can take, and on the
surface these three seem to be independent of one another.
In one direction I know the non-human world in which I live.
In the second direction I know the minds of other human beings, what they think and value. In the third direction I
know myself. But these three are not independent of one another. In developing knowledge of nature my own mind is
created. The more I know about nature, the more of a
mind I have. But most of what I know about nature I learn
from other minds. Thus, what I know about nature is in
great part knowledge of other minds. Also what I know
about myself is gained in great part by what I learn from
the way other people respond to me.

This union of the three ways of knowing is most vividly experienced after I have lived in intimate communion with
one or more other persons and in a physical environment
which we have shared together. After such a fellowship with
one another and with nature, all the familiar objects of that
scene which was present when we were together, speak to
me of those other minds; and my knowledge of their minds
is inseparable from the scenes which we have experienced together.

All our knowledge of nature, of self and of other minds
comes from the same source. The source is a creative interchange between self, nature and other minds. Insights,
generated in my mind by material things, I communicate to
others to find if they can observe what I observe when they
put themselves under the same conditions. This is most obviously the way scientific knowledge of nature is developed
but it is also the way we come to know a common world in
everyday life. The solitary thinker uses knowledge gained
from other minds when he thinks and when he views any
scene of nature and when he conducts inquiry to gain further
knowledge.

This threefold knowledge of nature, self and others,
when reflectively considered, gives me knowledge of God if
I understand God to be the creativity operating in human life
by way of creative interchange to create my own mind, beginning with the first days of infancy; at the same time and
by the same kind of interchange, creating other minds in
community with one another. Also this same kind of interchange creates the universe when universe means the view we
have of the external world. Even the most creative and imaginative scientist gets almost all his knowledge about the uni-

verse from other scientists.   Furthermore, what the natural
scientist called the universe in 1900, before the galactic systems were discovered, was very different from what it is today; and if revolutionary discoveries continue as they have
been occurring during the last fifty years, the known universe
will be very different one hundred years from now.   Thus our
knowledge of nature is derived from knowledge of other minds,
forming a shared vision which we call the universe.

If the name of God is given to the creativity which
transforms the universe by individuals learning from one another, at the same time transforming our own minds and the
knowledge we share in common with other minds, which is
knowledge of their minds, then I agree with the following:
"Social experience, then, becomes religious experience only
when it is at the same time experience of Nature power.
And nature experience likewise is religious only when Nature
becomes an object of social apprehension." 7

Experience of nature is religious only when I view it
as a form of communion with other minds, as in truth it is
when I take it for what it truly is.   This is so because my
view of nature is created, along with creation of my own
mind, by learning from others the accepted view of nature.
This accepted view is undergoing continuous transformation,
not only in science but in the view held by any community of
people, because the original perspective of the unique individual is communicated to others, if not in words, then in action.

This does not mean that everyone sees nature in exactly the same way as others do.   It does mean that we
could not coordinate our activities nor communicate intelligibly if what I see in nature did not have a great deal in common with others.   The tree, hill, road, and river as known
to me must be tree, hill, road and river as known to the
others; and the relation they have to one another in my view
cannot be radically different from the relation they have in
the view of others.   If this were not the case, we could not
coordinate our activities in moving about the country; nor
could we communicate with one another.

All this can be translated into Hocking's assertion:
The "...original source of the knowledge of God is an experience of not being alone in knowing the world."   But as I interpret these words, God is not merely one more additional
knower, added to the human knowers.   Rather God is that

kind of creative interchange between individuals whereby nature becomes a shared vision, so that, in knowing nature I
know the minds of those who share this vision with me.   In
contrast to this interpretation of the words quoted, Hocking
means to say that God is the all-knower, so that, to some
degree of approximation, in knowing nature I know the mind
of God.

My difficulty in accepting Hocking's idea of an all-
knower can be stated in several ways, but the following is
one way of putting it.   A "mind" which "knows" by instan-
taneous intuition the total cosmos across vast spaces requiring a ray of light millions of years to traverse, is not
"mind" and is not "knowing" as these words apply to human
beings.   The difference in what is designated is so radical
that "mind" in the one case is a different word from "mind"
in the other case, even though the spelling and pronunciation
are the same.   Also "knowing" in the one case is an entirely
different word from "knowing" in the other case.   Consequently there can be no all-knower.   There can only be an
all-X, because the word having the letters of "knower" in
"all-knower" is not at all the same word used when I say
that I know nature, meaning to know that small bit of objective reality which happens to come within range of my perceptions and my inferences, largely based on information
about nature which I have received from others.

"I cannot clear nature of selfhood although I can clear
her of my own self and of any particular self." [8]   Here
again is a profound insight which has been very fruitful in
my own thinking, although I interpret it differently from
Hocking.   Nature as I view it is saturated with self because
my view of it has been created in me by communications
with other minds.   This does not make it subjective but does
make it a selection from the total fullness of all being.
This selection has been developed by the insights of many
thousands of individuals, these insights communicated from one
to others and integrated into a comprehensive vision, this vision constantly changing as it is communicated from one person to another, from one generation to another, from one
age and one culture to another.

"No form of argument can be valid which finds God
at the level of thought only, and not at the level of sensation." [9]   Here again is a claim which has continued with me
through the years and which I have defended against much
opposition, although I have developed the suggestion in my

own way. God must be found at the level of sensation as
well as at the level of thought if God is that creativity which
creates our own minds in community with others. This is so
because sensation can reach consciousness only when it takes
on meaning; and the meaning which sensation has at the level
of perception is the anticipation of further sensations which
will occur if I gaze more intently, or change my position, or
listen or approach or touch or perform any of the innumerable activities by which sensations follow one another according to an anticipated sequence. If sensations do not occur in
the sequence anticipated, I recognize that my perception was
mistaken.

Of all the sensations I am able to have, only those are
selected which association and cooperation with other people
have endowed with anticipation of an orderly sequence of further sensations, when appropriate actions are performed.
For this reason people living in different cultures have different forms of perception, although the similarity of human organisms and social organizations produce perceptions in all
human beings which are more alike than the perceptions of
other animals are like the human.

If the name of God is given to that kind of interchange
between individuals which leads people to cooperate and understand one another and share a common vision to which each
unique individual can make his own original contribution, then
God is found at the level of sensation because only those sensations develop into perceptions which are endowed with anticipation of a further sequence of sensations, and this comes
from communication with others and from cooperation with
them. The spontaneous responses of the organism play a
part in this selection, but these responses are profoundly
shaped from early infancy by intimate association with other
human beings. The shaping of perception by interaction with
others is that creativity which creates my mind in community
with others and also creates what we call nature. In this
sense God is found at the level of sensation, if God is identified with this creativity.

"It is through knowledge of God that I am able to know
men: not first through knowledge of men that I am able to
know or imagine God."[10] I would amend this statement
slightly by saying that it is through God that I am able to
know men, and when I come to understand how I know men,
this understanding gives me knowledge of God. I know men
by way of the creative interchange discussed in preceding
paragraphs.

I now turn to another theme which is central to every philosophy of religion, although it takes on different interpretations in different philosophies. Hocking expresses it in these words: "It is because neither my world nor myself can serve as foundation for thought and action that I must grope for a deeper foundation."[11]

The previous discussion has shown the sense in which it is here claimed that the world as we know it cannot be self sufficient. Nor can any world ever to be known by any mind ever be self sufficient. This is so because of the nature of mind, of knowledge and of the knowable world. The knowable world is a selection from out of the totality of all being; and it is forever impossible to have any other kind of knowable world. This selection begins, as previously indicated, by selecting certain sensations and ignoring others, the ones selected being those which arouse readiness for a sequence of further sensations when appropriate actions are performed. Thus my mind and my world are created together and this creation is accomplished by selecting certain sensations and ignoring others, ordering these sensations into perceptions and ordering perceptions into structure by inferences under the guidance of theories imaginatively constructed.

The human organism limits to some degree the diversity of worlds which can be selectively created in the way mentioned. But if other planets somewhere throughout the galactic systems are occupied by organism different from the human, (which seems very probable), and if these organisms are able to form theories, universes can be created with them as subjects; and these universes might well be unimaginably different from any that human beings have ever known or could know.

What has just been stated is speculative, but it is not speculative to say that very different universes are known to human minds as we pass from age to age and culture to culture. The universe as known to a primitive tribe stands in contrast to the universe as known to modern science; and we cannot know what the universe will be as known to science five hundred years from now, if the revolutionary transformations in scientific theory and scientific discovery continue as they have been developing during the past century.

The point of all this is to assert that the plenitude of being, otherwise called the mystery of being, cannot be a universe of any kind and cannot be known to any mind because

every universe is a selection from the fullness of being;
and all knowledge is developed by selecting sensations, ordering them into perceptions and ordering the perceptions into far ranging constructions under the guidance of theories.
These theories can themselves be very diverse as shown by
the development of modern science and by the diverse worlds
known to different peoples in different ages and cultures.

The second point of this discussion is to show that the
universe as known to any mind is not self sufficient, not because it depends upon an all-knower, but because it depends
upon that creativity operating in human life which creates the
universe as known to any community of minds in any age and
culture. The totality of all that is, otherwise called the mystery of being, is not a universe and is not knowable by any
mind, not even by a divine mind, if the word "mind" applied
to God has any identity of meaning with the word "mind" as
applied to human knowing. Total reality is receptive to an
indefinite diversity of Whole Ideas. In this age of magnified
power, salvation lies not in the identification of any one Whole
Idea with ultimate reality and imposing it on others, but in
providing conditions under which diverse Whole Ideas can
modify and expand one another. The Absolute is this interchange creating wholeness out of conflict.

To say that the universe as known to any mind is created after the manner described, does not mean that the
known world is a subjective creation of human imagination,
although imagination always plays a part in its creation. It
does mean that every known world must necessarily be a selection from the total plenitude of being. The infinite fullness of being permits the creation of innumerable worlds by
the creativity which selects sensations for the formation of
perceptions and orders these perceptions in the form of theories which guide inferences to predicted consequences. When
the sequence of sensations ensue in accordance with the anticipations implicit in perception, we have true knowledge of
reality in whatsoever sense there is any truth and any reality.
When perceptions are ordered by theories guiding inference to
predicted consequences, we have true knowledge of reality.

Of course all knowledge is probable in the sense that
perceptions and theories can always be changed to make them
more precise and more comprehensive. But since the only
kind of knowledge any mind can ever have, and the only kind
of reality ever to be known, is of this sort, there is no
truth ever to be attained other than knowledge subject to cor-

rection and further development.

Since the knowable universe is thus dependent and transitory, some religious thinkers give the name of God not to any knowable universe but to the mystery of being out of which the universe is created after the manner above described. Since nothing is knowable except what is selected from the mystery of being in the form of perceptions, theories and inferences, the mystery of being is unknowable. That is one interpretation of the word "mystery" when applied to being. [12]

God, thus identified with the unknowable, permits the imagination, unchecked and unrestrained, to endow the mystery of being with whatever suits the religious fancy and the felt need of the worshipper.

When religion takes this form it becomes identified with the psychological effects of beliefs regardless of their truth when truth means belief supported by empirical and rational evidence. Beliefs of this kind cannot reliably predict the consequences of any course of action, because reliable prediction is the test of truth and is possible only by way of selections from the fullness of being as above described. Beliefs which cannot predict the consequences of action are unfit to guide the use of power, especially power magnified to the enormous proportions now attained in the form of scientific technology. Beliefs which cannot guide the use of power cannot shape the course of events, and therefore are negligible for all practical purposes beyond the psychological effects the beliefs may have.

This leads to an obvious conclusion. If God is identified with the mystery of being, then religious beliefs will be of no importance in shaping the course of events because they are not used to guide the use of power, or else they will be used to guide the exercise of power without being able to predict the consequences of that use. The power of man has now become so great that using it without predicting the consequences of its use will be devastating in its consequences. Therefore, when God is identified with the unknowable mystery of being, religion becomes either negligible or else the source of great evil through the irresponsible use of power.

The empirical philosophy of religion insists that religious belief should be shaped to direct the ultimate commitment of human life to what does in truth create, sustain, save and expand that coherence which sustains human life and deepens the appreciative consciousness to apprehend the greatest good human life can ever attain. I believe Professor Hocking and I are united in the claim that religious belief should not be about the unknowable but should be about what is empirically and rationally knowable. We differ on how religious belief should be directed to accomplish this end. I have tried to show where we differ, not to be controversial, but rather to make plain how my thought has developed out of his thought. I suspect most religious thinkers will contend that I have gone astray and have departed from the truth as found in Hocking's teaching.

Whatever may be true or false in my own empirical philosophy of religion, I do not know how I can honestly and fully show my indebtedness to Hocking except by indicating the course my thought has taken after long study of his teaching. I have done this in that spirit of comradeship which he expressed so many years ago, as I came away from my examination for the Doctor's degree, and he said to me with a cordial smile: "Some day we'll have a good fight together."

Notes

1. William Ernest Hocking, The Meaning of God in Human Experience, p. 31.

2. William Ernest Hocking, Experiment in Education, p. 226.

3. Op. cit., p. 283.

4. See The Source of Human Good and Man's Ultimate Commitment both in paperback, published by Southern Illinois University Press. Also The Intellectual Foundation of Faith, the Philosophical Library. Also The Empirical Theology of Henry Nelson Wieman published by Macmillan as the fourth volume in the Library of Living Theology, edited by Kegley and Bretall.

5. Hocking, The Meaning of God in Human Experience, pp. 232-3.

6. Ibid., p. 236.

7.   Ibid., p. 232.

8.   Ibid., p. 287.

9.   Ibid., p. 313.

10. Ibid., pp. 297-8.

11. Ibid., p. 312.

12. See Paul Tillich on this point, Systematic Theology, vol. I.

WHAT IS MOST IMPORTANT IN CHRISTIANITY?*

We are not asking what is essential Christianity as over against the accidental husk. Much less are we interested in what, if anything, is held in common by all Christians, for the most common is rarely if ever the most excellent. Least of all are we trying to point out something in Christianity which can be found nowhere else. We are seeking what is most important in our faith even though this most important feature might appear outside Christianity, as well as inside, and even though it might be displayed very rarely in Christian history and in the lives of only a few Christian people, and even though many might say that it is not inclusive of what is essential. On the other hand this most important element might be found nowhere save in the regions where Christianity has reached. It might be a deep undercurrent running through all Christian history and it might be what some would call essential Christianity. The point is that these are subordinate questions which do not concern us here. We only want to know what is most important in our religious heritage and must not predetermine or pervert our evaluation by these other questions.

We shall not take space to discuss all the different views that have been held concerning what is most important and then range our own along with them and show the agreements and disagreements. This would be a worthy and scholarly undertaking. But for the present we shall be content with stating as clearly as we know how what we think is most important and then let our presentation justify itself or provoke disagreement as the case may be.

We suggest at the start that the most important element in Christianity is the forgiveness of sin. A complex of events occurring in the Greco-Roman world, in which the life and death and resurrection of Jesus Christ were central, re-

---

*Reprinted from <u>Religion in the Making</u>, I (1940-41), pp. 149-166.

leased into history and into the lives of all men who are able
to receive it, a dynamic, creative process variously called
the Holy Spirit or the Living Christ, or the Grace of God,
whereby it became possible to overcome man's resistance to
God without destroying the resisters. This is the forgiveness of sin. It is the way of grace as over against the way
of the law.

Sin is anything in the conduct of human living which
resists the creativity of God. When sin is unforgiven, God
cannot overcome this resistance except by destroying the individual or group which does the resisting. When sin is forgiven the resistance is still present but God can overcome it
without destroying the individuals or groups concerned. The
one is sin unto death, the other is sin not unto death. This
second is the power of God unto salvation. It is the grace
of God in Christ Jesus whereby we know the power of his
resurrection, the fellowship of his sufferings, being conformed unto his death.

All this will not make sense until we clarify three
things: the nature of this creativity of God; the nature of
man's resistance to it which is sin; the conditions which must
be met in order that this creativity may overcome the resistance without destroying the resisters.

THE CREATIVITY OF GOD

Suppose Mr. Box and Mr. Cox are brought into association with one another. If the situation is at all favorable,
they will talk or make some signs. Not only that, but all
manner of interactions, conscious and unconscious, will occur between them. Much of this interaction will be quite unintended, impulsive and spontaneous but unavoidable in the
situation. In consequence of all this interaction the mind of
each will be transformed to some degree. Each will become
a participant in the life of the other. Habits, thoughts,
words, impulses and feelings of Mr. Box will become supplementary to those of Mr. Cox. The same will be true of
Mr. Cox in relation to Mr. Box. The behavior, feelings,
and ideas of each will become a fragment of a larger whole,
incomplete without the reciprocal and complementary behavior
of the other. The expressions of each will enrich the life of
the other, meaning by enrichment not merely pleasant feelings but greater vividness and variety of feelings, some of
which may be very painful. It is important to note that our

awareness of the badness of evil (which generally involves
the kind of feeling we call suffering) is just as great a good
as our appreciation of the goodness of what is excellent.
The point is that this interaction between persons widens and
deepens the appreciative consciousness. It makes us more
alive, it makes life more abundant, it increases the qualitative richness of conscious experience. Greater heights and
depths of positive and negative evaluation enter our experience because of such interactions. No other contact is so
enriching as this of interaction between persons when it is
free, spontaneous and abundant.

What we have been describing is creative of all that
is distinctively human in man. All the relevant sciences
would support us in this claim, particularly that science
which makes this matter its peculiar field of study, namely
social psychology. This kind of interaction creates and
transforms progressively the human mind, human purpose
and ideals, and all human value. We suffer great impover-
ishments and decline in all that is distinctively human when
we try to control it so as to fulfill what we are now able to
appreciate, because it creates and transforms our appreciations. We cannot harness it to our own purposes because it
creates and transforms our purposes. In that sense it is
more than human. It is going on in us and around us all
the time, although it may sink to a dying trickle or rise to
great volume. It is so commonplace that we scarcely pay
any attention to it. It is the most wonderful thing in the
world and yet is so intimately and persistently with us that
we scarcely ever take any note of it nor of what it is doing
to us.

Even enemies when brought into association interact
in such a way that the words, actions and feelings of each
generate and enrich the meanings, the feelings, the actions
of the other. Associated individuals may do everything in
their power to prevent and destroy the growth of these connections whereby they become members one of another and
may succeed in keeping this mutuality down to the minimum.
But unless they break off all association, or utterly annihilate one another, some such interactions, transformative and
creative of the personalities and groups involved, will develop between them despite all that they can do. Each will derive from the other meaning, imagery and qualitative richness of feeling which will widen and deepen his consciousness of good and evil. This interaction will recreate the
mind of both so that they will become adjuncts of one another.

Even when great modern, industrialized nations are
at war each trying to annihilate the other, this ineraction of
mutual support and enrichment cannot entirely be cut off.   It
is recorded that during the first world war France and Germany could not have continued to carry on the conflict against
one another if there had not been a continuous stream of interchange by way of Luxembourg whereby one provided coal
to the other, and the second gave iron to the first.   And
this is only a very small illustration of the material and
spiritual reciprocation which goes on all the while between
nations engaged in mortal combat whereby more abundant life
for each and both is created, even when each uses this enriched and magnified life to destroy life faster than creativity can create it.

Certainly this creative interaction between persons and
nations, between groups and sensitive organisms of every
kind, is by no means so full and free as it should be.   Perhaps nowhere in all the vast expanse of human and sub-human living do we find so tragic and awful a contrast between
what might be and what actually is, as we find here between
the amount of creative interaction which does occur and what
might.   Men, and all living things for that matter, are so
torpid!   They are so fearful of one another, and with good
cause!   They are so vain and self-centered, so preoccupied
with the impression they are making that they cannot interact
with the freedom and fullness that yields abundant life!   They
are so envious and so jealous!   They are so dull, so fixated,
so stupid in ways that could be remedied!   We are so secre-
tive and so covered with protective armor plate, that creative interaction is kept down to the minimum.   The fixative,
protective and malignant patterns of behaviors which dominate
all living seem at times to crush the life out of creativity.
And yet, when one is observant and thinks about it, it is
amazing how much of this kind of interaction is able to break
through all the obstructive and destructive armament of
life.

Let us state the nature of this creative interaction or
creativity in general and comprehensive terms and present it
in such a way that it becomes open to daily observation.   It
is the growth of connections between sensitive organisms, all
the way from cells and plant spores to human personalities
and groups, which transforms the participant individuals so
that they interact in mutual support and mutual enrichment.
The enrichment, of course, does not begin until the sensitive
organisms become conscious, for we mean by enrichment in-

crease in the vividness and variety of all the feelings which
make up the qualities of conscious experience.

This growth of connections which enriches life is subject to three kinds of obstructions or perversions. They
might be called the fixative, the protective and the malignant
perversions. We see all three most strikingly today in the
growth of connections between sovereign states. We see them
in the psychoses of human personality. The most common
example of malignant growth in the biological organism is
cancer. But individual personalities, groups and whole cultures have no absolute value. They should rise or fall, come
and go, live and die, according as may best serve the increase of creative interaction between individuals and groups.
We are not suggesting that any human individual, class or
other group is competent to judge when any other should be
sacrificed. We are only saying that such sacrifice is right
and good when creativity is thereby advanced.

Creative interaction is the one and only absolute good
against which all others must be measured because it is the
generative source of all value. It is the creative origin of
all richness of experience as well as of personality and society. It is precisely this creative interaction which, for example, transforms the biochemical organism of the human infant into a human personality. It is the creative work of
God in the world.

Nothing is truly good, no matter how much I desire it,
unless it contributes to, and is an expression of, this interaction between cells, organisms, personalities and groups,
whereby mutual support and enrichment are magnified. Anything and everything becomes evil when it obstructs the growth
of connections which sustain and stimulate such interaction.
If, for example, I cling to good health with such tenacity and
persistence that it prevents me from moving freely and fully
into all connections which sustain and enrich life, I not only
destroy my good health in the end, but whatever health I have
becomes destructive of other goods. On the other hand, if I
sustain and promote my health as it contributes to creative
interaction between cells, organisms, personalities and
groups, it is a great and growing good. The same can be
said of wealth, popularity, beauty, truth and every other alleged good. All specific values are in reality good only as
they are expressions and forms of the growth of these connections, and only when enjoyed and promoted as expressions
of creativity. They are good only as they are held subject
to the working of that interaction between individuals and

groups which sustains, generates and enriches the appreciative consciousness of each.

Even the continued existence of the individual is good only so long as it can undergo the transformations required by this enriching interaction between itself and others. When the individual can no longer undergo the transformation of creativity by reason of physiological or psychological or social inertia or decay or perversion, he should die, unless there is some hope that he can recover this capacity. As human personalities we are both originally and continuously generated by God's creativity. We belong ultimately and absolutely to that creativity. There is nothing else to live for save for it. There is no ground or reason for our existence except as we belong to it. We destroy our humanity and all the meaning and value of life when we break connections with it.

This creativity of God which we have been describing is not, of course, peculiar to Christianity. It is to be found at work everywhere that man exists and even beyond, whereever sensitive organisms exist. But we must understand this working of God in order to see what is the most important element in Christianity. We said that this most important component is the forgiveness of sin which means the setting up of conditions whereby it is possible for God's love to overcome man's resistance without destroying the resister. God's love is this creativity.

God's "judgment" or "wrath" is inseparable from his love. It is, indeed, the same thing but working under different conditions. God's love is the growth of connections whereby individuals and groups become mutually enriching members of a shared life. It is what we have just been describing as creativity. God's wrath is the mutual destructiveness of such individuals and groups when they are drawn closer together by these connections but resist the transformation which is required by the life of mutual enrichment within these closer bonds of interdependence. Such mutual destructiveness (the wrath of God) is an obvious fact in the world today. The closer draw the cords of love, the more destructive of one another do men become when they resist the transformation imposed by these closer connections and required in order to interact within these closer connections with mutual support and mutual enrichment. The present war is an excellent example of this.

God's forgiveness is accomplished by setting up conditions whereby it is possible to circumvent this mutual destructiveness and transform sinners despite their resistance to God's love. To see how this is accomplished by the life and death and resurrection of Christ when joined with the continuing practice of confession and repentance of sin, we must look a little closer at the nature of man's sin.

MAN'S SIN

Sin is any blockage to the creativity of God arising from the way man conducts his living. The most deadly sin is that which is unconscious and unintended. If one wishes to reserve the word sin for conscious and deliberate transgression, then we must invent another word to designate that evil arising out of man's way of living which is most destructive of life and of all the goods of life, in the clutch of which man is most helpless and from which he most desperately needs salvation. All this is so because it is quite obvious that when man is fully conscious of doing what is obstructive to the generative source of all good, he is well on the road to deliverance from it. It is the unconscious, unintended resistance to God's love which has on man the hold of death.

Sin is the clinging to anything, or the striving after anything, when such clinging or striving prevents one from undergoing the transformations involved in creative interaction. When connections have been formed between individuals and groups requiring such interactions, they become mutually impoverishing when they resist the transformation which they must undergo to interact in the required way. Any social structure, any ideal or moral code, any institution or other order of existence, which men uphold or promote, becomes sinful just as soon as that upholding or promoting obstructs creativity, which is to say, obstructs the mutual transformations of enriching interaction. Obviously in a world like ours a vast amount of this obstructiveness to creativity is inevitable, due to the inability of individuals and groups to undergo the transformations involved in creative interaction.

The art of living plainly indicates that this creativity must be the one and only object of absolute religious commitment. Everything else must be sought or held or relinquished according to the requirements of this. If need be one must come to love what now he hates, seek what now he dreads, fight what now he

cherishes, destroy what now he upholds.   No other tie can
be absolute save only this commitment to creativity.   This
alone can be sovereign over life.   For the Lord thy God is
a jealous God and human life can have but one ruling devotion.   No other loyalty, no other love, no desire, satisfaction, hope, fear or dread must stand against this.   One must
be free to move with creativity, giving up anything or taking
anything.   In this way only is found freedom and all the riches of value.   Any other way leads to impoverishment and
destruction of value.   Every other way is the way of sin.
Plainly our hope is not that we shall be sinless but that our
sins shall be forgiven.

      This necessity of making creativity sovereign in any
life which would experience value abundantly, and the correlative necessity of being able to give up any specific good according as creativity may require, can be illustrated by a
rather mechanical device.   Suppose a lofty and spacious building from the ceiling of which is suspended a cable.   At the
end of the cable is a parachutist's harness in which you are
strapped.   The game is to swing high and wide on this cable
for it represents creativity or the forming of connections between individuals whereby they are so transformed as to be
mutually enriching in their behavior, their feelings, thoughts
and words.   To swing on the cable, however, one must have
pull-ropes.   So ropes extend inward from the sides of the
building to where you hang suspended.   Each rope has on its
end a ring which you can seize and thus pull yourself this
way and that.   One rope represents the specific value of
health, another that of wealth, another popularity, another
good looks, another knowledge or education, another some
specific love, another some friendship, and so on indefinitely.
Now as long as one can pull on his health or his wealth or
any other of these ropes, and then let go of it, he can swing
wide and high and free.   But if he holds fast to these specific values, he cannot swing with creativity.   If, worst of
all, he takes a cord and ties himself to health, to wealth, to
popularity, to any or all of these, it is plain that he cannot
swing.   He can only jiggle about in one locality.

      One must be able to let go of every specific good if
he is going to live under the sovereign control of creativity.
And the strange thing is that when one holds fast to his popularity or some particular friendship or love or specific loyalty with such persistence and tenacity that he cannot move
with the ever changing formation of connections which yield
enrichment, he is much more likely to lose that good to

which he clings than when he is not so bound to it. Stranger
still, perhaps, he cannot fully appreciate and enjoy the values
of health and wealth and love and all the rest when he is ov-
erly anxious about them or considers any of them a necessary
good. Only when he can let go of them, only when he can
draw upon them and then release them, as may be required
by the forming of connections which transform him and others, can he experience the real value in all these so-called
values. As a matter of fact they are not values at all except as they promote the forming of those connections which
elicit interactions which sustain and enrich. When death contributes more to creativity than continued life, then death is
better than life. A human personality absolutely committed
to creativity and to nothing else, can in this way die with
joy. We are always delivered unto death for Christ's sake,
said Paul.

I must die to all specific goods in order to be born
again with this one and only tie whereby I hang suspended on
one cable only, free to move with creativity through all
things, whether it be life or death, or things present or
things to come, or any other creature. Then I can do all
things through Christ which strengthened me, meaning that I
can let go of anything or take hold of anything as creativity
may require. Then nothing can separate me from the love
of God, for the love of God is precisely this forming of connections between me and others and between them and me
whereby we are transformed from day to day and from glory
unto glory.

THE FORGIVENESS OF SIN

In order for the working of God to overcome the obstructions to creative interaction which are set up by inertia,
fear and malignancy of men three things are required.

(1) Creative interaction between persons must be released from confinement to any one set of structures or order of life in the sense that it shall be able to transform or
create whatever organization may be required for mutual enrichment when wider or deeper association between individuals and groups may occur. This first condition for the forgiveness of sin was partially met in the Roman Empire by
the intermingling of races, the interpenetration of cultures,
the interchange between diverse tribal patterns and races.
In this way the individual and the group was somewhat re-

leased from the coercive and absolute control of any one order of life, which for the Jew meant the law. In this way
it became possible (although by no means fully actual) that
persons could interact differently from the prescribed ways
of the ancestral pattern when creativity might require. It
was a situation favorable to the creation of new orders and
to meet the requirements of wider, freer, richer creative interaction between members within the same group or with
men who under other circumstances would be considered
"outsiders."

But in itself alone all this was not sufficient. A second condition was required and after that a third.

(2) The second condition which had to be met in order that sins be forgiven was that a psychological, social historical process get under way which would make creativity
potent and sovereign over the lives of a few (at least) so that
no hope or dream, no ideal or order of existence could exercise equal control over them. This was accomplished by
the life, crucifixion and resurrection of Jesus Christ.

Jesus during his life developed in a small group a
height and depth and richness of creative interaction that was
unique. Perhaps he attained one of the high points in history
in this respect. In any case it was something more wonderful than anything those simple peasants had ever experienced.
Nevertheless it never broke free of the established patterns
of their Hebrew heritage as long as Jesus lived. They continued to dream and hope that Jesus would establish a kingdom and they with him would sit upon thrones and rule the
world as Hebrew tradition prescribed.

The crucifixion cracked this structure of existence and
possibility, this order of dream and practice, which had been
the framework within which their creative interaction had heretofore occurred. It did not destroy the control which was exercised over their lives by the law and order of Hebrew tradition, but it loosened somewhat further its absolute coercive-
ness and sovereignty. It did this by destroying their hope
and even, for a little while, the creative interaction which
they had had in fellowship with one another when Jesus was
with them. With the crucifixion Jesus failed them utterly.
They had hoped that he was the messiah. But he died mis-
erably upon a cross and was wholly unable to be or to do
what their Hebrew way of life prescribed for him. It was
one of the most complete "blackouts," one of the most mis-

erable "washouts," that men ever experienced. Hope and
promise was so high, disillusionment so complete. Everything was gone. Nothing was left for them to live for. The
hope of Israel and the marvelous creative interaction which
had been theirs, all disappeared in the black-out of the crucifixion.

But after the numbness and the despair had lasted for
about three days, a miracle happened. That kind of interaction which Jesus had engendered among them came back.
They found themselves interacting with one another and with
other people in that marvelous way which had only happened
when Jesus was in their midst.

This was the resurrection. Jesus had initiated a kind
of creative interaction which went beyond anything men had
known before, or at any rate beyond anything these men had
known before. But now, after it had seemed to be destroyed
by his death, it rose again from the dead and was with them.
It was not the resurrection from the grave of one hundred
and sixty pounds, more or less, of the flesh and of the blood
of the Nazarene. No, it was not the resurrection of the
poundage of meat and bone which pertained to the man Jesus,
but it was the resurrection of that height and depth and richness of creativity which only the physical presence of Jesus
had heretofore been able to engender. But more than that
was involved. The power of the resurrection was the power
of a creativity on the way to being liberated from bondage to
the law, which is to say, liberated from any limitations imposed by any structure of society, any organization of personality, any form of existence. That does not mean that there
can be creative interaction apart from some social structure,
some organization of society, some form of existence. But
it means a creativity that can transcend any structure, organization and form by transforming what has heretofore been attained and creating structures which have never yet been experienced and doing this without known limit.

Thus the new creativity which issued into history from
the crucifixion and the resurrection was a creative interaction
which could break through the bounds of the law and thereby
forgive sin. That is to say, it could overcome man's resistance to creativity without destroying the resisters, providing they met one further condition which is repentance, to be
discussed later. It was the unlimited grace of God. It could
occur not only between the circumcised but between the circumcised and uncircumcised, which is a symbolic way of say-

ing that it need not be confined to any one way of living, any
one order of society, any one kind of people, any one set of
ideals. It could occur between Jew and Gentile, Greek and
Barbarian, bond and free, rich and poor, foolish and ignorant, high and low. It could be creative and transformative
of every structure of existence and way of living to whatsoever measure might be required by the utmost mutual enrichment of creative interaction.

It took some time for the theory and the established
practice of this new way of living to become formulated and
recognized. Hence the vacillation of Peter and the contro-
versy between Paul and the Judaizers and, for that matter,
all the vacillation, compromises, regressions, fixations,
heresy hunting, witch-burning and other sorry spectacles of
Christian history. We repeat, what here concerns us is not
what is universal among Christians but something which is
the most important element in their history, no matter how
rare it may be, nor how faint and discontinuous may be the
thread of its historic existence.

One further thing should be said about this matter of
the resurrection. When people have had a strange and wonderful experience in dealing with a certain person, the vivid
recurrence of that experience, even when the person is no
longer physically present, will give them a profound sense
of the real presence of that one. If the experience is sufficiently vivid and unique, and if it has never heretofore occurred except in association with that one person, then its
occurrence will almost inevitably create the illusion that the
person involved is now physically here. In such case, some
will very likely think that they see and feel and hear the
face and hands, the body, wounds, and voice of this person.
This is a well known characteristic of human psychology.
After the experience has been retold several times by a sequence of reporters, the illusion will become like an established fact of history. But the important thing about the
resurrection was not an illusion. The important thing about
the resurrection was not the avoirdupois of flesh that had
been crucified, but it was the resurrection of a creative interaction free to overcome the resistance of men without destroying the men and groups who resisted. It was the power
of God unto salvation.

The creativity of God had at last broken free and now
issued into history by way of a continuing social process of
creative interaction. It had broken free of every social

structure, form of existence, system of values, goal, hope
and ideal of men. It was free of these, we repeat, not in
the sense that it could operate apart from some such structures, but free in the sense that it could now transform and
create structures suited to its need. It was no longer confined to the law, meaning any established system of social
organization and patterns of behavior. It could transcend
any and all of these in the sense of creating whatever modifications it might require. Again we must repeat that such
new creations can never be the work of human intelligence
because human intelligence naturally is limited to that totality of ideal structures available to it at any given time, while
creativity is precisely the introduction of new structures not
previously available to intelligence. Such innovations come
by way of creative interaction between individuals and groups.
This is a common fact of experience and generally recognized
by all the relevant sciences.

The creativity of God had at last broken free of the
law and issued into history with power to save beyond the
law through the co-working of the social situation in the
Roman Empire with the life, death and resurrection of Jesus
Christ. After this any man might cry: I count all things to
be loss for the excellency of the knowledge of Christ Jesus
my Lord, for which I have suffered the loss of all things
and do count them but dung, that I may win Christ (the unlimited creativity of God) and be found in him; not having a
righteousness of mine own, even that which is of the law,
but the righteousness which is through faith in Christ, a
righteousness from God by faith; that I may know him and
the power of his resurrection and the fellowship of his suffering, being conformed unto his death.

CONFESSION AND REPENTANCE OF SIN

There is, however, a third condition which must be
met before the power of God unto salvation is free to work
without limit in delivering men from that sin which is unto
death. It is repentance. Why it is a necessary condition
becomes apparent as soon as we see what is involved.

The confession and repentance of sin means three
things. It means, first, to recognize that my personality at
depths far below the reach of consciousness at any given
time is patterned and structured by an organization which
does resist the transformations required for that fullness of

creative interaction demanded by the connections I have with
other people. Since I do not undergo the required transformation, I interact with them in ways that are mutually impoverishing and mutually destructive. Some of this destructiveness I see. Much of it escapes my focus of attention and
my capacity for sensitive appreciation. But I know enough
about life and about myself to know that it does occur. To
recognize this fact about myself, and to realize the depth
and tragedy of evil that is involved in it, is to confess my
sin.

Confession and repentance of sin mean, in the second
place, that I shall resolve repeatedly, and with all the depths
of sincerity that is in me, to hold myself subject to every
transformation creative interaction may require, no matter
what pain, death or loss such changes may involve. I do
this because I know that in this I am gainer in every way
along with God and everyone else who may be involved. I
and all are gainers because in so far as I do yield to such
transformation, and in so far as I am the responsible agent
in each situation, I become the medium and the expression
of that creativity which is the generative source of all the
values that can ever be experienced.

Confession and repentance of sin mean in the third
place that I shall search out every habit, every object of desire, fear, hope and dread, that I can at all suspect to be
recalcitrant to creative interaction, and resolve that each one
shall be taken from me or given to me, according as creative interaction may require. Nothing shall be mine except
as I receive it from the creativity of God. Nothing shall be
held back by me when the creativity of God would take it
away. Everyone who practices this kind of commitment to
creativity will become aware of certain desires, habits, propensities in himself that resist the transformation necessary
to fruitful interaction with things and persons and groups.
These specific patterns of behavior in himself he will not
fight directly, for that may only make their hold upon him
more tenacious. But he will take them one by one and resolve that each shall be given over to the creative process of
transformation as it arises in the concrete situations into
which he enters day by day and hour by hour. He will seek
to formulate and develop whatever habits, propensities and
cherished objectives may produce in himself the kind of personality that can move freely and fully with all the transformations and fulfilments of creativity in each concrete situation as it develops.

If this interpretation of the confession and repentance of sin be correct it should be apparent, without further argumentation, that it is a third condition which must be met before the creativity of God is free to work freely and fully beyond the bounds of the law to save each sinner from that sin which is unto death.

We have tried to point out what we hold to be the most important element in Christianity. We have called it the forgiveness of sin. It is to be understood, however, not in the form of some static decree nor as a juridical pronouncement. When it is so understood, it is falsified, we think. Rather it is a dynamic reality working in history, in society and in each personality who has been touched by this dynamic, social, historical process and who meets the condition of repentance.

Let us summarize. The life, crucifixion and resurrection of Jesus Christ released the creative work of God from obstructions which had elsewhere limited its operations. The creative work of God is the transformation of individuals and groups by way of interaction so that they progressively sustain and enrich one another. Interaction may be impoverishing and destructive but creative interaction is the opposite. It generates the qualitative riches of conscious experience with all the meanings, imagery, feeling and vivifying sense data of consciousness. It releases the appreciative consciousness from bondage to special goods so that it may range more widely and deeply. Its work is obstructed and perverted by the inertia of the world and the sin of man. In order to overcome these perversions and obstructions it must have a medium through which to work in the form of a community of persons, however, few they may be. This community must be made up of persons who commit themselves absolutely to the transformative working of the creativity of God. The Roman Empire, combined with the life, death and resurrection of Jesus Christ and the practice of repentance, created such a community of interacting persons. This community is not the church as an institution but it is made up of certain interacting individuals who have made this absolute commitment.

Thus the released and unlimited creativity of God reaches us through Jesus Christ. Perhaps it may be found through other religions. Perhaps not. It is not our part to pronounce judgment on that point. We only say that Christianity is the way by which it reaches us and that it is the best and greatest reality to be found in our Christian heritage.

PART 4:
THE PERSON, SOCIETY, AND CREATIVE INTERCHANGE

INTRODUCTION

The editor is well aware that Wieman's statements
with regard to the person, society, and creative interchange
are not limited to these three essays. As in the case with
other "topics," Wieman's analyses of this one range throughout his books and essays. The essays gathered here are
representative of how he has approached and analyzed this
topic, however.

These three essays show how Wieman analyzes the
power and salvation of creative interchange as it functions
throughout history, from its creation of the level of existence
called human, to the emergence of the individual human organism out of a matrix of plurality of individuals, to the relational achievement of the person through its responses to
the relational achievements of other persons, and to the
emergence of culture and history. These analyses indicate
how the function of creative interchange is frustrated by the
inertias latent in the individual, the person, society, institutions, culture, and history.

It is only through ultimate commitment to creative interchange that persons in relations can expect to find the
standard by which to distinguish between the good and the evil
in the alternative actions for which they are "responsible."
When the good is chosen at such times, "speech" in the existential situation, personal and social stability, and education for social direction are achieved.

SPEECH IN THE EXISTENTIAL SITUATION*

The problem to be considered in this essay can be stated in these words: How can the resources of the existential situation be used to communicate awareness of the good and evil in the alternative courses of action calling for decision? I shall try to show that this problem is of paramount importance for the conduct of human living generally and especially for the time in which we live.

The existential situation is the actual, present set of conditions in which the speaker utters what he has to say. It is made up of three parts: (1) the total expressiveness of the bodily presence and personality of the speaker; (2) the total responsiveness of the bodily presence and personality of the listener or listeners; (3) the events leading to the present from which arise the alternative courses of action determining the good and evil in the lives of those involved.

The kind of speech which communicates the sense of good and evil most effectively is here called "creative interchange" to distinguish it from other forms of speech. By creative interchange we mean that kind of communication which does three things: (1) creates an understanding in the listener of the viewpoint of the speaker; (2) integrates this viewpoint into the perspective of the listener so that he has a more comprehensive understanding; (3) communicates the sense of good and evil so that each can be aware of the way the other values the alternative possibilities arising out of the situation.

The viewpoint and the values thus communicated may be in error. Nevertheless this kind of communication is of great positive value because knowledge of misdirected striving in the lives of associates is indispensable to any effective, intelligent action. The discovery of error, and the effort to

---

*Reprinted from Quarterly Journal of Speech, Vol. XLVII (April, 1961), No. 2, pp. 150-157.

correct it, is one of the most common ways leading to more comprehensive and reliable knowledge. Furthermore, it may be I who have the error and I who judge the evil to be good. In this case, interchange of the sense of good and evil between me and the other person is the way in which my mistaken standard of judgment is most likely to be corrected. Regardless of the truth and error involved, and regardless of the mistaken sense of good and evil communicated, this kind of interchange is a basic good in human life. It is the chief way in which error is corrected, knowledge expanded, values purged, insight deepened, and appreciative understanding established among individuals, groups, and peoples. Creative interchange cannot be complete until the viewpoint of the other is integrated into my own perspective. This integration may be positive, affirming the truth and virtue involved in the communication, or it may be negative. In either case this integration expands and deepens the sense of values and the knowledge had by each.

All thought, all striving, all knowledge, all action, all decision, indeed the whole of human life is directed and controlled by what men judge to be good and evil. Therefore, the all-important part of any communication is the view of good and evil involved in it. Logic, information, evidence, knowledge, and rationality take on great value when they serve to communicate a profound sense of good and evil and clarify the distinctions between them. But when information, technique, and rational order are not put to communicating this profound intuition, or when they are treated as ends in themselves, they become trivial in the sense that they make no appreciable difference in the conduct of human living. Nothing can make an appreciable difference in human life unless it motivates thought, feeling, and action. Since the sense of good and evil alone can motivate, all knowledge and all forms of reason are trivial unless they carry with them this driving sense.

But values cannot be communicated effectively and profoundly apart from the resources of the existential situation. In order to communicate effectively the sense of good and evil, the total expressiveness of the bodily presence and personality of the speaker is required; also required is the total responsiveness of the bodily presence and personality of the listener. This expressiveness and responsiveness must be joined with awareness of the events leading to the present and must reveal the fateful alternative possibilities issuing from these events.

This points to a very important conclusion about a dominant drift in modern society. Communication is being taken over more and more by machinery, which excludes the expressiveness of the bodily presence and personality of the speaker and reduces the responsiveness of the listener. These mechanized forms of communication include print, radio, television, recorded speeches, and teaching machines. Such mechanized communications reduce the sense of events that created the present and reduce the possibility of realizing the fateful consequences of the future.

Television does, of course, present the visual image of the speaker, but this is not the same as the bodily presence. Television productions are generally show pieces, artfully designed and lacking the spontaneity of bodily presence. Even when not artfully designed, the individual in the wholeness of his being, charged with his compelling sense of values, is not before us. As for the listener, sitting alone or with a few friends in his home amid conditions designed for relaxation rather than total responsiveness, watching a production interspersed with commercial advertisements and trivial skits, he is in no condition to respond to the values involved in compelling and fateful issues. The existential situation necessary to communicate a driving sense of good and evil is even more clearly absent in other mechanized forms of communication so that radio has fewer aspects of the existential situation, while printing, recordings, teaching machines, all fail to create the best conditions for creative interchange.

A serious danger threatens our society as mechanized communication prevails and the speech of creative interchange declines. The danger is that men will lose the sense of the great values at stake in human existence, thus becoming apathetic, preoccupied with trivial matters, unable to experience the driving passion of those men who have lived greatly, whether in defeat or in triumph. This apathy and triviality will be the consequence of excluding speech in the form of creative interchange, because the great values must be built up in the individual by this kind of communication. No infant is born with these values; he must acquire them by integrating many visions into a profound and comprehensive vision.

By no means are we saying that speech with bodily presence in the existential situation always communicates the sense of good and evil among the parties concerned. There are many kinds and forms of speech. In many cases,

speech communicates values no better than a machine does.
But creative interchange, which requires the existential situation as we have defined it, does communicate values more profoundly and effectively than any other form of speech.
The great art in speech is to communicate values at deeper levels than is possible without this art. Values at deeper levels are those that underlie and sustain a great number of other values. Words alone are ineffective in communicating values, but speech in the threefold existential situation may bring the maximum sense of awareness of the good and evil implicit in alternative choices. In such a situation, creative interchange would be lifted to dominance over counter processes.

On the other hand, it should be noted that creative interchange is not an ideal. It is an actuality that is always occurring to some degree, even when suppressed, obstructed, and reduced to a minimum by other kinds of communication and by distracting interests. Although creative interchange is not an ideal, one may have ideals about it, just as one may have the ideal of lifting it to a higher level of dominance.
The process of creative interchange is prior to all ideals.
One must first have the sense of good and evil before he can have ideals. Since creative interchange creates the sense of good and evil at the human level, it is the creative source of all ideals. Therefore, instead of ideals bringing creative interchange into existence, the reverse is the truth of the matter. Moreover, if ideals are to have their scope extended or if one is to be moved by values at deeper levels, creative interchange must first awaken the ideal or value. In the development of both human individuals and human cultures, creative interchange advances the ideal rather than the ideal advancing creative interchange.

For these reasons, ideals should be subordinated to creative interchange and made to serve it. When the reverse occurs, great evils follow. When the ideal is set up as supreme and human life is shaped to meet the demands of the ideal, this sovereignty suppresses and inhibits the creativity which should correct the ideal and expand its range of values. In addition, the sovereignty of the ideal prevents such correction as might occur if the ideal were forced to meet the demands of different individuals, problems, and conditions. When the ideal is supreme, it cannot be transformed to take into consideration those deeper values and wider reaches of good and evil which can be brought about through creative interchange.

In failing to understand the necessity to make creative interchange superior to ideals, many have made tragic errors. The religious humanist sets up the ideal as supreme. The tragic error of the social sciences is that they repudiate the moral obligation of seeking out the social conditions most favorable for the effective operation of creative interchange among individuals, among organized groups, and among all conflicting divisions of society, including the diverse nations, cultures, and races now compelled to live on this planet in intimate interdependence. This moral irresponsibility of the social sciences is one of the most dangerous features of our American society. The social scientists claim that their responsibility ends with providing the knowledge that can be used as a means to the attainment of any end, no matter how evil that end may be. Thus the exploiters, the deceivers, the propagandists, the racketeers, and the destroyers are served as readily and effectively by research in the social sciences as any who might seek to promote the greater good. This moral irresponsibility may not characterize all social scientists, but it is the position taken by the sociologists with whom I have conversed and argued.

Speech, both as a field for research and as a practicing art, carries a special moral responsibility for promoting the kind of communication which expands the range of what men can appreciate as good and distinguish as evil. If creative interchange is not the best name to distinguish this kind of speech, some other name can be devised. The name is not important, but this kind of communication is, since all distinctively human values are created by creative interchange, beginning with early infancy and continuing throughout the life of the individual. If creative interchange does not occur effectively between parent and child, the child becomes neurotic or psychotic or otherwise unfit to live with other human beings in ways of mutual trust and mutual support.

To the measure that this kind of communication dominates over the counter processes going on in our interpersonal and social relations, life is good. To the measure that it is obstructed, reduced, or subordinated to other processes, life becomes evil. This claim is based first of all on the fact that this kind of interchange creates the human level of existence in the infant. To the measure that it prevails over counter processes, it sustains the human level over against all that tends to tear down and destroy mutual support and creative transformation in our relations to one another. This kind of interchange renders conflict constructive rather than

destructive since it expands the range of our sense of values
to include those of the other party. It is the only way that
conflicts can be resolved insofar as resolution is possible.
When conflicts cannot be resolved, this kind of interchange
makes the conflict a source of new insights and constructive
action, provided that the conflicting parties give priority to
this kind of interchange as being the source of greatest good.

This is not a blueprint for utopia. No suggestion is
here made that all evil will disappear and all good prevail
if and when the moral priority of creative interchange is accepted and is promoted by research in the social sciences
and in the art of communication. Our only claim is that this
is the way, and the only way, in which human life can be
made less evil. No one knows how much good may be attained, and how much evil may be reduced or how much the
reverse may occur. But there is a way to promote the good
so far as it can be promoted. If we fail and life sinks to
even deeper levels of evil, the claim still stands: Creative
interchange is the way to promote the greater good in so far
as it is possible to promote it. To what degree it can prevail, nobody knows. But this is the road to the greater
good, whether or not we are able to travel it.

More than any other animal, man is addicted to
courses of action leading to self-destruction. Other animals
may fail to cope with environmental conditions, but they do
not develop ever-increasing power organized and directed to
their own destruction. Men have been occupied in such destruction throughout human history, whether they did it by
exploiting and grinding down to miserable poverty the mass
of workers or by wanton destruction and exhaustion of natural resources or by military conquest and slaughter of fellow
men.

The chief danger that has always threatened human existence, becoming more dangerous as human power increases,
is this propensity for self-destruction. The only way of deliverance from the fatal consequences of this propensity is
the kind of communication by which we get the values of the
other person, group, or class of people, and integrate them
into our own perspective. This is the thesis I shall try to
demonstrate, first by stating the distinctive characteristics
of the human level of existence and then showing that creative interchange creates this human level, sustains it, saves
it from self-destruction, and develops its constructive potentialities to the measure that it prevails over all that oppose it.

Excepting the biological organism of man, everything distinctively human is created and sustained by the use of language. The human level is distinguished from every other form of existence by the indefinite expansion of the range of knowledge, of control, of values appreciated and evils distinguished, and by the depth of subjectivity which the individual finds in himself and senses in other human beings. But all this is the consequence of using language when language means signs which carry meanings sufficiently independent of the local situation to expand and develop in the ways just mentioned. Even the biological organism peculiar to man, while not directly created by language, could not occur without it. The new born human infant is so helpless for so long a time that it could not be kept alive and developed to become a language-user without the elaborate, intimate, and long continued care made possible by the use of language between the parents and other associates upon whom the infant depends for survival.

Culture and history are distinctive characteristics of the human level of existence, but they could not arise nor continue without the use of language. Culture is the sharing of knowledge, techniques, and values; and this sharing could not occur without the kind of communication made possible by the use of language. History is the accumulation and communication of resources for human living through a sequence of generations, and this also depends on the use of language. These uniquely human activities require for their origin that language, at least in some degree, be used creatively to expand the range of knowledge, the perception of values, and the awareness of deep subjectivity in one's self and others. But language can be used in other ways that prevent creative interchange.

Creative interchange should be sharply distinguished from that use of language by which one party dominates and controls the other without any consideration for the values sought and cherished by the dominated individuals. Many kinds of propaganda used to exercise political control or sell goods are of this sort. Language can be used in this way to reduce individuals to brain-washed puppets. Still another kind of communication to be distinguished from the creative is the deceptive. Language is commonly used to protect one's own self esteem by building up a false picture of the self, thus constructing an image deceiving others and also one's self. Then there is regulative communication by which activities are directed and coordinated without generating any

new insights or awakening appreciative consciousness of the
values cherished by the individuals involved. Traffic rules
are of this sort, as are all rules when there is no creative
transformation of the mind and no expanding range of evaluation.

Of course, rules and many other kinds of communication have their place in the conduct of human society. But
they stand in contrast to creative interchange when it uses
all the resources of the existential situation to communicate
from one to another the sense of good and evil. Religion,
morality, art, love, friendship, devotion, passion, vision,
and statesmanship all grow out of this kind of interchange
creating progressively the range and depth of values that
people can experience. Life is mean or noble, destructive
or constructive, miserable or blessed, according as the value-sense of individuals is developed by this kind of communication.

The living presence of a person committed to the im-
port of his utterance, and relatively free of inner conflicts
and inhibitions, is a presence with powerful "hidden persuaders." The impassioned and dedicated person has hidden
persuaders in the sense that a great part of his expressiveness reaches us persuasively below the level of consciousness. We become aware of his thought, his mind, his purpose, of the kind of person he is, in ways we cannot analyze.
We say it is intuitive. The human mind is always fallible,
and these intuitions may be in error, but it is amazing how
accurate and right they are in many cases. Small children
especially, with very undeveloped intellectuality and very little self-consciousness, have these correct intuitions arising
from unconscious response to the subtle and complex expressiveness of another person. Members of the family in intimate association are frequently communicating with one another below the level of consciousness. The communication
is expressed in their reciprocal behavior toward one another.
Words are used, but the meaning conveyed by these words is
not at all derived from the verbal context. It is derived
from the existential situation, including the unconscious expressiveness and the unconscious interpretation of this expressiveness on the part of the persons in the situation.

The most profound and important evaluative understanding of other persons comes to us in this way from unconscious resources in the existential situation. At this unconscious or semi-conscious level, a speaker communicates

with the listener and responds to him when conditions are favorable and when speech utilizes the resources of the existential situation. What we get from the other person in this way is not a descriptive statement about him, for such statements fall hopelessly short of conveying this "understanding" of him. This understanding is our ability to respond appropriately to his unique individuality and to his intentions, purposes, and passions. Our response may be negative in opposition, or positive in cooperation, but it is profound beyond the reach of descriptive statements.

In all these cases the existential situation is potent over the verbal context in determining the meaning communicated. Sometimes the existential situation submerges the verbal context to such a degree that the words take on a meaning wholly foreign to the "proper" or dictionary meaning, as in the following story from A Tree Grows in Brooklyn.

It was the night before Christmas, and the family was too poor to buy a Christmas tree. But the little girl of ten and her brother, nine years of age, knew of a custom prevailing in the locality. They knew that late on the night before Christmas the men who sold Christmas trees would give a tree to any person who would stand up and have a tree thrown at him and not fall down when hit. So brother and sister went out that night to the yard around the corner where the man was selling trees and asked him to throw a tree at them. They stood up hand in hand to support one another while the man threw a tree. They did not fall and so claimed the tree. Then the man said to them: "And now get the hell out of here with your tree, you lousy bastards."

Such were the words the man used. But children have the strange capacity to get a meaning different from the words, a meaning derived from the person and the situation. So the little girl understood that when the man said, "Get the hell out of here," in a certain tone of voice on Christmas Eve when hearts are tender and when the rough men in the locality had no other language, what he really meant was, "Goodbye--God bless you." But the man could not use such language, and the little girl knew it. He used the only kind of language he knew how to use, and the little girl understood the meaning derived not from the words but from the social-historical situation called Christmas time combined with expressiveness of personality.

The written word and mechanized communication have their own kind of superiority over the spoken. When the meaning is derived from the verbal context to the exclusion of the existential situation, the statement can retain its identity of meaning when time passes and new situations arise. The existential situation, giving power and depth and scope of meaning to the spoken word, is swiftly transitory. Hence, the meaning derived from it cannot be recovered except as the original situation, or a typical situation of the same kind, is imaginatively reproduced. But such reproduction is only a pale reflection of what actually happened where the existential situation was most potent in giving depth of meaning to what was said.

The written word does not exclude entirely the meanings derived from the existential situation. For example, a pamphlet or essay written to promote a cause in the heat and turmoil of a great social struggle can take on much of its meaning from the existential situation. But it can never do this with the sweeping power of the spoken word rightly uttered at such a time. Literature as a fine art can also quicken the imagination so that an existential situation is imagined. But here again this falls far short of the actual situation in respect to its effectiveness for stirring men to action, transforming the mental attitude, and recreating organization of personality. Furthermore, this imagined situation depends for its effectiveness and content upon actual situations that have been experienced by way of the spoken word.

Complex social-historical situations cannot pour their full meaning into the life of the individual or into the life of the people without the spoken word to interpret this meaning and communicate it. The spoken word may be spoken to oneself; but without speech, the depth, the transforming power, and the far reach of values to be derived from the swiftly passing existential situation can never enter human experience and shape the conduct of human life. This is the genius and high vocation of speech in contrast to the written word and all mechanized forms of communication.

The human level of existence is created by the use of language with all the meanings that language can carry. This human level is dangerously self-destructive. It becomes self-destructive when there is obstruction to the kind of interchange which creates appreciative understanding of one another. It is constructive when this communication of the values of each to the other can be most full, free, and pro-

found, thus expanding indefinitely the vision of good and evil
involved in the situation calling for decision and action to
avoid the evil and attain the good.

We are all in the predicament of being human. He
who says that the human level of existence is not good does
thereby demonstrate that he has not found it good. Psychological studies indicate that he who has not found it good to
live at the human level, is one who has not found among his
fellows an appreciative understanding of himself nor has acquired such an understanding of them. On the other hand,
he who finds human life good is one who has been able to
engage in this kind of interchange with the experience of expanding horizons of good and evil through learning from others a widening range of what can be evaluated.

We live in an age when communication of values has
declined giving place to mechanized communication of knowledge and techniques of control. The consequence is that
knowledge and power of control have increased more rapidly
than the sense of values by which this knowledge and this
power might be directed and controlled. For this reason we
do not know how to use our magnified power constructively
and wisely. When power is swiftly and vastly increased without proportionate increase in the range and depth of values
discerned and appreciated, the power becomes destructive in
the hands of those who do not know how to use it for their
own good. This is the predicament of modern man. His
salvation lies in that kind of interchange which increases the
range and depth of values discerned and appreciated.

Here is the high vocation and major responsibility for
the teacher of speech. First of all it is a problem for research. Then it is the cultivation of an art. The problem
and the art are to make speech expressive of values by using the resources of the existential situation. This is the
kind of speech we must have to be saved from self-destruction when our power has become so great that it cannot be
controlled nor directed by the sense of values now prevailing. We must have a more profound, comprehensive, and
accurate discernment of the good and evil involved in the social developments of our time. This must be created in the
minds of men by the kind of speech which communicates
from one to another the deepest discernment of value each
has attained. In this way the integration of many visions into
one profound and comprehensive vision might show us the
way to use our power constructively. Furthermore, this is

the only way that democracy can be sustained and communicated to others.

We have gathered knowledge and magnified power in many areas, but we have neglected to seek knowledge concerning the conditions under which the value-sense of the individual and the values shared in community can be deepened, widened, corrected, and made to remove the barriers of estrangement and hostility among peoples and cultures. To express these values and remove these barriers is the opportunity and responsibility for the teacher of speech.

ACHIEVING PERSONAL STABILITY*

When a person possesses what he regards as most important, he has personal stability. When he is cut off from what is most important to him, he suffers instability. Many a man today feels that what is most important to him is being destroyed or is becoming inaccessible or is otherwise threatened. For such a one the river of life no longer flows in full volume. Will he be able to keep his home? Can he keep his family together? Will his son be killed in battle? Will he have to live in a society where he cannot think and act according to his true convictions? If the things threatened are to his essential for living significantly, or if they are connected with what is essential, so that if he should lose them life would cease to be worth the striving, stability is impaired or destroyed.

Every person seeks stability; yet it is not always good. In fact, it may be very evil. If what I feel to be most important for me obstructs the good of human living as a whole, my stability may be worse than instability. If my continued sense of worth in living requires that I be the star on every occasion, the center of attention and admiration, my personal stability becomes a nuisance and may be devastating. Or, again, personal stability may be based upon something very trivial. If what I feel to be most important for me is only an inconsequential detail in the story of man, not closely related to the central plot and underlying theme, then the more stability I achieve, the more shallow and superficial I become. Personal stability may be very insecure. I may be perfectly stabilized, and yet that on which my stability rests may be taken away at any time. I may feel perfectly secure because I know nothing of that likelihood; but, if what gives me the sense of worth in living is destined to fade away with the onset of pain and loss, of defeat and ig-

*Reprinted from Religion and the Present Crisis. John Knox, (ed.) Chicago: University of Chicago Press, 1942, pp. 69-86.

nominy, of old age and death, then my personal stability is
itself insecure.

The problem, then, is not merely to achieve personal
stability. It is rather to achieve that kind of stability which
can also be the basis of stability for society, for history,
and for humanity. What gives this kind of stability to the individual must be identical with what gives stability to democracy and to the planetary enterprise of man. That reality
which the individual feels is most important for him must be
identical with the reality which is truly most important for
all human living. The deepest foundations of personal stability are also the foundations of social stability.

There is a story running through all of human living.
It gives meaning and worth to all the disasters and tragedies
as well as to all the triumphs and fulfilments. When one
discerns the central theme of this story, one finds that it
gives meaning to pain and loss and age and death as well as
to their opposites.   Furthermore, when this underlying theme
of all human existence becomes most important to me, not
merely in theory or in belief, but vitally and personally, so
that it controls my living, then I have the ultimate stability.

But, before we discuss this underlying theme, let us
look at several ways in which men actually seek stability.
We shall then be in position to designate, without attempting
to set up theoretical norms, the way which gives what I have
just called the "ultimate stability."

I

May I indicate with an illustration the first and most
common of these ways of seeking stability? Here is the
head painter in an automobile factory. His sustaining interest is his job. He has worked his way up to his position,
and it makes him a respected participant in the way of life
of those whose good will is important to him. He is associated with people whom he respects and by whom he is respected. He can talk to them, and he knows that they are
interested in what he says, and he is interested in them.
He belongs to a certain arrangement of things, and the interest of each man who benefits from this arrangement supports
and augments the interest of all the others. He has personal stability because he belongs to this particular established
order of life.

If you asked such a one if he was happy, he might very correctly say, "No"; but we are not talking about that elusive thing called "happiness." This particular painter, let us say, is not happy because his wife is sick and his children misbehave frightfully. Besides, he broke his arm and for a while could not earn enough to provide for the family. His automobile was stolen, and on Hallowe'en those Polacks from across the tracks broke the window panes in his house. "How can I be happy in a world like that?" he demands. In fact, he goes so far as to say that he does not believe in happiness. But his personal stability endures so long as that order of life endures to which he and the people who count in his esteem belong.

But let us suppose the head painter loses his job and cannot get another. Suppose he has to leave town and go among folk who do not honor the things which are right and good in his eyes. Suppose his children not only misbehave but do not even respect his moral standards. Suppose he is out of touch with any who appreciate very deeply what makes life worth living for him. In a word, suppose he is, for any reason, separated from the order of life which to him is most important--then the sustaining interest of his life will fail and his personal stability with it.

Many people today are having the experience we have just described. Such a person may sneak around like a shadow, trying to conceal his inner self because that inner self is made up of appreciations which no one seems to care about. He may take to drink in order to forget it all. He may resort to various devices, such as pretending to be something different from what he truly is. His stability has always depended upon living within the sustaining arms of a certain order of life. That order is breaking into fragments, and with it his sense of worth in living also fails.

Let us leave him, then, and look at another way of achieving stability. Here is a man who has not been born into an established and honored way of life, but he has been born and reared under conditions which have developed in him the resources and the confidence to achieve what he regards as most important. Perhaps he has been trained to endure hard knocks of all kinds and has had enough initial success in the face of difficulty to give him the confidence he needs. His sense of worth and his personal stability depend upon self-confidence. This way of seeking stability is not necessarily any more ignoble than the first; some admir-

able examples of it are known to all of us.   But the task of
preserving self-sufficiency is becoming more and more difficult with every week that goes by.   Self-confidence tends to
become more desperate, more destructive, and generally
more evil as it becomes more difficult to maintain.   The
great dictators of our day are perhaps the outstanding examples of stability grounded in deliberate self-sufficiency.

Still another way to personal stability is that of idealism.   No one particular established order is most important
to one who follows this third way, nor is his own self-confidence, but rather the greatness and the worth of some ideal
order which he has envisioned.   Not what he has, nor yet
what he is able to achieve, but the importance of what he
serves in the form of an ideal gives him personal stability.

But people today are not so sure of their ideals as
they once were.   We have come to see that the highest ideals
are merely the highest conceivable by a very limited human
mind, namely, our own--a mind which is culture-biased,
vanity-ridden, blind-spotted.   Some of the worst pests and
destroyers are persons most sure of the nobility of their
ideals.   The mutually destructive conflict between huge, dynamic organization of men, each striving for the highest in
its own esteem, has made us question the effectiveness of
this way to stability.   The Nazis seek one ideal order with
amazing devotion and commitment.   The communists seek
another with a completeness of self-giving no less astounding.
Is this the way to the ultimate stability of the individual?
Is this the way to the ultimate stability of society and of human history?

Unsatisfied as yet, we turn to a fourth way of achieving personal stability.   It is the way of faith, as that word
is most commonly understood.   It is personal stability found
by way of a belief which cannot be supported by rational and
empirical evidence.   If I see that there is no established order which can be securely held as most important for me,
if self-confidence either becomes pernicious or is weakened,
and if I cannot be sure that the highest ideals as envisaged
by me or anyone I know are most worthful for all human living, then may I not turn to supernatural revelation or un-
tested intuition or dogmatic authority?   Beyond the bounds of
what we can experience in this world is there not another
realm?   Many thousands of people assure me that there is,
and that I need only faith, unsupported by ordinary evidence,
to make it mine.   In this place by horror haunted is there

balm in Gilead?   Quoth the Raven, "Yes."

     This way of faith that goes beyond the evidence may
not be directed to what are ordinarily called "religious objects," although that is most common.   It may be nothing
more than belief in good luck.   It may be the belief of Mr.
Micawber who was always very sure that some good turn of
fortune was just about to happen.   Something would surely
turn up!   Personal stability may be centered in unsupported
belief in fate or luck or God, but in any case it is belief
which cannot be held except by what is called "a leap of
faith."

     This way to personal stability, popular and sporadi-
cally effective as it has always been and probably always
will be, is having serious difficulties in these times.   It is
true that the more the other ways to personal stability are
blocked, the more this one is resorted to.   On the other
hand, it is not so easy for the modern man to hold beliefs
of this sort with the sureness which personal stability requires.   These beliefs are being shaken by the spread and
influence of science, by penetrating analyses with powerful
intellectual instruments, by psychological and sociological
studies into the cause and source of such beliefs, and by the
general empirical-mindedness that has tended to pervade our
world.   If a modern sophisticated mind is going to achieve
personal stability by way of such a faith, either the belief
must be defended by very intricate and subtly rationalizing
logical devices or else such a mind must repudiate reason
and intelligence and evidence when matters regarded as most
important are concerned.   Since there are many of us, however, who feel that either alternative exposes us to great
dangers and evils, we turn away again to seek still a fifth
way of achieving personal and social stability in our time.

     This fifth way is that of adaptation.   Instead of striv-
ing to conserve some specific order felt to be most important, or striving to keep one's confidence that one can achieve
what one needs, or clinging to some ideal order or resort-
ing to the leap of faith, one simply uses one's ingenuity to
adapt to whatever order may present itself.   The finest modern exposition I know of this way of achieving personal stability is to be found in the last chapter of Walter Lippmann's
Preface to Morals.   This way of adaptation has also been
nobly upheld by the great Stoics, by Spinoza, and by others.
At its best, it yields a certain greatness and goodness; but
its limitations are obvious.   At its worst, it degenerates in-

to the use of clever tricks to win one's way to social accept-
ability in whatever group happens to be dominant. It may become more opportunism and expediency. This, like all the
other ways to personal stability which we have examined, has
both its noble and its ignoble forms. But in the last weigh-
ing, it is always found wanting.

II

So far we have described five different ways in which
men have sought and found access to what they felt to be
most important. They do not always take the form of a religion; but every one of them, and every possible combination of them, has been interpreted and practiced as a religion. I would go further and say that every one of them,
and every possible combination of them, has been interpreted
and practiced under the name of Christianity. Every one of
them has been described as the way which Jesus taught and
practiced. But the way to ultimate stability, not only for the
individual but for society and for all of human history, is
different from all of them. It is my belief, also, that this
way which I shall now try to describe is the most distinctive
and important element in Christianity, although Christianity
has no monopoly on it. This way--which is man's destiny,
which connects him with the central theme of the story of
man--is personal commitment to the creativity of the living
God. The creativity of God is not something outside this
world beyond the reach of our surest knowing. It does not
require the leap of faith. We can prove its reality. We can
know it and experience it. Faith is required, to be sure,
but not faith in the sense of a leap beyond the evidence. It
is faith in the sense of giving one's self over to the control
of this creativity after one has proof of its reality and its
importance.

This is not to say that there are no difficulties in
achieving stability in this last way. But the difficulties grow
out of our immaturity, not out of misplaced trust.

The first of the difficulties which obstruct this way to
ultimate stability has to do with the original nature of man.
No child in the beginning can find personal stability by committing himself to the creativity of God. Every young child
must find stability in one or more of the first ways which we
have considered. He must find his stability in his membership in the established order of the home. If a child is to

have a wholesome, integrated personality, he must have a
sense of belonging to that small group of people who love him
and care for him.   He must feel that he belongs regardless
of any merit on his part.   If he feels that he must earn his
right to belong, if he feels that he must make good or else
be cast out from the inner circle of the home, he will become anxious, neurotic, and may suffer all his life from a
deep instability.   But unless his parents see that the growing
child must gradually find a new basis for his stability, he
may always seek this way of locating a congenial group in
which he can have membership, no matter what sacrifice of
integrity this membership may require.

        The second difficulty which obstructs the way to ulti-
mate stability in the creativity of God follows naturally from
this first.   Every individual, we have just seen, must first
become stabilized in the established order of the home.
Then, normally, he should develop self-confidence in constructing some order of his own.   Also, he will develop
ideals and be controlled by them.   All this is required for a
wholesome and well-developed personality.   Now, if a man
becomes fairly well stabilized in these more elementary and
temporary ways, he will not seek any other way to stability.
This comes necessarily from the very nature of stability.   If
he has achieved stability in something other than the creativity of God, he cannot turn to the creativity of God to find stability.   He already has it and therefore will stay where he is.

        Now it is true that the creativity of God is never
wholly absent from the foundations of any man's stability if
he has found it by attaching himself to any truly good thing.
The creativity of God is not absent from the established order of the home or from any other good order which may
give him stability.   It is not absent from self-confidence, nor
from ideals which give a man a sense of worth in living.
All this is true.   But there is another truth which is not so
commonly seen: The good gifts which are bestowed upon man
by the creativity of God may beguile the soul of man to fas-
ten upon the gifts and turn away from the giver.   Most commonly men find their stability by attaching importance to
some gift which they have received, while ignoring the giver,
this giver being always the creativity of God.   Sometimes,
indeed, men find a sense of worth by devotion to what is a
perversion of what God has produced.   In any case, having
found stability in something less than the creativity of God,
they will not turn to this creativity until they undergo some
catastrophe and so become unstabilized in the old ways.

Their regularly established order begins to fail, their self-confidence begins to weaken, their ideals show themselves to be false guides, the leap of faith is seriously questioned, the way of adaptation becomes unsatisfactory. Until their stability in the old ways has been disturbed, they will not seek the ultimate stability.

What I have just been saying applies not only to man's relation to God but also to his relation to everything else. So long as a man is quite satisfied with a model-T Ford, he is not going to try to get a Cadillac. When he feels that the elementary grades in school give him all the learning he wants, he is not going on to high school and college. Whenever and wherever a man finds personal stability in the sense of gaining access to what he feels is most important for him, he is not going to seek anything else. Since the requirements of childhood and infancy demand that each person first find personal stability in some gift of God's creativity and not by giving himself directly to that creativity itself, no man will seek and find the ultimate stability until these other stabilities are disturbed. No bird will learn to fly if it is content to stay in the nest where it is hatched. Something must force it to leave the nest. So it is with man and his relation to the creativity of God.

It is on this account that those who have the best and greatest gifts are often the last to find ultimate stability in the creativity of God. Often these talented ones never find it at all. Therefore the first shall be last, and the last shall be first. Therefore, not many wise, not many strong, not many noble, are chosen. The wise, the strong, the noble, the gifted, generally have ingenuity and resources for finding the utmost possible stability in these other ways. The nest which they make for themselves and inhabit is so secure and so satisfying that they never learn to fly. So it has been said that the meek shall inherit the earth and that the poor in spirit shall possess the kingdom of Heaven. Those who mourn shall be comforted, and those who are reviled and persecuted and have all manner of evil said against them falsely shall be blessed.

A homely woman is likely to know more about all the devices and resources for achieving beauty than does the gorgeous creature who walks in beauty and does not know how it happened. A man who has had to encounter great personal difficulties may know more about the ultimate sources of personal stability than more fortunate persons. There is a wis-

dom had by the foolish which the strong and the wise cannot
possess unless they become greatly humbled. The oppressed
and the impoverished can know some realities which the rul-
ers and the wealthy cannot discover. There are truths revealed to babes and sucklings which the great intellect by
reason of its very greatness may not find. The kind of civilization and the kind of education we have today have developed the minds most exposed to them, which usually means
the best minds, in ways which render it difficult for them to
detect the most important realities. To say this in the
midst of a great university in the most powerful and prosper-
ous country in the world may seem terrible. But some
truths are terrible.

Being in trouble over the failure of the lesser stabilities, however, does not necessarily lead to the finding of ultimate stability. Men can suffer all manner of impoverishment, pain, ignominy, disaster and despair, and still not find
the way to ultimate stability. They may be cut off from
what they feel to be most important for them and continue in
this state indefinitely without ever finding intimately and com-
pulsively the supreme importance of God's creativity. Indeed, all these troubles are likely to make their last estate
worse than the first, for in their panic they tend to fall back
upon some mean and wicked established order, or their self-
confidence becomes demonic, or their idealism degenerates
into a resolution to superimpose an ideal order by force, as
by tank and gun upon all of Europe. Or they make the leap
of faith with increasing disregard of reason, intelligence, and
empirical evidence. In short, there is a third requirement
which must be met before one can find ultimate stability in
the creativity of God. Not only must a man be born into the
nest of an established order, and not only must he be forced
out of that nest, before he can learn to fly in the creativity
of God, but he must also be associated with people who have
learned to fly. He must ordinarily have had personal association with people who have found this ultimate stability in
riding the winds of God's creativity. If he does not have association with people who are living this way, he can scarcely secure any experience of this other way of life. How,
then, can he gain access to it?

The people who live in commitment to the creativity of
God and who are, therefore, transmitters of this way of life
to others are a peculiar community. This community has a
remarkable historic continuity. Furthermore, this community is nameless. It is nameless because the name we have

for it inevitably conveys the wrong meaning. The name we have for it is "church." "Church" means many things: an ecclesiastic organization, a social institution, institutionalized Christianity. It means the officers and the committees, the ceremonies and the doctrines. For the most of us, church does not mean the community and historic continuity of those who live under the dominant control of the creativity of God. Therefore this community and continuity must for the present remain nameless. What we are saying, however, is that no man, except by happy accident, can find this ultimate stability in God's creativity except he be introduced to this way of living by the community and historic continuity of those who live in this way.

Something still further must happen to the man seeking ultimate stability in the creativity of God. Some judgment must be generated in him of the difference in worthfulness between his old way of living and the new. This judgment may not be articulate. It may not be formulated into a neat proposition. It may be more a feeling and a subconscious propulsion. But he must have some appraising apprehension of the comparative worth of these two ways. This judgment of value emerges out of the interaction with other persons who are living sincere and meaningful lives.

Finally, he must <u>decide</u>--definitely, sincerely, wholeheartedly--that he will give himself to this new way. Then he must practice the disciplines required to continue and develop this way of living.

In this new way he will find stability through having access to what he feels is most important to him. That is true of every way of finding stability in so far as it is effective. But the difference between this new way and the old is that what one now feels to be most important is not a human structure. It is not an established order; it is not self-confidence in one's ability to achieve an order thought to be good; it is not one's idealism, nor one's leap of faith, nor one's adaptations. It is nothing else than the creativity of God.

III

Here, however, we come again to an insistent question which cannot longer be put off. What do we mean by this creativity of God? We must see it in terms of common,

everyday experience. It is not something far off. It is
something we are experiencing all the time and must experience as long as we are human beings because it alone makes
us human. By "creativity of God" we mean, it is important
to notice first of all, something that is done to us, not by us.
We can provide the conditions needed for its operation, but
we cannot do the work itself. That work is to make us mutually aware of one another's interests. We cannot make ourselves aware of the interests of others any more than we can
make cartilage turn into bone in the growing child. But when
we meet the required conditions, we become aware of what
the other is thinking, feeling, hoping, fearing. These interests of others emerge, first of all, in our minds as intuition.
When we talk with another person and observe him, we become aware of what he is seeking and avoiding, what he is
remembering and imagining, provided we keep ourselves in
attentive readiness to be inwardly transformed by these intuitions as they emerge.

Watch an infant when it first begins to react with understanding to the signs and symbols used by its parents and
others. One will see the creativity of God at work bringing
into existence a human mind and personality, community and
history, and unfolding in that infant all the values that are
distinctive and constitutive of the life of man. Watch that
baby just as mind is dawning in him. That dawning mind is
the emergence in him of his intuitions of your meanings when
you make certain signs. These intuitions are not the result
of the infant's using his intelligence; his intelligence operates
to test, apply, and interpret them.

An intuition taken by itself is neither true nor false.
It is just a happening in the mind where it occurs. Most of
our communion and the most precious experiences of our lives
are of this sort. They are not propositions which are found
to be true or false. They are experiences in which, when we
are most sensitive and responsive to one another, a great
wealth of ideas and feelings is generated in us by the creativity of God.

Steinbeck in his Grapes of Wrath tells of how the people in the dust bowl, especially the women and children, got
this awareness of thought and feeling through such sensitivity
and responsiveness. The dust had ruined the corn,

> drying fast now, only a little green showing through
> the film of dust. The men were silent and they did

not move often.   And the women came out of the
houses to stand beside their men--to feel whether
this time the men would break.   The women studied the men's faces secretly, for the corn could go,
as long as something else remained.   The children
stood near by, drawing figures in the dust with bare
toes, and the children sent exploring senses out to
see whether men and women would break.   The
children peeked at the faces of the men and women,
and then drew careful lines in the dust with their
toes.   Horses came to the watering troughs and
nuzzled the water to clear the surface dust.   After
a while the faces of the watching men lost their be-
mused perplexity and became hard and angry and
resistant.   Then the women knew that they were
safe and that there was no break.   Then they asked:
What'll we do?   And the men replied: I don't know.
But it was all right.   The women knew it was all
right, and the watching children knew it was all right.
Women and children knew deep in themselves that
no misfortune was too great to bear if their men
were whole.   The women went into the houses to
their work, and the children began to play, but
cautiously at first.

Under proper conditions we become aware of the hope
and fear, joy and sorrow, hate and love, in the minds of
one another, and this is what makes us human.   What we do
with this awareness of the interests of others may be very
evil, but the getting of this awareness is the source of all
human good, and it is the creativity of God.   He who gives
himself to this without reservation will find the ultimate stability.

This creativity of God, we hold, is what was released
into history with magnified power and scope by the cross of
Christ.   Commitment to this creativity is what we find expressed in the New Testament.   Perhaps nowhere do we find
it more vividly and jubilantly proclaimed than in the writings
of Paul.   Paul called it the "living Christ,"--Christ risen
from the dead and living in our midst, Christ not after the
flesh but after the spirit.   This creativity is not a set of
principles, not even the principles of Jesus.   It is not an
idea, or an ideal, or a teaching.   It is the living and creative source of ideas and ideals and teachings.   In its deepest
and most distinctive character it is not ethical living.   To be
sure, it issues in ethical living.   Ethical living is the fruit

of it, not the root, for the root of it is living under the control of that creativity which generates our ethical ideals along with all else that is good. It is living under the control of that living God who creates and transforms our ideals, for it is precisely this mutual awareness of one another's interests which does this. We can see the truth of this in the contrary case. Living under the dominant control of our preconceived ideals will blind us to the interests of others and cause us to perpetuate great evils. For the human mind is very vain in its judgments of what is highest and best for God and the world and fellow-man.

IV

This way of living, I have said, is not only the way to personal stability; it is also the way to social stability. Our American democracy is desperately in need of some basis of stability which is trustworthy, which will give access to what is most important, and which will not be destructive of America's own good and that of other peoples.

There is a faith to be formed and reared here in America which was never lived in any other time or age. I do not mean that it will necessarily be superior to all others. I mean that it must be characteristically American and therefore different. Every age and people must have its own formulation of the Christian faith, just as every individual must. Certainly each age and people must draw from the materials of the past. In one sense the faith must always be the ancient faith; but it must also be a people's own, reformulated so that it works freely and pervasively in all that is done and thought and sought by that people. Otherwise the people will stumble and blunder and fall, trying to wear Saul's armor.

Heretofore America has been trying to wear Saul's armor, so far as concerns the Christian faith. Certainly the Christian faith is our heritage. But we have not learned how to express it and live it in our own way. We have not yet formulated it so that we can readily make it a part of our everyday living. It comes to us clothed in a structure of thought which we cannot make our own without separating ourselves from much of the rest of our life. This is fatal. We have not formulated our Christian faith in such a way that it can possess us and we can be possessed by it. That is one cause for our present instability both as individual personalities and as an American people.

But the instability we have as yet experienced is slight, compared to what we are doomed to experience if we will not or cannot develop such an American formulation of our faith that we can live it fully and powerfully in the new age which is swiftly coming. We cannot live by those formulations which Europe was using when she went down to her death as a dominating center of world-culture. The great religious problem of our time is not to take over the established forms of the ancient past for the sake of ecumenicity. If American faith tries to fit itself into those forms, it will not have the power of spiritual life required in these days to come.

For this reason we must distinguish between the various formulations of Christianity now advocated in our country. Some of our most prominent religious leaders are chiefly engaged in transmitting to us the thought-forms of Europe. They are performing an invaluable service. They are sifting and transmitting to us the best of European religious thought so translated that we can assimilate it. But they are American translators of foreign formulations. They are not American creators. If the Christian faith is to live on into the future as a central shaping propulsion in the life of this planet, giving stability in the creativity of God to individuals and peoples, it must be Americanized. This must be because America will have to bear the chief responsibility for putting it into the planetary life which will supersede the segregated regional existence we have known.

Tomorrow America will have to stand up beside Russia and China. These three giants will dominate the earth. Even if Russia should be utterly defeated by the mechanized army of the invader, she cannot be permanently dominated and controlled as a people. With her enormous expanse of territory, with her vast natural resources, with a population of so many millions now awakened to a sense of their power, and with the resources of modern science at their command she cannot be kept a subject country. After the war Russia will rise quickly, as China also will do; and the three great peoples--American, Chinese, and Russian--will be the chief shapers of history. Of these three, America alone will have the Christian faith. If this faith is not so shaped as to become intrinsic to our life, enabling us to move freely and powerfully in the Christian way, so far as any people can, the faiths of Russia and of China will be stronger, more vital, and more adroit. Shall we have our faith so fitted to our power and to our genius that we can express it in our litera-

ture, in our science, in our industry and business, in our
political action, so that it may become a quickening power
in the world?

We must not break community with any other people
anywhere who have this stability in the creativity of God.
But Christians in America have a peculiar responsibility.
The chasm of this war and the days to follow must be
bridged for the Christian faith by the power of America.
Over this bridge the meek of all nations who shall inherit the
earth may pass to their distant kingdom.

Since this is our responsibility, the bridge which we
rear must be strong. Our faith must be shaped so that it
can get into the daily life of our homes and schools. It is
not enough to fit it for the pulpit. Through the home, through
the school, and through the local community it must be carried, with the power that is America, into the world that is
to be.

Heretofore the American people have found their stability partly by way of an established order, partly by self-
confidence that they could construct any conceived order,
partly by idealism, partly by the leap of faith, and partly by
clever adaptation. All these they must continue to practice.
Perhaps all these are inseparable from the human way of living. But none of these can henceforth be the chief means to
personal and social stability on any wide scale.

What we have heretofore held most important must be
made subject to something else. This something else, which
alone can give us stability if we hold it most important, is
that creativity which makes us mutually aware of one another's interests, which enables the thought and feeling, hope
and fear, of each to become creative in others. This alone
can give stability to our hope, to our democracy, to our history, and, through us, to all other peoples. This must give
us our prophecy, our language, and our song.

EDUCATION FOR SOCIAL DIRECTION*[1]

Two facts now before the American people force the problem of education for social direction more vividly into consciousness and make it more urgent than it was ten years ago. One of these two facts is a movement gathering momentum among educators; the other is the developing world situation.

Among educators has appeared the National Policies Commission. It was appointed by the National Education Association and one of its purposes is "to prepare recommendations on education for moral and spiritual values." I have a recent letter from John K. Norton, Chairman of this Commission, in which he is asking a number of men what they think moral and spiritual values are, and what is their source and sanction. Apparently the National Policies Commission and the National Education Association are trying to swing the educational system of our country into the service of a way of life which may give character, direction, and unity to the American people and--if the hope be not too ambitious --contribute to the shared life which all men henceforth must live in common.

The world situation so far as it bears upon this problem might be characterized by three terms: the cold war, the Asiatic peoples, atomic energy. Let me briefly state the significance of these three, so far as they indicate the urgency of organizing and directing education to the end of establishing in the minds and sentiments and habits of each generation a way of life that is broad enough and good enough and cooperative enough to be a highway for all men.

The educational system from the kindergarten to the

---

*Reprinted from Perspectives on a Troubled Decade: Science, Philosophy, and Religion, 1939-49. Lyman Bryson, Louis Finkelstein, R. M. MacIver, editors. (New York: Harper & Row, 1950) pp. 493-506.

top levels of the university could be the most powerful agency in the world for promoting a way of life, if educators
could agree on the broad principles defining such a way, and
would assume responsibility for promoting it, each in his own
field and province.

The first of the three features of the world situation
is the cold war.   Two powers dominating the rest of the
planet are struggling with one another to determine what way
of life shall be followed by the human race.   Modern technology is binding all parts of the world together so that the outcome of this struggle will shape the life of all.   America
cannot swing her weight in this conflict until the way of life
which we would promote is much more clearly defined, widely
established, and unanimously supported in our own country,
than now it is.   No agency at our command is so well fitted
to clarify and establish moral and spiritual values in the
thought and habit of each generation as the universities, and,
under their leadership, the other schools in our educational
system.

If my interpretation of the world situation is correct,
the course of future history will go in one direction or another, according as the universities assume this responsibility or do not.   The problem is not to "defeat the strategems
of the Kremlin."   To envisage the problem in such terms is
puerile.   The problem is to find and to establish a way of
life which all men can follow to the good of all, while living
on a planet that is swiftly contracting.   The universities and
with them the other schools must make this the primary aim
of education in the United States, otherwise America cannot
meet the demands of this critical moment in the world's history.

The second fact in the world situation which likewise
points to the urgency of this educational task is the rising
power of the Asiatic and colored people.   Up until the past
decade or so these millions outside Europe and America were
an inert and helpless mass.   We of the West could walk
across the earth and do about as we liked.   We could push
these other peoples around and they could do very little to resist.   But this condition is rapidly changing.   The science and
technology that has given us our superior power is swiftly being transmitted to these other peoples.   In forty years, when
the generation now in school reaches full maturity, these other peoples will be standing on their feet and looking us
straight in the eye with a power comparble to our own.   When

that time comes we must be living and promoting a way of
life that is broad enough and good enough and wise enough to
invite them to go with us down the highway of history.   If
we are not sufficiently united and equipped morally and spir-
itually to do that, it might be better if our children and
grandchildren were not living then.

There is a third fact pointing to the same task to be
done by the universities.   It is atomic energy.   This new
kind of power is a knife so big and so sharp that we shall
surely cut our fingers, if not our jugular veins, when we try
to use it, unless we have established a way of life sufficiently wise and good to be able to operate such a power.

By reason of the three facts mentioned, the "moral
and spiritual values" can no longer be neglected by the universities for the sake of concentrating upon special fields of
knowledge and technology.   We must do the latter to be sure,
but general or liberal education must be no less clear and
definite in its aim.   It must help to establish and improve a
way of life that is competent to carry the East-West struggle
to a successful issue, to join cooperatively with the Asiatic
peoples, and to operate constructively with atomic energy.

What must be the basis of a way of life having this
threefold competence?   We suggest three kinds of ability necessary to it.   If these three are essential, they should be
the ruling aim of general education.   Student and teacher
should seek above all else to cultivate this threefold ability
through the study of literature, history, philosophy, psychology, and the social sciences.

If our analysis is correct, the aim of general education should be to develop in every student the following:

(1) The ability to get the other fellow's viewpoint.
This does not mean necessarily to agree with him nor approve what he proposes, but it does mean to understand him.
It means to see and feel the situation under consideration
within the bounds of the other man's perspective.

(2) The ability to communicate to the other man one's
own viewpoint so that he will see and feel the situation within the bounds of one's perspective.

(3) The ability to adjust these different viewpoints to
one another.   This adjustment may eventuate in my view cor-

recting his error or his mine; or the adjustment might result in mutual correction of errors. It might even produce
a synthesis yielding a much more penetrating and comprehensive view of the matter which engages the associated individuals. The adjustment might be some kind of compromise; it
might result in any one of an indefinite number of different
outcomes. In any case this third kind of ability is to adjust
diverse viewpoints and interests to one another, so as to
make an integrated whole sufficient to carry on the collective
life of society and preserve the integrity of the individual personality.

Many teachers and men of research in their professional capacities repudiate all attempts to "make the world
better," or to "do good" and "improve people." Who are we
to say what people ought to do and ought not to do, say they.
Any attempt to "save the world" becomes a matter of ridicule among them. We can give you the facts, say they, but
what is better and worse in the situation to which the facts
pertain, or in the purpose for which the facts may be used,
is not for us to judge. Any such judgment would be subjective, and we must not be guilty of that.

This manner of teaching cannot continue. Either the
educators will themselves strive to sustain and promote a way
of life which they judge to be best, or some ruling authority
will take them in hand and make these objective teachers
serve the subjective ends of this authority. Several different
kinds of groups are watching eagerly for the opportunity to
take over the educational system to this end. Some of these
groups are political, some industrial-financial, some religious. The educational system as a tool to serve the interests of such a power hungry group would be a temptation too
great to resist, should opportunity offer itself. The opportunity is fast approaching because of the growing need of our
common life for unity and direction. The refusal of educators to assume this responsibility plays directly into the hands
of those groups who want to take over. The need to shape
and direct our common life is too desperately urgent to allow
our universities to continue their social irresponsibility.
Some kind of authority compelling the schools to impose upon
our common life a dictated unity, or the united action of the
teaching fraternity to promote the democratic way of life, are
the alternatives before us.

The teaching profession cannot as a unit support any
specific act of social change when it is controversial; but they

can promote a way of life based on broad general principles
such as those outlined above.

If this overall aim of education were adopted as a
master plan, no revolutionary change in education would be
required, because, we believe, this aim is already implicit
in the entire educational procedure. It only needs to be
made explicity, deliberately and widely adopted as the recognized aim of education, and intelligently pursued.

Other proposed aims of education may seem to disagree with this one, but analysis may reveal that the difference is in wording more than in substance. One statement
of the aims of education often heard is the following:

(1) To gain knowledge of our cultural heritage
(2) To add to the sum of knowledge
(3) To communicate (1) and (2).

The individual is acquiring his cultural heritage
throughout his life. The amount of it he can get during four
years in college is very small compared to the continued
learning of a lifetime. The chief task of the college is to
aid society in transmitting to each individual what the past
has to teach which may be of value to us all. This heritage
is acquired by each through understanding other minds. Always the transmission must be from one mind to another by
way of some medium of communication, whether it be ancient
documents and other signs and symbols of that kind, or the
"great books" or two men talking. Hence the chief service
rendered by the school is not only to communicate to the student what it can of this cultural heritage, but above all to develop in him the ability to understand and appraise the communication of it as it comes to him throughout the rest of his
life from any source whatsoever, living or dead, past or present. But if the school does this it must adopt as its ruling
aim the ability to understand and to feel the other man's ideas
and valuings, to communicate one's own, and to bring these
diverse views into the working unity of one's own striving,
thinking self.

We now come to number (2), which is to add to the
sum of knowledge. This requires a new insight of some
kind. But a new insight always involves some new integration in the mind of the individual of ideas and valuings derived from various sources. This is one part of the aim I
first proposed for education. So we see that this proposal,

when analyzed, is seen to be not really an alternative to my
own proposal, but resolves itself into the same thing, namely, to get the other man's view, to communicate one's own,
and to adjust the views gathered from different sources into
the growing, working unity of one's own mind.

If my analysis is correct, this alternative proposal
concerning the aim of education, while diverse in form, is
practically equivalent to the one I first set forth.

BENEFITS RESULTING FROM THIS AIM

No matter what goal is adopted for education some
people will refuse to be helped by it, some will be hurt by
our attempts at education, and none will be made perfect or
even approximate perfection. Also we must remember that
society outside the school is far more powerful in shaping
life than is school; but power and responsibility of the school
increases with advancing civilization. With these reserva-
tions, the following benefits ought to result from an education having the aim I have proposed:

(1) Success and happiness in life for the individual depend more upon "getting along with other people" than upon
anything else, and this, in turn, depends upon the threefold
ability.

(2) All the values of civilization and culture are to be
found in human minds and nowhere else. Hence one is an
outcast from the culture and civilization of his society or any
other, except as he develops the ability to understand others
and to adjust diverse views and interests.

(3) Conflicts can be resolved to the benefit of all parties only when this threefold ability is developed and practiced. Not all conflicts will result in this happy consequence,
of course, but when they do it will be because the participants have this kind of ability.

(4) Progressive expansion of the mind in scope and
vividness of qualities enjoyed, truths understood, and activities controlled, results from this threefold ability.

(5) Freedom of the individual combined with spontaneity and initiative, and with responsibility for other persons
and for the welfare of society, can occur when people have

this threefold ability; but without it, there can be neither freedom nor intelligent responsibility in a complex society.

(6) Inner conflicts and inhibitions that produce neuroses and psychoses can be relieved and often prevented and overcome in this way. Psychiatry and case studies show that these psychic ills arise out of maladjustment between associated persons. The threefold ability is directed to preventing or correcting such maladjustments.

(7) To the measure that people live together under control of the threefold ability, the world comes alive to each person because the meaning of what he is doing acquires scope and vividness through the kind of interchange we have described. Dull routine, mechanical performance, and meaningless activity disappear; performance takes on fullness of meaning to the measure that people live together in this way whether in factory, home, or elsewhere.

(8) The human kind of mind along with self-knowledge is attained in this way. We understand ourselves as we see ourselves through the eyes of others, especially through the eyes of the wisest men who have lived.

(9) Free constructive cooperation requires the threefold ability; otherwise coercion under a dictatorship or antlike coordination of routine habit are needed to achieve cooperation in a complex society.

(10) As civilization advances, we become increasingly dependent upon greater numbers of people. One way to diagnose our troubles is to say that interdependence has advanced more rapidly than our ability to understand one another and adjust our differences. Hence the importance of education adopting the aim here proposed. It might be demonstrated that one cause for the recurrent breakdown and disintegration of civilizations is the failure to develop among the people by way of universal education this threefold ability to meet the demands of increasing complexity of interdependence and increasing power of action exercised by associated groups. If this should be true, the critical nature of the present moment in history for our own civilization should be apparent; also the need for education to adopt the aim proposed.

THE NEW SOCIETY

The kind of society being brought into existence by the worldwide spread and intensive development of mass production magnifies the importance of the kind of social interchange and personal integration which we have been proposing as the aim of education. An article by Peter F. Drucker that originally appeared in Harper's Magazine shows how our way of living is being transformed by mass production and the assembly line.

> The world revolution of our time is not communism, fascism, the new nationalism of the non-western peoples, or any of the other 'isms' that appear in the headlines; these are reactions to the basic disturbance, secondary rather than primary. The true world-revolution... is the mass-production principle. Nothing ever before recorded in the history of man equals in speed, universality and impact the transformation that modern industrial organization has wrought in the foundations of society in the forty years since Henry Ford developed the mass-production principle to turn out the Model T.... Today the representative, the decisive, industrial unit is the large mass-production plant, managed by professionals without ownership-stake, employing thousands of people, and organized on technological, social and economic principles (entirely different from) the typical factory of 1910. [2]

Mr. Drucker shows that this method of organization is not peculiar to manufacture but is pervading the whole of our society. It applies to agriculture as well as to industry, to finance and banking, and also to clerical work, to scientific research and to military action. The Russian collective farm and the vegetable cooperatives in California show how it is done in agriculture. The check-sorting and check-clearing operations in a big bank are examples of it and also the sorting and filing of orders in a mail order house. The Sloan-Kettering center for cancer research and the production of the atomic bomb show how it works in scientific research. In the Mayo clinic medical diagnosis operates on the principle of the production line and the same was manifest in the preparations for D Day when allied armies invaded Europe.

This manner of human action is not essentially a matter of machines; it is a newly discovered way in which men coordinate their activities to do anything, whether with machines or without. It consists in breaking down the total undertaking into very small and accurate operations and then integrating these minor unit-operations into a total pattern. It is this pattern of a great complexity of small unit-operations that produces; no individual human being produces anything. Human individuals create the pattern, repair it, keep it going, and improve it. Some individuals perform some of the minor unit-operations but these are increasingly taken over by the machine and in time all of them will be.

This kind of cooperative action does not eliminate skill. On the contrary more skill is required to create and keep going this complex pattern of integrated operations than was involved in earlier forms of productive work. The new skill is the ability to see and understand the pattern of integration and so be able to act intelligently to keep it going, to repair, improve, or recreate it. This kind of skill requires imaginative ability of high order, something like that of the artist, says Drucker.

The consequences of this new way of living and acting together in all areas of life are revolutionary. Unemployment or the threat of unemployment becomes intolerable because the individual can no longer produce anything. He can be a productive and hence a valued and respected member of society only when he participates in maintaining some part of the pattern of complex operations by which almost all the goods and services for human living are produced. Furthermore, the family ceases to have any part in this productive process which is the substance of society and in that sense is separated from society. Finally, this way of ordering society introduces new social classes and imposes tasks upon government far beyond the capacity of the traditional forms of government. Thus it opens the way for the tyrant if the required governmental forms are not developed to meet the need.

Now we come to the main point so far as it bears upon the problem of education. To the measure that society is organized after the manner described, the pattern of complex operations is the only agent that produces anything outside art and the professions. Therefore the individual can have no social status, no social prestige, no social power, and can find no meaning in what he does, unless he can understand and im-

aginatively grasp the pattern of complex operations which he
helps to sustain.   Therefore, if the individual is not to become a rebel or a derelict, he must have two things.   First,
he must be reasonably certain that he will not be cast out
from society by involuntary unemployment.   Second, he must
be able to grasp imaginatively the pattern of operations which
he works to sustain, create, repair, or improve.

The second of these two imperatives is especially relevant to the problem of education.   The school cannot teach
the individual the pattern of complex operations in which he
will participate, partly because it is always changing from
year to year and job to job, partly because one can truly
learn the nature of the pattern only as he participates in tending it.   But one thing the school can do, and must do: it
must develop in each individual the capacity to get the other
man's viewpoint, to communicate one's own view to the other,
and to integrate these diverse perspectives into a comprehensive pattern of what is going on.

Mass production is driving society swiftly into an order of existence wherein this threefold ability becomes the
very foundation upon which everything depends.   So long as
the individual can produce a product by his own efforts, or
can work in a relatively small organization where he can see
and understand what is produced, the imaginative grasp of
pattern by way of communication with other participants is
not so necessary.   But with mass production it is the only
way by which the individual can find any meaning in what he
does or achieve any sense of status, prestige, and power.
Without this ability the world in which he lives becomes a
meaningless jumble in which nothing makes sense, in which
rational or intelligent conduct becomes impossible, and where
moral principle and social responsibility become words without application to anything at all that he can grasp.

Again I quote from Drucker in the article above mentioned.

> ... the inevitable development of history (is) not to-
> ward the victory of the proleteriat but toward the
> victory of the secretariat....   This is the new
> class whose members have yet to see the whole of
> which their work is a part.   Their blinders are a
> menace to the functioning of modern industrial so-
> ciety, and for their enlightenment we have only the
> feeble devices of publicity or that magic abracadab-
> ra of modern management, the 'organizational chart.'

> Actually this middle class of technicians is the off-
> spring of the mass-production principle; they are
> not orphans but the true inheritors of a revolution
> which they scarcely recognize, much less under-
> stand.... Precisely because this mass-production
> technology is a corrosive acid which no pre-indus-
> trial culture or social worker can resist, the world
> requires a working model of the political and social
> institutions for an industrial age. Without such a
> model to imitate and learn from, the mass-produc-
> tion revolution can only produce decades of world
> war, chaos, despair, and destruction. If the mod-
> el is not furnished by the West, if it is not a mod-
> el of a free industrial society, then it will be the
> model of a slave industrial society.

Developing in each individual so far as possible the
kind of threefold ability we have been describing is, we believe, the only way in which a society organized for mass-
production can possibly be free. Of course the right kind of
education cannot alone provide what is required. All our
basic institutions, political, industrial, financial, religious,
must be shaped to meet the demands of a society organized
on these lines. But the school from kindergarten to gradu-
ate work in the university is one of these institutions. I have
tried to show what I believe the school must do to meet its
responsibility in such a society, along with the political, industrial, religious, and other institutions. The school must
adopt the aim and the methods required to develop in each individual to the limit of his capacity the ability to understand
and feel the thoughts and desires of the other fellow, to communicate his own so that the other can understand him in like
manner, and to integrate the diverse perspectives thus gained
from others into the working and growing unity of his own
mind and personality.

METHODS FOR ATTAINING THE PROPOSED AIM

1. Acceptance of the proposed aim by a considerable
number of students and faculty would in itself help to attain
the end sought, because the subject matter of instruction in
our schools is already fitted to this end in no small part.
We are helped to understand the likes and dislikes of others
through the study of literature, history, philosophy, psychology, language, art. The sciences put knowledge into the form
in which it can be most widely and freely shared.

2.   A common body of literature, history, philosophy, language, art, psychology, and the sciences, studied by all, with material specially selected for this purpose and with instruction conducted to this end would provide bases for more profound mutual understanding, and permit discussion to reach deeper levels.

3.   The method of discussion should be given a large place, providing it is practised with the purpose of attaining mutual understanding and organization of the mind of each in orientation to the other, and not practised for self-display or to win the argument or for mental gymnastics.

4.   The study of social and psychological problems with a view to finding how best to organize society and conduct the life of the individual so that social interchange and personal integration of diversities can reach the maximum, would also conduce to develop in the student the kind of ability sought.

5.   Recognition that this kind of interchange between persons requires the individual to hold the organization of his personality subject to progressive organization by what he gets from others.   This, in turn, requires a kind of religious commitment to this way of life, because otherwise the personality cannot voluntarily undergo such transformation, not knowing what it will become, except only that its vision will be widened, its understanding deepened, its range of enjoyment and suffering made more far-reaching.   The private practice and the public practice of some ritual of commitment would greatly aid the undertaking, if this could be done in the right spirit.   Indeed, rightly interpreted, confession and repentance of sin are indispensable to this way of life. The trouble with most religionists is that they call for this, in order to conform to some set of regulations imposed by the church, or else, like the neo-orthodox, to the attainment of nothing that can be specified in terms of our daily living. Hence, it produces either a sanctimonious moralism or, in the second case, a confused state of morbid uncertainty. Here, however, the confession and repentance are directed to the attainment of something specific, namely, the more or less continuous transformation of personal organization and social order involved in the interchange and integration (or other adjustment) of diversities between persons.

6.   Certain psychological treatments akin to psycho-analysis might help individuals liberate themselves from many

of the self-protective devices which obstruct the deeper levels of mutual understanding and prevent that kind of progressive reorganization of personality involved in the interchange and integration of diversities.

7. The social and psychological sciences, if they applied themselves to the problem, could help to show the way to this goal of education, once it was widely adopted by the universities.

8. Demonstration to the student of the high importance to himself and the great values to be personally and socially attained by developing ability to engage in this interchange and integration of diversities, is a necessary part of the method.

9. The conduct of extra-curricular activities, housing of the students, and all manner of free associations outside the class room, can also develop the threefold ability as much as the regular studies.

THE PROBLEM OF INTEGRATION

The problem of integration in education is misconstrued when it is thought to be merely achieving some kind of systematic unity of the materials of instruction, so that the student can grasp it all as a whole. Rather the problem is to enable the student to preserve the integrity of his own mind and personality while absorbing diverse ideas and incentives from many different sources. This must be, of course, a kind of progressive integration, sometimes involving radical transformations of mind and personality along the way. This is a delicate and difficult problem. However, it is not merely the problem of student and teacher in school. It is the heart of the problem of human life, especially at the present time.

1. Integration in the mind of the student of what he gets from different courses (and other sources) is most likely to occur when the material in each course is so presented that the student feels: here is something I need and must get in order to live effectively and happily.

2. Integration in the mind and personality of the student is most likely to occur if the material of instruction is so presented that the student is always asking and the teacher

is always answering, although the student's questioning will not ordinarily be spoken (or may not be).

3. Integration in the mind and personality of the student will occur, if the material of instruction is so presented that the student becomes intensely interested in the problem of human living common to his time and society, and is made to feel that what he is getting is indispensable to any intelligent treatment of those problems.

4. Integration in the mind and personality of the student will occur most creatively for himself and for society, if the entire university and all courses are organized and directed to serve a goal which the student himself can adopt as the chief concern of his own life. This coalescence of aim in personal living and in educational procedure would make the university a powerful agent in creating a culture of growing attainment.

5. Integration in the mind and personality of the student will occur if an influential group (or groups) of the faculty should meet regularly, at times with one another and at times with students, to discuss the purpose they all can have in common in the work of education, and the best means of attaining that purpose. This would keep the overall aim of their cooperative undertaking constantly alive in the minds of all, constantly subject to reinterpretation, clarification, and refinement. It would make possible the constant improvement in method both of the teachers and the students, and would enable them all to cooperate more effectively. It would help to prevent lapse into dull routine both in teaching and in studying; it would help to prevent that confusion and crosspurpose which results when teachers and students do not know what they severally are doing or trying to do in the undertaking called education. Above all, it would engender a growing unity of purpose and a stimulating interchange which would produce in the university a powerfully creative community, even in the midst of great diversities and disputes.

6. Number five in the previous section dealing with the general problem of method should be repeated here. Integration when most difficult can be attained only by religious commitment to this way of life, based on creative interchange and progressive integration of diversities in the life of the individual and in society. This involves the practice of ritual and the confession and repentance of sin to the end of undergoing the transformations of personality brought

on by creative interchange between persons, and the progressive integration in each of what he gets from others.

Notes

1. This paper is a reconsideration of my "Education for Social Direction," Approaches to National Unity, Lyman Bryson, Louis Finkelstein, R. M. MacIver, editors, Conference on Science, Philosophy and Religion in Their Relation to the Democratic Way of Life, Inc., New York, 1945.

2. Peter F. Drucker, The New Society: The Anatomy of the Industrial Commonwealth, Harper & Brothers, New York, 1950.

PART 5:
WHY RELIGION, SCIENCE, AND PHILOSOPHY
NEED EACH OTHER

INTRODUCTION

Here Wieman is especially concerned to show how vital to the survival of humanity is the interdependence of religious inquiry, science, and philosophy. The need for this interdependence has been implicit to Wieman's career as a religious philosopher. He began his career in that cluster of events known as the end of the nineteenth century--World War I with its causes and aftermath. The end of the nineteenth century saw the collapse of many of the traditional and "modern" world views from which persons and societies gained their raisons d'être. Not only did the nineteenth century come to an end and world views collapse because World War I betrayed the "idea of progress," but a new age emerged at this juncture.

This new age can be characterized best by its predominant elements, which have determined world events over the past six decades so radically: science, technology, nuclear power, and the interdependence of world communities. The effect that the new age has had on history has been so immense that the new age itself has been called "post-industrial," "post-modern," "post-civilization," "post-Christian," among other names. Various religious responses have been made to the challenge and dangers of this new age, Wieman's being one such. As Wieman has indicated in personal correspondence to the editor, the reason religion, science, and philosophy need each other is because only through their interdependence can mankind go about "seeking a faith for the new age."

SCIENCE AND A NEW RELIGIOUS REFORMATION*

Science is the way we achieve knowledge and power; religion is the way we give ourselves in supreme devotion to the best we know. If knowledge and power are not merged with supreme devotion to the best we know, they will not be used effectively to serve the best we know. If supreme devotion is not guided, informed, and empowered by the most penetrating method of inquiry at our command, our devotion will stumble and blunder in relative futility. I think we are generally agreed that the resources of science and the resources of religion must be united if the human race is not to destroy itself or sink to desperate futility just when it reaches its highest peak of power.

Karl Jaspers, in a recent book called The Origin and Goal of History, speaks of the axial period in history. It was the time when those insights and convictions entered human consciousness which created all the great world religions now prevailing. At no other time before or since in recorded history have there occurred such depth and power of creative insight in answer to the question asked by the religious consciousness of man. In Israel, in India, in Greece, in China, in Persia men appeared who proposed answers to the religious question more profound and adequate than any known before that time. The religious question is this: What has such character and power that it will transform man, to save him from the worst and lead him to the best, if he commit himself to it and meet other required conditions?

All the great world religions constantly go back for renewal and purging to their origins in the axial period. No outstanding leader in any of these religions has ever claimed to depart in any radical way from those insights and from the way of life which first appeared in the original source. It is true that Christianity and Islam do not go back to the

---
*Reprinted from Zygon--Journal of Religion and Science, Vol. 1:2 (June, 1966), pp. 125-139.

time which Jaspers calls the axial period, when religious creativity brought forth the great religions. But Jaspers claims, with much to support the claim, that Christianity and Islam did not introduce anything so radically different from the teaching of the Hebrew prophets as their teaching was from what preceded them. These two religions certainly introduced innovations, but Jesus and St. Paul, on the one hand, and Mahomet on the other, got their most important insights from the Hebrew prophets. Consequently, Jaspers dates the period of revolutionary religious creativity from about 800 B.C. to 200 B.C. The exact dates are not important. If Christians insist on extending the period to include the lives of Jesus and Paul and the first Christian disciples, the main point of the argument is not changed. The main point is that at a certain time in human history the social, psychological, and historical conditions were present which made it possible for the creativity, always latent in human life, to bring forth a better answer to the religious question than any ever before known. Jews and Christians give the name of God to this creativity. Some of the other religions do not. But regardless of names, the actual fact seems to stand that, under certain conditions, human thought and behavior are creatively transformed.

Until recently these religions have dominated and inspired the cultures where they existed. Recently they have lost this power. They continue to attract individuals and sustain religious fellowships. But their power to inspire and direct the course of government and politics, industry and commerce, education and art, science and literature, family and major social groupings has declined toward the vanishing point.

By "axial period," I understand Jaspers to mean the most revolutionary turning point in the history of the human race. The first civilizations arose long before this time, developing in and around the first cities. But the period in history called "axial" is given that name by Jaspers because at that time the moral standards and religious commitments came into being which made possible the subsequent development of civilization and culture. These further social developments could scarcely have ensued without some marked change in the evaluation men made of their fellows. The axial period originated the moral standards and religious devotion which made possible this wider distribution of responsibility.

As said before, no idea in the New Testament and no
idea in Christian history since the New Testament depart in
any revolutionary way from the teaching of the Hebrew prophets. So also with the other great world religions. Any innovation appearing in them is always rooted in the original
founders and appears as a further interpretation of the originating insights. Every revival of new vitality in the faith is
a return to further appreciation of what arose in the axial
period in human history.

This constant return to the originating sources is not
to be condemned. On the contrary, the revolutionary transformation during the axial period that occurred in the minds
of a few people was of such an order that two thousand years
and more have been required to carry it to others and to absorb it into the lives of men generally. Over two thousand
years have been required to study and interpret and better
understand the way of life which emerged in the axial period
--a way of life more fully controlled by creative interchange
than was ever before possible. The time extending from the
axial period until now has been required to extend this way of
life as widely as possible among men and bring the basic institutions of society into some form of conformity to it and
service of it.

CREATIVE INTERCHANGE

We use the expression "creative interchange" or the
equivalent expression "creativity" to distinguish that kind of
interaction between persons and peoples whereby their diverse
activities are brought into relations of mutual support by each
acquiring some sense of the value in the activities of the others. Each activity has its own value because a value is any
goal-seeking activity. But diverse and complex activities
which are interdependent and carried on by many different
people can be related in three different ways: (1) They may
frustrate and conflict and thus nullify their value. (2) They
may be brought into relations of mutual support by coercion,
deception, exploitation, and unconscious conditioning of the
persons involved under the control of a ruling group. (3) Or,
again, they may engage in creative interchange so that the
valuing consciousness of each is expanded to comprehend the
value of the whole system of interdependent activities.

This third way is the way of creative interchange.
When it occurs with sufficient scope and power, each partici-

pant in the total system of interdependent activities becomes a free, sustaining, and creative member with a consciousness of values capable of indefinite expansion.

Doubtless, the first civilizations arose by bringing many diverse and complex activities into a system of mutual support by conquest, deception, exploitation, conditioning, and subordination of the many to the service of a few. But these civilizations could not have continued to develop, and certainly could not have increased the values of life for the vast majority, if the religions of civilization had not arisen in place of the tribal religions to direct the ruling commitment of their adherents to the creative interchange. The tribal religions did this in a way fitted for tribal life; but they could not do it in a way fitted for civilization when interdependent activities were much more diversified, much more complex, and when the power of technology was greatly magnified.

Religion, when fulfilling its proper function, can now be further defined as those rituals, symbols, and beliefs by which the ruling commitment of human life is directed to what creates our humanity, saves it from its own self-destructive propensities, and transforms it by expanding indefinitely the valuing consciousness of each individual in community with others.

What does this is a creativity operating in human life by way of creative interchange. This creativity is often given the name of God. In Christianity, God is often identified with love. But when love is thus applied to God, the word must be understood to refer to something far more profound, pervasive, sustaining, and creative than what is ordinarily meant by this expression. In short, when love is applied to God, it must be understood to mean that creativity operating by way of creative interchange to create a valuing consciousness capable of indefinite expansion in community with others. This kind of valuing consciousness is the essential nature of our humanity.

The great religions of civilization, arising in the axial period to take the place of the tribal religions, symbolized this creativity in various ways. In Christianity, it was called the "living Christ." St. Paul called it "Christ in you." In Judaism, it was called the "one God," superseding the tribal gods. This one God should be served and worshipped by all peoples in all ages, according to the teaching

of Judaism. Other of the world religions arising in this period symbolized this creativity in other ways.

Regardless of the way it was symbolized, the reality
symbolized was a creativity operating in human life to widen
and deepen the range of that kind of community wherein individuals and organizations interchange and integrate their goal-
seeking activities. Individuals and peoples committed to this
creativity live not for themselves alone and not for any established system of values but for what breaks through the
limitations of every established system to expand indefinitely
the range of values by which and in which human beings live
in community with one another. At least this seems to have
been what the great founders of these religions had in mind
and what is indicated by their outstanding representatives.

But the problem is to have the teaching, the symbolism, and the understanding required to present this creativity in a way to induce people to live for it and in it so that,
in times of major decision, they will choose that alternative
best fitted to provide the conditions under which this creativity can operate most effectively throughout the whole of human existence. When conditions undergo great change, especially when there is great diversity, complexity, and power
of goal-seeking activities to be brought into mutual support,
the teaching, the symbolism, the understanding, and the methods required to present this creativity in a way to induce
commitment to it must undergo a corresponding change.
That is the reason the tribal religions were unfit for civilization.

The same creativity operated in tribal life as operates
in civilization to create the valuing consciousness of individuals in community with one another. But the teaching, the
symbolism, and the understanding required to do this for the
mentality of tribal life were not fit to do it for the mentality
and other conditions prevailing in civilization. Hence, conquest, coercion, control by military organization, deception
practiced by the priesthood, all manner of exploitation of the
many by the few, were the methods used by the early civilizations to maintain the social order. Of course, these methods have always been used by all people in all ages. But
this is a matter of degree. There is evidence to indicate
that the early civilizations did this with more deliberate in-
tent and organized power than was possible in the primitive,
food-gathering tribe.

The great religions arose to correct this evil condition of civilization. It was evil in the sense that it narrowly limited the range of the valuing consciousness of the masses who were suppressed, coerced, deceived, exploited, and reduced more or less to puppets. It also restricted the range of the valuing consciousness of the ruling few because they had to maintain an organization which obstructed the free, full, and open expression of the values of unique individuality. This limited the range and variety of values each could get from others, and thereby impoverished the integrated system of values accessible to the valuing consciousness of each. Not only did it limit creative interchange between members of the ruling group but what was much more serious, it prevented all other members of society from making their own unique contribution to that integrated system of goal-seeking activities called the "culture" of that society. It also prevented that continuous increase of power exercised co-operatively by all segments of society that is necessary to sustain a society in which activities become increasingly diverse and complex.

THE DEMANDS OF POST-CIVILIZATION

With this understanding of the basic problem of human existence, which is also the basic problem of religious commitment, we see how it applies to the revolutionary transformation of human existence now occurring. Just as agriculture and the city transformed primitive tribal life into the life of civilization, so now scientific research and scientific technology are transforming civilization into a way of life as different from the civilization of the past five thousand years as civilization was different from the tribal life which preceded it. Just as the symbolism of tribal religions had to be transformed into the symbolism and intellectual understanding of the world religions to sustain the values of life when that first great transition occurred, so now the symbolism and intellectual understanding of this creativity as found in the religions of civilization must be transformed into a religion fit to sustain the values of human life in post-civilization.

The expression "post-civilization" is taken from the book by Kenneth Boulding, The Meaning of the 20th Century: The Great Transition. One may insist that the new way of life now emerging will still be a form of civilization. But that is not the point. The point is that we are midway in a

transition as great as the one which brought civilization into
existence. Therefore, the way of life now emerging will be
as different from that of past civilization as civilization was
different from tribal life.

Just as agriculture and the city distinguished civilization from tribal life, so today the magnified power of scientific research and scientific technology distinguish post-civilization from the civilizations of the past. As in civilization
creativity had to be symbolized and understood in ways to
show how it operated in life dominated by agriculture and the
city, so in post-civilization this creativity must be symbolized and understood to show how it operates in life dominated
and controlled by scientific research and scientific technology.

This creativity operates throughout the whole of human existence at all levels from the physical, the chemical,
and biological through the psychological, social, cultural, and
the historical. In this context "the historical" means the accumulation of symbolized meanings through a long sequence
of generations, these meanings carried by language to form
a culture in which the values of human life are embodied.

With this understanding of the proper function of religion as directing the ruling commitment of human life to the
creativity operating throughout the whole of human existence,
it is plain that any religion fit to do this in post-civilization
must be united in close co-operation with all the sciences.
This is so because only the sciences can search out the conditions at all levels of human existence which must be shaped
in such a way that creativity can operate most effectively to
expand the valuing consciousness of each individual in community with others. The responsibility of science is to provide
this knowledge along with the technology required to use the
knowledge effectively. The responsibility of religion is to
maintain throughout society a ruling commitment to this cre-
ativity--leading individuals, organizations, and institutions to
use this knowledge and this technology to provide these conditions for the effective operation of the creativity which creates, sustains, and magnifies the values of human existence.

This kind of religion and this union of religion with
science are needed today as they were not in other times because of the enormous power of scientific research and scientific technology. If this power is not used to provide conditions for the effective operation of the creativity which creates and sustains and expands the valuing consciousness of

individuals in community of mutual support with one another,
it will be used in other ways. As has already been noted,
there are two other ways this power can be used. One way
leads to the extinction of the human race by conflict, confusion, and chaos of goal-seeking activities equipped with the
power of scientific technology. The other way this power of
science can be used is to superimpose a mechanized order
enforced by tyranny, reducing the mass of humanity to puppets as has been predicted by Aldous Huxley in Brave New
World, by George Orwell in his book 1984, by Michael Har-
rington in the Accidental Century, and by David Riesman with
his concept of "the other-directed man," which is the first
mild beginning of this reduction to puppets.

A NEW RELIGIOUS REFORMATION

With this understanding of our need for a new reformation of religion in relation to science, let us look at the
conditions which must be present for such a development.
One of these conditions is a vivid and widely prevalent recognition of the limitation and inadequacy of religion as it now
exists and operates.

Another required condition is the emergence of the religious problem from beneath the thick layers of ritual and
belief. Religion must begin to appear to many minds, not
only as a body of doctrine and a way of life to be accepted
or rejected, but as a question to be answered and a problem
to be solved. Not otherwise can important religious innovation occur. Unless men search, they will not find; if they
do not ask, no answer will be given them.

Doubt and rejection of prevalent forms of religion are
not enough to bring forth a more profound and effective faith.
Nothing creative can come out of such a negative attitude.
Creative insight emerges, not by rejecting a way of life, but
by recognizing the problem which underlies it; and, seeing
that this problem is incompletely solved, yet of utmost importance for human existence, by calling imperatively for a better solution than any now in practice. Whatever the social
and historical conditions may have been in the axial period,
they must have produced this state of mind in the leaders
who brought forth the great religions of the world. Everything we know about Hebrew prophets, about Socrates and
Plato, about Buddha, Confucius, and Zoroaster supports this
assertion about the state of mind which possessed them.

If Karl Jaspers is correct in saying that now again, after 2,500 years, we are entering a period when a further advance in religion will occur comparable to that of the axial
period, then the first sign and evidence for such a claim
must be the appearance and spread of that attitude toward religion which we have just been describing. Religion must
again begin to appear to the minds of a considerable number
of people, not merely as something to believe or doubt, accept or reject, and not merely as something to reform by
going back to the founders of the faith, but as a problem of
utmost importance to be solved more completely than any solution now available--by a solution which reaches more deeply into the intricacies of life and higher into its possibilities.

Here, then, we have the first condition which must
prevail if our time is to be one of opportunity for further development in religion. Does religion begin to appear to increasing numbers as a problem to solve in the sense indicated? I think we can answer that question in the affirma-
tive.

But, when we speak of religion presenting itself to the
mind as a problem, we must distinguish the basic problem
from many other problems which engage the minds of men in
matters religious. In one sense, religion is always a problem for everyone all of the time. But very rarely does this
problematical character of religion reach the level of what is
here called the basic problem. Some of these other problems must be noted here in order to distinguish them from
that problem which generates the revolutionary religious insights when men struggle with it.

One problem which occupies many religious thinkers
at the present time is the problem of formulating and establishing those beliefs which give peace of mind or enable the
individual to get what he wants in the form of health, wealth,
honor, and other achievement. It is the psychological effect
of beliefs which is sought and not any other actuality operating to transform creatively. The most popular books today
in the field of religion and the most popular religious leaders
are working on this problem; but this is not the one which
can bring forth the insight we seek.

Another problem which engages fruitfully the great
minds in the field of religion today is that of recovering the
whole truth and depth of the teaching and the power of the
originators of Christianity and other religions as they are to

be found down through history. Certainly there can be no advance in the depth and truth of religious insight and commitment if the best achieved to date is not conserved or recovered. Only by building on the best attained so far in human
history can there be any advance over the past. Consequently, the work of scholars and thinkers engaged in this enterprise is a necessary part of what we need. Without their
work, the next step in religious development can not occur.
But this recovery of the best the past has to offer, indispensable as it is, is not itself the next step. This recovery of
the best is one of the necessary conditions which must be
present; and the fact that it is being done so effectively in
our time is further evidence supporting the claim that another
axial period may be on the way. But we must distinguish
this problem of recovery from the problem which brings forth
the innovation.

Another problem engaging the minds of many religious
leaders at the present time is to discover or achieve a ruling
concensus of dominant religious thinkers. This effort is
called the "ecuminical movement." Viewed as strategy to
gain power by closing ranks and uniting forces, this may be
a significant endeavor; but it moves in the opposite direction
from that struggle with the basic problem out of which may
arise a religious commitment with more power to transform
human life than any now practiced. The Hebrew prophets,
Socrates and Plato, Buddha, Confucius, and Zoroaster could
never have brought forth the great religions of the world if
they had been trying to reach some consensus with other religious leaders of their time. Indeed, if they had been caught
into a powerful ecumenical movement, the innovations brought
forth by them could never have occurred, and the religions
of the world now prevailing for over two thousand years
would never have come into being.

The list of problems engaging the minds of religious
thinkers and inquirers to which great scholarship and whole
lives are devoted might be extended. But the ones mentioned
may serve to illustrate those problems which are not to be
identified with the basic problem. They cannot give us that
fuller understanding of what it is that calls for the ultimate
commitment of man.

THE BASIC RELIGIOUS PROBLEM

The most promising development in our time which in-

dicates that we may be entering a period when further creative insights will occur is the increasing awareness of the
basic religious problem out of which innovating insights can
emerge when men struggle with it. This increasing concern
with the underlying religious problem, in contrast to the other religious problems mentioned, might be traced back to
Descartes and the seventeenth century. Since Descartes, the
outstanding figures who have treated religion as a problem to
solve, rather than as a body of doctrine and practice to accept or reject, have been Immanuel Kant, Søren Kierkegaard,
and today the existentialists. A progression can be traced
from Descartes and Kant to the existentialists of our time in
the ever fuller exposure of the problem which underlies religion and the increasing intensity of the realization that the
problem is not solved and no answer to date is altogether
satisfactory.

      This recognition of the problem and the intense con-
cern about it appear most strikingly in the writing of Martin
Heidegger and Karl Jaspers in Europe and Paul Tillich in
this country. Jean-Paul Sartre rejects all religious solutions but recognizes the problem in all its urgency and struggles with it constantly. According to him, man stands before the abyss of nothingness and creates himself with each
act of will. Regardless of agreement or disagreement with
Sartre, he does expose vividly and dramatically the religious
question, namely, what, in truth, has the character and power to create, sustain, save, and transform the total being of
man?

      It is true that existentialists from Søren Kierkegaard
down to contemporary figures, while exposing the religious
problem in all its depth and urgency, deny that any rational
solution of the problem is possible. The only way the problem can be solved, they say, is by an act of faith, where
faith is understood to be an ultimate commitment without
guidance of knowledge. This rejection of reason and knowledge as a guide at the frontier of religious commitment is
not the point we are defending. So far as concerns us here,
the important thing about these religious leaders is that they
are awakening the minds of men from their dogmatic slum-
ber, to use Kant's expression. They are compelling thinkers
in the field of religion to recognize that religion is ultimately a question, rather than a set of answers; and this question, while it has received many answers, has received none
which is both rationally defensible and at the same time satisfactory. That is tantamount to saying that religion is an

unsolved problem. This state of mind is a necessary first
condition for any struggle with the problem which can hope
to bring forth the answer we seek.

A RATIONAL ALTERNATIVE TO EXISTENTIALISM

The ability to deal rationally with the ultimate religious problem requires a cultural development of the mind
which I believe we are approaching. To understand this cultural development and the state of mind enabling men to deal
constructively with this problem, let us trace the stages of
this development.

These stages are not stages through which all humanity passes--not by any means. Perhaps the great majority
of humankind are still at the lowest level so far as concerns
this particular line of development. "Lowest," as here used,
does not mean lowest in every particular and does not necessarily carry any suggestion of meanness or contempt. It
is simply the level where the mind begins to move toward the
level where it is possible to deal constructively and rationally with the ultimate religious problem. Millions, I should
judge, are still at the first and second levels to be described.
Other millions are at the third and fourth levels. But social
processes are not at work which, if war does not overwhelm,
will carry many beyond the "lowest" level. That does not
mean that they will reach the "highest" level. But they make
it possible that an increasing number might reach the level
where they can deal constructively and rationally with the ultimate religious question.

At the first level in this cultural development, the mind
is obsessed with the struggle to obtain the necessities of biological survival such as food, shelter, reproduction, care of
the children. Religion at this level, along with all other resources available to man, is chiefly directed to obtain protec-
tion from the enemy, food and shelter, health and long life,
children and their normal development. Even when material
goods are in abundant supply, this state of mind may still
persist because the organization of personality, the structure
of consciousness, and the traditions of the culture do not
change so readily as material conditions. But today rapid development of a powerful productive industry extending throughout the world could reduce the number of people living at this
level.

At the second level of cultural development, the mind is no longer obsessed with the necessities of biological survival but continues to live under the dominant control of an authoritative religious tradition which people at this level do not venture to challenge.   The dictates of this religious tradition are supposed to have a supernatural source and hence to exercise an authority and contain a rightness which no human mind can question.   But powerful forces are at work in the world today to carry people beyond this level.   Just as the power and spread of industrial production promises to deliver great numbers from preoccupation with the necessities of life, so communication, travel, and voluminous interchange and intermingling of all the diverse religious traditions of the world combined with the rising power of science tend to weaken the domination and authority exercised by any inflexible tradition over the minds of any people.

At the third level of cultural development, people are no longer preoccupied with the struggle to obtain material goods and no longer dominated by the unquestioned authority of a religious tradition.   Hence, they feel free to decide for themselves what is worthy of man's ultimate religious commitment.   But here they are caught by a bondage as confining and misleading as any to be found at the first two levels. It is the bondage imposed by an illusion.   It is the illusion that the individual with his own private judgment is competent to solve the most profound and difficult problem which ever confronted the mind of man, namely, the problem of what, in truth, does have the character and power to transform man.

At this third level, there is no intensive study of any great religious tradition.   Consequently, the individual is not even so well informed concerning this problem as he might be under the dominant control of one of the great traditions. For this reason, the religious convictions and commitments of people at this level tend to become superficial, uninformed, and relatively irresponsible.   These convictions and commitments cease to have any great unifying and directing power for society because they are so diverse, conflicting, and superficial.   As a result of this diversity and superficiality, religion loses its power, although it may become increasingly popular because people can readily flock together to celebrate symbols which have no common meaning and no great power to control and reshape their lives.

Since people at this third level have no depth of communion in shared conviction and shared commitment concerning matters most important for all human living, a sense of loneliness and isolation gradually creeps into the mind. It may be kept out of consciousness by various devices, but it cannot be stilled, and it cannot be stopped so long as this condition of religion continues.

Also the superficiality and diversity of religious commitment produce a sense of insecurity. The most powerfully sustaining security comes only when the individual is very sure that he has given himself quite completely to what creates, sustains, saves, and transforms toward the best possible. But the ordinary person cannot be sure of any such thing unless his beliefs are reinforced by finding that others who truly count in his esteem share with him much the same belief and self-giving. Also, under the conditions now being considered, the individual cannot count on any revered and unquestioned authority to reassure him; the diversity of religious beliefs tends to weaken his convictions about any of them. Hence the creeping insecurity which invades the mind.

Much the same causes which produce the loneliness and insecurity also increase the feeling of personal insignificance. One can feel that his own person and his own striving have high importance only if he believes that his life is caught into some development or design which includes society and history. But since the individual, for reasons stated, can have no strong convictions or assurance on this matter, and since no deep communion of shared commitment unites him in strong bonds of mutual support with others, the sense of insignificance and relative worthlessness and lack of meaning tend to creep over him.

This state of mind at the third level of cultural development, marked by loneliness, insecurity, insignificance, loss of direction, and lack of meaning, has been called by the existentialists "dreadful freedom." It is the kind of freedom from which men in time try to escape, according to Erich Fromm. Consequently, at this third level of cultural development, we find people recurrently trying to put themselves under control of the ancient, authoritative, traditional forms of religion.

This brings us to the fourth level of cultural development in dealing with the religious problem. At this level, the religious problem is recognized in all its depth and urgency, but it is interpreted to be an unfathomable mystery

which the human intellect cannot penetrate. These are the
religious existenialists and the neo-orthodox. The reality
which concerns religion, so these men say, transcends time
and space and all existence; it transcends the reach of human
reason. It can be brought to conscious awareness by means
of appropriate symbols, but it cannot be brought within the
bounds of human understanding. Any attempt to deal with this
problem by way of abstract concepts is a species of idolatry,
according to men at this level. The most sophisticated, outstanding leaders of religious thought in the Western world today are at this fourth level of cultural development in man's
struggle with the religious problem.

The great virtue of this fourth level is that it brings
the unsolved religious problem to the forefront of conscious
awareness. No longer is religion identified at this level with
a system of doctrine giving conceptual knowledge of what determines human destiny at the deepest levels of our existence. No longer can any set of practices and symbols be accepted as authoritative. All of these, doctrines, symbols,
rituals, and practices, are subject to revolutionary transformation, since none of them are based upon assured knowledge.

This fourth level is, I believe, the consequence of
psychological conditions produced by the third level, namely,
the loneliness, insecurity, insignificance, loss of direction
and meaning in life resulting from the attempt to hand over
to uninformed private judgment the most profound and difficult problem ever encountered by the human mind. This
fourth level is a reaction to the opposite extreme from the
assumed self-assured competence of private judgment to set-
tle this religious question. It is a rebound from one extreme
to the opposite. But it is, I believe, transitional to a fifth
level in the cultural development of the human mind in its
struggle with the religious problem.

THE NEW CULTURAL THRESHOLD

Once religion is seen to be a problem and not a set of
unquestioned beliefs or assured knowledge or symbols authori-
tatively imposed, the way is cleared to advance to the fifth
level. To be sure, this further step cannot be taken so long
as impenetrable mystery is held to be the ultimate concern of
religion. At this fifth level, one seeks knowledge to guide religious commitment and so cannot stop with mystery. At this

fifth level, mystery is recognized as the frontier of knowledge
but not as the barrier beyond which intellectual inquiry cannot pass, even though there may always remain further mysteries. Transition from the fourth to the fifth level of cultural development is accomplished by redefining the problem
of ultimate religious concern. One need not challenge the
claim that there is a mystery of Being which never can be
fully or finally penetrated by intellectual inquiry; but when
one comes up against that blank wall, one can redefine the
problem so as to open a way for intellectual inquiry in other
directions where something of importance can be discovered.
If any satisfaction or virtue is to be had by contemplating the
mystery beyond the reach of all knowledge, by all means let
us contemplate it. Let us accept everything which this ultimate concern with mystery may have to offer. But let us be
on our guard against using this appeal to mystery as a device for holding fast to cherished beliefs which we know can
never be sustained by evidence.

Against this background of analysis and survey of conditions, may we summarize the basic religious problem of
our time as we see it. It can be put in the form of a question, thus: How can religion and science be united to make
human existence at all levels more fit for the effective operation of that creativity which expands indefinitely the valuing
consciousness of each individual in community with others
when this community must itself expand indefinitely to include
all the diverse goal-seeking activities of human existence insofar as they can be brought into relations of mutual support
at deeper levels of mutual understanding across wider ranges
of diversity?

This will require a change in the motivation of science
as well as a change in religion. It will require that scientific research be motivated by commitment to this creativity,
seeking out the conditions for its most effective operation.
It will require a change in religion, seeking a more intelligent understanding of this creativity by joining with science
to get the needed knowledge.

Today, talk about "the death of God" by theologians is
symptomatic of the great change religion is now undergoing.
What form religion will take in the future we do not know.
We have here tried to indicate the direction which we believe
this change in religion should take.

CO-OPERATIVE FUNCTIONS OF SCIENCE AND RELIGION*

INTRODUCTION

We cannot take religion as it is and science as it is and put them together in co-operation to promote the good of human existence. We must distinguish that form of religion which can co-operate effectively with science; and we must distinguish that application of science which can co-operate with this form of religious commitment. Otherwise the two cannot work together.

Two other concepts are involved in this problem. We must have some understanding of human existence relative to these issues and some understanding of the good to be attained for human existence by this co-operation of science and religion. Hence the following discussion will examine these four--religion, science, human existence, and greatest good--so far as they are involved in this problem.

It is here proposed that the kind of religious commitment fit to work with science to attain the greatest good is a commitment to a creativity operating in a fourfold way as follows: (1) Individuals and peoples interact, creating in each party an awareness of the needs and interests of the other. (2) Each party integrates the needs and interests of the other into his own, after due modification. (3) This enables the interacting parties to work co-operatively for the needs and interests they share in common, developing the unique individuality of each person and each culture thus interacting. (4) Out of this develops an expanding system of mutually sustaining activities, institutionally maintained, endowing each participant with a growing good encompassing the lives of all.

*Reprinted from Zygon--Journal of Religion and Science, Vol. 3, No. 1, (March, 1968), pp. 32-58.

Creativity operating in this fourfold way is most fully developed only in human existence. If it comes from the ground of all being, so be it. It certainly does not pervade all existence. But let us not be diverted from our problem by these controversies about ultimate reality. If we become involved with questions about a creator transcending all existence, controversies over metaphysics, cosmologies, and ontologies will divert us from the problem before us, which is to show the form of religious commitment that is fit to work effectively with science.

The fourfold creativity just described is always present in human existence at some level, because otherwise we could not communicate as we do. But other processes are also in human existence, and these counter-processes often dominate, defeat, distort, and submerge this creativity. Hence the basic problem is to bring this creativity to a higher level of dominance over these counterprocesses. This is the central problem to be discussed throughout this writing.

With this understanding of the problem we can state in a brief introductory way the co-operative functions of science and religion.

The function of science is to search out the conditions which must be present for this creativity to rise to dominance over counterprocesses and to create the technology and other methods by which these conditions can be provided.

The function of religion is by rituals of worship, preaching, and private devotion to bring people to practice in daily living a ruling commitment to this creativity so that, in every time of major decision, they will use this knowledge and technology provided by science, along with all other resources, to choose that alternative best fitted to provide the conditions under which this creativity can operate most effectively in transforming human existence toward the greatest good.

This does not mean that religion depends on science for all the knowledge it can have. That would be as foolish as to say that getting wholesome food depends on science for all the knowledge needed to get wholesome food. Vital necessities, including food and religious commitment, had been provided in human culture long before modern science arose, and we have a store of knowledge from this long experience. But, for reasons to be explained later, all human activities

in the modern world need, in addition to traditional knowledge, the service of science. This applies to guidance in
religious commitment as well as to guidance in getting wholesome food.

This creativity is a distinct entity because it is a
process having a distinct structure. Every existing entity is
a process having a structure by which it is distinguished
from what it is not. Creativity runs continuously through human existence, ignored and submerged as it often is. It can
be called creative interchange or dialogue or sensitive negoti-
ation or reciprocity or love or empathy or creative interaction. But none of these words with its ordinary meaning ac-
curately designates it. It can be called Holy Spirit, or
Christ with us, or even God with us. But here also the conventional meanings do not fully satisfy.

The reason for using these traditional words is that
the transformation in human life, traditionally ascribed to
Christ or the divine presence, is the creative transformation
which we here call creativity or creative interaction. When
we examine empirically what actually happens in human personality and society in cases that are called the work of the
divine presence, we find this creative transformation occurring. We do not mean to suggest that this creativity occurs
only in Christianity. But we do find it occurring very con-
spicuously in the fellowship of Jesus as portrayed in the New
Testament.

This creative interaction does not operate only by
verbal communication of concepts; we also apprehend the
needs and intentions of others by feeling awareness. Indeed,
it seems in many cases that feeling awareness plays a larger
part than abstract concepts in apprehending the values that
distinguish the unique individuality of the other person. The
same applies to apprehending the values of an alien culture
when we live among the people who embody it. This creativity works at all levels of the human personality, conscious
and unconscious.

THE FUNCTION OF RELIGION IN AN AGE OF SCIENCE

When we speak of the co-operation of science and religion we do not mean to suggest that these alone must co-
operate to save our civilization from destruction. Government, politics, industry, commerce, education, the arts,

the family--all the major activities of human life--must have
some order and direction and yield some essential values for
our lives.   But there is a special reason for considering science in relation to religion.   Science as research to acquire
knowledge, along with its applications in technology, has become the supreme instrument of power in our civilization.
No governmental, industrial, commercial, or educational institution in the world today can exercise power relative to
the others if it does not bring science into its service.

This applies also to religion.   A form of religion unfit and unable to bring science into its service will be unfit
to give order, direction, and meaning to human life as now
lived.   Science, both directly and through the other agencies
that use it to attain their goals, is shaping our thoughts,
feelings, purposes, and activities down to the bottom level of
human personality.   If this powerful and pervasive influence
cannot be shaped and directed by our religious commitment,
then our religion is futile and can avail nothing in directing
our lives and the course of civilization.   For this reason we
must develop a form of religion that can bring science into
its service and also point the way to man's salvation and
creative transformation.

We are not concerned with reconciling the findings of
science with the affirmations of faith.   We are not concerned
with the kind of religion that would have this conflict with
science.   At the same time, we reject that form of religion
which deals with problems entirely beyond the reach of scientific inquiry and with an area of experience entirely independent of the sciences.

Rather the form of religion here to be considered is
a ruling commitment that can work in close co-operation
with science.   It is a ruling commitment which human life
must assume if human existence is to be saved from self-
destruction in the age that is now beginning.

Religion must assume different forms to deal with different problems as they arise in different periods of history
and in different cultures.   Religion is always the same in the
sense of being a ruling commitment that should take first priority in every time of major decision.   But the ruling commitment is differently interpreted and takes on different forms
as human life undergoes the great transformation to which it
is addicted.   Religion betrays its truth, and becomes an evil,
when it refuses to undergo the changes required to deal with

the basic problems of human existence as these change from
age to age.

One primary function of religion is to direct mankind
to what transforms human existence toward the greatest good,
whether this transforming power be called God or Christ or
the law of karma or be given some other name. If people
generally have no understanding, no conviction, no agreement
on what has this transforming power, science cannot be used
to promote it, precisely because there is no agreement on
what it is. In such a case the pervasive and profoundly
transforming power of science will be used for whatever ends
may happen to possess the minds of men who are in posi-
tions of control. This will lead to conflicts which cannot be
adjudicated because adjudication means to decide that some
course of action and way of life is better than others. This
requires some agreement between conflicting powers concerning what is the better way at some basic level of commitment. Conflicts that cannot be adjudicated, when equipped
with the power of modern science, will drive inevitably to
annihilation. Agreement at some basic level of ultimate commitment is religion.

In the past, the different divisions of human cultures
were sufficiently under the control of native unifying traditions so that each could seek the greater good as this was
interpreted by the tradition of that people. Whether or not
their judgment of greater good was right, they did not have
the power of modern science to implement their error.
Therefore, their errors of judgment were not made fatal by
the powers of scientific theory. They could recover and learn
something from the mistake they made. But today basic error concerning what transforms toward the greater good is
implemented with such power that we cannot survive serious
misuse of it. This power is modern scientific knowledge
and technology.

In the past, traditions that were unfit to sustain human life would eliminate or alienate the people adhering to
them. Thus, those traditions survived that did meet human
need more or less adequately under the conditions. But today all the different peoples and all the diverse traditions
must live in one single community that is rapidly drawing
ever tighter the bonds of interdependence. No one of these
diverse traditions is fit to govern the life of this world community. Furthermore, none of these traditions, including
the religious, has been developed in a way to guide the use

of modern science and its technology, because modern science did not exist when these traditions were in process of formation. We cannot develop the needed kind of tradition by allowing the unfit to destroy themselves by misuse of science, because the unfit will be the entire human community.

The basic problem here to be considered cannot be solved by religion alone but only by religion in close co-operation with science unless religion assumes the form fitted to deal with this problem and fitted to work with science. Traditional forms of religion are not fitted to do this unless they undergo revision.

What is said of religion applies also to science. Science cannot work with religion on this problem unless scientific research, scientific knowledge, and scientific technology are applied to the problem of religious commitment as being of even greater concern than equipping war with more deadly weapons or exploring the far regions of space or controlling the masses to serve industrial production. That is to say, science cannot work with religion on the religious problem unless it gives first priority to this problem rather than to others that work against it.

The basic problem of our time, requiring the union of science and religion to solve, can now be stated: <u>What form of religious commitment and application of science can enable the diverse peoples of the world to live together in community of mutual support when equipped with ever increasing technological power and brought into ever tighter bonds of interdependence</u>?

In other words: How can world community be created without eliminating diversity and conflict but by so modifying the diversities and so controlling the conflicts that they serve to widen and deepen community while at the same time expanding the range of what men can know, control, and value?

This is the problem to be solved by the union of science and religion. Other agencies, such as politics, economics, art, and education, are included when we speak of science and religion uniting to solve the problem, because science gives to each of the other agencies its power to act and religion gives then the ruling purpose of their existence, which guides their use of this power.

To state the problem most simply: How attain a

world community in which goal-seeking activities support one
another across conflicts and diversity?

I am convinced that such a community cannot be created by any direct action. It cannot be created, for example,
by an arbitrary social organization imposed on the peoples of
the earth, suppressing the diversities and the conflicts arising out of these diversities. Any attempt to do that would
bring on a tyranny so oppressive that men would not endure
it.

How, then, can this problem of world community be
solved if not by direct action and social organization? Our
title suggests an answer: The Co-operative Functions of Science and Religion. A world community must, of course,
have a social organization, but the organization must develop
in terms of the realities of the community. It cannot first
be imposed on the world and thereby produce a world community. The futility of this procedure is exposed in what we
are attempting to do in Vietnam today.

Wherever a community of mutually sustaining activities has been created--whether between parent and child and
husband and wife or in any association in village, town, nation, international relations, or empire--it has always been
created and sustained primarily by a kind of interchange between the participants whereby the needs and interests of the
various parties were communicated back and forth and to
some degree were recognized and met by the interchange.
Community created in this way has always needed the support
of social organization. But to avoid the social organization
being oppressive to the point of intolerable enslavement and
self-destruction, we need interchange of the sort mentioned,
which is religious in character.

What makes our age different from the past and generates the basic problem here under consideration is that this
minimum of creative interchange sufficient to sustain human
society in the past will no longer be adequate. If the newly
interdependent worldwide population of humanity is to survive
in the midst of rapidly evolving knowledge, technology, and
ways of life, it must attain a new level of commitment to
the creativity that creates community and at the same time
maintains respect for diversity.

In summary, we have reached a period in the historic development of civilization when we are confronted with a

problem so basic that the continued existence of the human
species depends on solving it; and this problem cannot be
solved unless religion assumes a form fitted to deal with it
and unless science also is applied in a way to search out the
needed knowledge and develop the needed religious art of technology.

Generally this creativity that creates a community of
mutually sustaining activities has operated without any understanding of it by the people involved in it. It has sometimes
been called love, but the word "love" gives no adequate knowledge of it and has many other meanings besides. This creativity has sometimes been called God, but the word "God"
gives no adequate understanding of it and has carried meanings even more diverse and remote from what is here under
consideration. "God" often refers to what is beyond the
reach of scientific inquiry.

We must now have a far better understanding than was
ever before required of this creativity that creates the human mind and personality in freedom and in mutual support
of others. The ruling commitment of our lives, called religion, must be given more directly and with more understanding to this creativity than was ever before necessary for
our salvation and creative transformation.

If the ruling commitment of our lives is not given to
this creativity, we will not apply scientific research to find
out how it operates in human existence and what conditions
must be present for its most effective operation. If the ruling commitment of our lives is not given to this creativity,
we will not use the technology and knowledge given to us by
science to provide the conditions--physical, biological, psychological, and social--which must be present for this creativity of interaction to prevail over counterprocesses. Without this ruling commitment of our lives called religion, we
will not seek to organize society in a way to promote creative communication between conflicting parties whereby the
opposing interests are brought under the control of mutual understanding and mutual concern. Without religion we will
not conduct our daily lives in such a way that, in times of
major decisions, we shall seek that alternative best fitted to
promote this way of dealing with conflict. For these reasons,
science must be joined with religion if this problem is to be
solved.

In the new age now coming upon us, co-operation of

human beings with one another can be as deadly as conflict,
if it is managed by people or computers so that each individual does his part without any concern for the common
good or the interests of his associates. In such case, some
individuals will seek sensuous enjoyment to make life livable
by use of drugs and by stimulating the brain to create blissful experience without responsibility for the conduct of human life. Some will seek the centers of power to control
the masses with the machines available. Some, driven by
the quest for power but unable to reach the centers of control, will seek power for their own ends by the destructive
use of violence. Still others will turn to hobbies and specialized occupations without concern or responsibility for the
major problems of human existence.

If the rebels could be kept under control, such a deadly system might be the outcome of the new age of scientific
control that is now beginning. But considering the restive
spirit and drive for power with which many are endowed, it
seems that such a worldwide condition of mechanized existence could not long endure without rebellion, anarchy, and
the self-destruction of humanity.

In sum, if humanity is to survive in the new age, science and religion must unite to seek a better understanding
of and a more profound commitment to what does actually operate in human existence to create community with freedom
and responsibility.

To carry further our understanding, we must explain
the meaning we attach to such key words as religion, science, human existence, and the greater good. Without clarity on what meaning we attach to these words, there can be
no understanding of the problem we are considering.

RELIGION

The word religion has so many meanings that some
have sought to escape the confusion by speaking of Christianity as something different from religion. But Christianity
has been interpreted with great diversity. Some try to narrow the field by speaking of biblical faith. But here again
we have all the different interpretations of the Bible. We believe our definition covers the most important features of all
the great world religions, including, of course, Christianity.
This definition exposes the great evils and errors of religion,

including those of Christianity. This exposure of evil and error in religion by any useful definition of it is necessary, because the purpose of getting religion before us is to distinguish what is true and right in it from what is false and wrong. Christianity is just as much in need of this kind of critical examination as any other form of religion.

It is not necessarily arrogant or presumptuous for a man critically to examine the form of faith given to him in his inheritance. Not only is this examination every man's right, it is his duty; otherwise he is evading his responsibility in accepting what is evil and false in the faith by which he lives.

Religion, then, as the word is here used, will mean a ruling commitment practiced by a community of individuals to what they believe creates, sustains, saves, and transforms human existence toward the greatest good.

Religion thus defined includes a vitally important belief. Every such religious belief can be in error. There is no way to make the human mind infallible. Even when a man takes his belief from what he thinks is an infallible authority, still it is his belief that the authority is infallible, and that particular belief may be in error. Furthermore, his interpretation of the authority is his own interpretation.

But a man's religion is not merely a belief; primarily it is a commitment, that is, a decision to live for a reality which, he believes, creates human existence and transforms it toward the best that human existence can ever become. The important thing about the belief is what it guides a man to do. It is not the belief that creates and transforms; it is the reality that does that. To have a ruling commitment to such a reality means that, in every time of major decision, the individual and his community of faith will seek to choose that alternative which, so far as they can discover, provides the conditions under which the reality can operate most effectively in transforming human existence, including oneself, toward the best that is possible.

Yet a man's faith is not determined merely by his private belief. It is determined by the community in which he lives, by the tradition which that community inherits, by all the great thinkers and leaders, together with all the great perverters and deceivers, who have shaped that tradition through the centuries. In this sense a man's faith is given

to him.   It is revealed to him.   I do not mean merely that
the Christian faith is revealed.   Every man's faith is revealed insofar as it is given to him and insofar as it informs
him and shapes his life after having been communicated to
him by the community of faith from which he gets it.   Every
man's faith, and not only the Christian faith, is revealed to
the individual insofar as it takes hold of him and shapes his
life.

Nevertheless, my point is that the faith as we find it
in our lives, given to us by our community, whether we call
it Christian or something else, calls for searching criticism,
as much as anything else involving all the values by which
and for which we live.

Especially is this required in a time of revolutionary
transformation.   This does not mean, when human life undergoes great change, that the reality that calls for the ruling commitment of our lives itself changes.   That may not
change.   But we change: the concepts by which we think of
it become different.   The way we approach it becomes different.   The old concepts, the old forms of thought, can no
longer guide us as once they did, even if they were free of
error for their own time and place.   But, giving the traditional system of belief every benefit of doubt, still we cannot think of the same reality with the same structure of
thought embodied in that tradition, because our minds no
longer can think with the same structure of thought.

But here we are chiefly concerned with the relation of
religion to science.   Science has changed, and is changing,
the structure of thought by which we apprehend all kinds of
reality.   Therefore, if the traditional forms of religious
thought do not change to fit into this new structure created
by science, they will lead us astray regardless of how right
may have been their guidance in the past.

Three forms of religion that are unfit to co-operate
with science should be noted.

First, religion that merely merges with science and
makes a religion out of science cannot co-operate with science to solve the basic problems of our existence.   A form
of religion that merely adds an emotional glow to the scientific vision or provides religious motivation to scientific research is unfit.   Religion must have work of its own to do
before it can cooperate with science.   In this respect it can

be compared to other institutional interests. Industry, for example, co-operates with science by giving to scientific research some industrial problem to be solved. Industry does not merely follow along after science and sing praises and express wonder over the vision of the universe that science is exposing. Industry unites with science to do its own job, which is to increase the quantity and quality of economic goods. Government, too, has its own distinctive work to do and assigns to science problems in government for resolution. The same is true of education and the military.

The only form of religion that can thus co-operate with science is a religion that directs its faith to a reality accessible to scientific inquiry, where scientific knowledge can help religious inquiry get a better understanding of what is required in religious commitment and what must be done to provide conditions most favorable for the effective operation of that to which men are religiously committed.

A second form of religion unfit to co-operate with science directs religious commitment to what is beyond the reach of all scientific inquiry, a form increasingly popular today in sophisticated circles. Obviously, such a commitment cannot co-operate with science in getting a better understanding of what it seeks to know, nor can it assign to science special problems. The outstanding theologians of our time, from Karl Barth to Paul Tillich, from Bultmann to the followers of Whitehead, represent this kind of religion. Whitehead comes closer to science than the others, but the primordial and consequent natures of God set forth by Whitehead are at best speculative rather than necessary assumptions of science. In any case, they are not directly accessible to scientific inquiry.

The third form of religion that is unfit is the religion which holds beliefs that are contrary to, if not contradicted by, scientific findings. This we need only mention, since few people interested in the problem here under consideration would adhere to it.

This brings us to a fourth kind of religion that can co-operate with science and thereby meet the need of our time. Discussion of this form of religion will continue as we examine "science," because we must understand the possible religious significance of science in discussing the kind of religion fitted to co-operate with it. At this point we can only say that, not only must the form of religion we seek di-

rect the ruling commitment of our lives to a creativity operating in human existence to transform the minds of men
together with the social order so that freedom and love can
prevail over counterdevelopments, but also it must involve
beliefs that are relatable to those of science. This creativity is such that it cannot operate effectively unless required
conditions are present. In such a case, the various sciences, each in its own field, must be able to search out
these conditions and also help create the techniques and technology by which these conditions can be provided.

This does not mean that this knowledge from science
and these techniques and technology can themselves transform the minds of men and the social order so as to bring
freedom, love, and justice to a higher level of dominance.
This can only be done by the creativity in question. One can
call this creativity "Christ" or "Holy Spirit," provided he
does not interpret it so as to put it beyond reach of scientific inquiry. Science with its knowledge and technology, when
these are applied to the problem, can help show how some of
these conditions can be provided, thus enabling the creativity to create the better life.

This can be compared to the problem of good health.
Medical science cannot itself provide good health, but it can
show how to provide some of the conditions that must be
present so that the life- and health-creating biological process can create good health.

Perhaps it should be added at this point that those
who fear we are driving out mystery from religion need not
be disturbed. Scientific inquiry can never eliminate mystery.
All that scientific inquiry or any kind of intellectual inquiry
can do is to give us abstract concepts about actual existence.
Actual existence itself, in all its concrete fullness, can never
be comprehended by these abstractions.

SCIENCE

We now turn to an examination of science. We want
to get some understanding of scientific knowledge and the way
it is attained to show commitment of a religion fit to deal
with the major problems of our age.

To get this view of scientific knowledge before us, I
shall quote from Ian Barbour, who is himself a physicist but

also interested in the problems of religion. I accept his interpretation of scientific knowledge, although I do not altogether agree with his understanding of religion. The view of scientific knowledge presented by Barbour is not peculiar to him. I believe many today who study the nature of scientific knowledge would agree with Barbour:

> ...there is no simple separation between observer and the observed because one deals always with relationships and interactions rather than objects in themselves. Objectivity thus cannot mean 'the study of an independent object' for a strictly independent object can never be known...there are no completely uninterpreted data in science... All data are to some extent 'theory-laden.' The processes of measurement and the language in which results are reported are influenced by the assumptions and concepts of the investigator. The totally neutral observation language which the positivist sought seems unattainable. For 'data' are always a selection from personal experience in terms of one's purposes and expectations. What the scientist looks for, and to some extent what he finds, is influenced by the traditions and paradigms of the scientific community. Attitudes change as to what problems are worth investigating, what kinds of questions are fruitful, and what types of concepts are likely to be promising. By the objectivity of the data, then, we can only mean its reproducibility within a scientific community sharing a common set of assumptions and concepts. This provides a basis for communication and agreement; but it does not imply that the data are independent of either the observer's experimental operations or his interpretive categories.[1]

The point to note here is that scientific knowledge, like all knowledge, is created by interaction between the sensitive organism and what is to be known. In the case of science it is interaction between what is to be known and the sensitive organism equipped with all the instruments, traditions, symbols, and accumulated theoretical structures of science. This makes knowledge not subjective but exactly the contrary. To simplify, take perception by the eye. What is to be perceived interacts with the eye of the organism to create the form and color that is perceived. What is perceived is truly there when related to the eye of that organism. To

be sure, what is there would be different if a different kind
of organism with a different eye were interacting with it.
The organism with its sensitivity makes its own contribution
to what is perceived. If that were not the case, if the perceiving consciousness were like a mirror, giving us a subjective reproduction of what was there independently of the
perceiving organism, this would indeed be a subjective creation, and there would be no way of comparing this subjective
image with what is being perceived. But if, on the contrary,
what is perceived is created by interaction with the organism, then what is perceived is the reality as it truly is when
related to that organism.

When a different organism is introduced, a different
form of reality is known. Or, if the organism is equipped
with all the equipment of modern science, the interaction
creates a form of reality different from that created when
the organism is not so equipped. Therefore, what is known
in a given situation by ordinary common sense is very different from what is known by science. This does not mean
that one is true and the other false. It only means that the
reality known is different when the organism and its equipment are different, because the reality known is known, not
by reflecting it without analysis or meaning for the organism
as a mirror does, but by interacting with it to create meaning. Of course error occurs. We have error when we do
not predict the future correctly or do not correctly infer,
from what is present, what is remote in space and remote
in the past. But this prediction and inference must be based
on what is created by interaction between the organism and
what is known.

If we do not adopt this view, then we would have to
say that when science uses more powerful instruments and
rejects the less powerful, knowledge based on the latter was
not true knowledge. But this leads to total skepticism, because science is constantly inventing new equipment and new
theories so that what is known at one time is always being
transformed. Such being the case, there would be no time
when we could say that what science knows is true, because
there would always be in time some new equipment, new theories, new focus of interest, and new individual genius.

In sum, the reality we know is not something independent of the knowing mind but something interacting with it.
The knowing mind, including the biological organism, always
makes its contribution to the reality that is known. Every

other alternative leads to hopeless skepticism.

But what the organism in the wholeness of its being
is experiencing at any one time is always vastly more than
what is consciously known at that time in that situation.
This can be demonstrated by focusing attention on different
parts of the body or engaging in some other purpose that will
bring to consciousness what could not reach consciousness
until this new goal of endeavor directed attention to it.   Yet
it was being unconsciously experienced all the time.   Therefore, what we know is determined by our goal-seeking activities, because every goal-seeking activity, if successful,
brings to consciousness items relevant for the goal.   Also,
when we know any object, much more must be active in the
knowing mind than what reaches consciousness.   That is to
say, in any case of knowledge much of what is known is below the level of consciousness, to be brought forth when difficulties arise requiring this unconscious knowledge to bring
forth what is sought.   Also much activity in the organism
sustaining our knowing mind is unconscious at levels that cannot be brought to consciousness, except in the form of feeling.   Feeling carries a wealth of guiding awareness that cannot be put in the form of language.   We feel the concrete
fullness of the reality far beyond what can be described.

The purpose of this discussion of scientific knowledge
and of knowledge in general is to demonstrate that in science
there is a creativity operating to transform the world, together with the human mind and human society, into forms
that are progressively accessible to knowledge, to evaluation,
and to control.   Furthermore, this creativity operates below
the level of consciousness even more than in consciousness,
although it transforms consciousness also.   The unconscious
part of it controls the consciousness more than the reverse.
In the third place, this creativity involved in scientific inquiry operates in a community of inquiring minds where each
must trust the other very fully, where each tells honestly and
completely what he thinks he has discovered relative to the
problem under inquiry, and where what each discovers must
be integrated quite completely into the community of knowledge after due criticism and discussion.

This creativity operating in science to create a community of mutual trust, along with full and honest interchange
within the limits of research, is the same in nature as that
creativity which operates in any association of individuals to
the measure that they attain a true community of mutual

trust, complete and honest communication, and integration of the findings of each into a common body of knowledge, value, and control.

This is similar to the creativity calling for religious commitment. But in religious commitment the whole self and the whole society are involved, not merely that fragmentary part of the individual and the society engaged in scientific research on a restricted area of knowledge. In the age of science, the whole self and the whole society cannot be fully committed to anything unless obstructions to this commitment are removed. For example, after describing the massacres that are going on throughout the world, perpetrated in the name of morality and religion, John F. Wharton writes,

> The new method (of science) would begin by observing how human beings actually behave and the forces that have changed their behavior, and then, reasoning from such observations as to what a human being really is, determining how further changes might be effected. In fact, there exists today a school of psychiatry which asserts that we now have the tools to build such a method and only our blindness to its potentialities keeps us from going to work.... We have today for the first time in world history, the basis for a psychology of human behavior, but we use it only as a therapeutic device to help a few thousand neurotic and psychotic unfortunates. [2]

The author goes on to say that we should have an "Academy for Man," following the suggestion of Dr. K. R. Eissler, to study human behavior and apply methods for changing the motives of behavior. Whether or not this is the right way to go about it, this quotation is offered as a suggestion of what is needed.

To submit human life to scientific control is just as futile and dangerous as to submit it to religious control, unless the scientific control is directed to providing the conditions under which that creativity which creates freedom and love can operate most effectively. Thus science and religion must work together, religion giving us the ruling commitment, science providing the tools and the knowledge required to render our commitment intelligent and creative.

We have seen that science is peculiarly fitted to do this because it operates under the control of this same creativity within the narrow limits of specialized research. In this sense, science might be called a pathfinder and scouting party, going ahead to explore a trail that the rest of human life can follow. The rest of human life would follow if religious commitment were given to this same creativity as it operates not only in science but also throughout the whole of human existence.

As said before, science and religion are not the only agencies that must serve this creativity which expands the bounds of freedom, community, and mutual control. Art, education, government, and industry all have their parts to play.

Finally, philosophy has an indispensable part in this undertaking. Philosophy should be the overseer, surveying the entire project, keeping the comprehensive vision clear, and showing how science and religion, art and morality, and other such agencies can work together to bring the whole self of each individual into a community of each with all, expanding indefinitely the range of what each can know, control, and value.

We may never reach an end of this task of advancing life, but striving for it seems to be our assigned task.

HUMAN EXISTENCE

A further key concept involved in the basic problem we are considering is human existence. Human existence can be distinguished from every other kind of being by three outstanding features. First, human existence breaks free from confinement to more limited systems of living activities. The second feature is self-conscious individuality, critical and anxious about itself. The third is conscious conflict that can be creative.

The first feature of human existence is the expansion of life's activities beyond the biological. The demands of the biological process must be met, but the human being is not limited to them to the degree that other forms of life are. Symbolized meanings, pre-eminently in the form of language, make possible a complex and far-reaching social organization of co-operating individuals, accumulating these meanings

through history. These accumulated meanings are organized
into systems that create the world and values known to the
human mind. They create culture or civilization.

The human individual can confine himself to any one
or more of the subsystems within the range of his culture.
He may confine himself largely to the needs of his biological
organism, or to some narrow group of associates, or to
some economic or political process, or to some art or profession. This propensity to restrict oneself to a narrow system of activities without regard to the comprehensive creativity that sustains all systems in mutual support carries the
danger that these systems then develop in ways that conflict
with one another, resulting in frustration and mutual destruction.

The way of salvation from this danger is a commitment to the overall creativity pervading the entire range of
human existence. This may keep alive a ruling concern for
human life as a whole and for that mutual support which all
specialized activities and limited systems must have if they
are to be sustained. Participation in the religion of the
community provides this salvation.

The second distinctive feature of human existences is
the individual who is conscious and critical of himself. Without this consciousness or awareness of self and world based
on symbolic intercommunication or exchange, we could not
have that indefinite expansion of activity which was the first
mentioned characteristic distinguishing human existence.

This second distinguishing feature carries its own
danger. As the self-conscious individual becomes increasingly conscious and critical of his evils and errors, his limitations and humiliations, he is addicted to anxiety. This anxiety may lead to despair if not brought under control. This
carries many evils. One of the worst is the creation of illusions to keep self-criticism and despair out of consciousness. One common way to do this is to create the illusion
that I and my community have a moral righteousness superi-
or to other people. If one can feel morally superior to some
other person or people, he need not be so self-critical and
anxious about himself. This illusion of superior moral
righteousness against some minority group can lead to massacres of the cruelest sort, because it seems morally justified by the illusion. Examples of minorities thus persecuted
are Jews in Nazi Germany, Hindus in India under a Moslem

regime, Moslems under a Hindu regime, American Indians when the Christian white men came to this country, and most recently the Communists in Indonesia.

Here again salvation lies in commitment to the creativity that operates to bring all men into a community of mutual support and expanding system of shared values. But this commitment is relatively futile unless the sciences are applied to show how this commitment can be made to prevail among men.

The third distinctive feature of human existence is creative conflict at a conscious level. Human existence is more addicted to conflict between individual members of its own species and between organized divisions of its own species than is any other form of life. But conflict can be creative as well as destructive. Creative conflict leads men to discuss their differences, thereby learning to understand one another and acquire from one another new insights. Out of this mutual learning and reorganization, of both personality and social relations, they can integrate their differences to form a wider and deeper community wherein a wider range of activities can sustain each other. Thus out of conflict a common good may be created that brings the parties together more profoundly and extensively than was possible before the conflict. This is creative conflict.

Any given case of conflict can be in part creative and in part destructive. Even the great wars, with all their destructiveness, have also been creative of new communities. The two world wars have created a wider and deeper community between the United States and Europe, among European countries, between the United States and Japan, and between other parts of the world.

I do not mean to suggest that we should practice war for the sake of the community it creates. The destructiveness of war today is far too great to compensate for the creativity that may also operate in it. I am only trying to show that conflict can be creative; and even in the most destructive forms of conflict some element of creativity may be present. The problem is to control conflicts so they can be creative to the maximum degree and destructive to the minimum.

Here again the way of salvation is by commitment to creativity and by the application of the relevant sicences to

the problem to find how the conflict can be kept within the
limits of creative communication, mutual learning, new discovery, and consequent reorganization of individual personality and of social relations.

During the next several decades, the chief danger will
probably arise from one of two alternative developments, either one of which would be a disaster. The outbreak of dis-
ruptive conflict might reach the point of destroying civilization. Yet the establishment of a worldwide system of control
to prevent such a conflict might at the same time suppress
individuality, diversity, creativity, and freedom. These two
alternative dangers will arise from three developments now
going on.

1. Diverse ways of life are becoming increasingly interdependent, each equipped with increasing power either to
impose its way of life on others or to resist such an imposi-
tion with destructive conflict.

2. The impoverished and relatively deprived people of
the earth are becoming increasingly aware that a more just
distribution of wealth and privilege is possible but not being
attained; this awareness is combined with their acquisition of
enough modern technology to fight for what they want.

3. There has been a failure to develop a religion that
directs our ruling commitment to what actually operates in
human life to create a wider and deeper community, a religion that is accessible to scientific inquiry as well as to commitment. This is the only kind of religion fit to meet the demands of the new age we are entering, because it alone is
able to work most closely and co-operatively with science on
the basic problems determining the good and evil of human
existence.

Often in time of danger there comes to the religious
mind the notion of supernatural intervention. God will inter-
vene to save his people is the affirmation of this kind of
faith. But this engenders a passivity that is itself one of the
great dangers. If this passivity based on the hope of divine
intervention should prevail, it will be as fatal as the other
dangers we have mentioned. In the past, this propensity to
passive trust was not so lethal, because men did not have the
power to act with such magnitude of destruction or construction. Today, they do have this power. Consequently, passivity which refuses to use the available power constructively

will expose us helplessly to its destructive use, and this can
be fatal.

We are rapidly moving into that critical period in human history when decisions concerning how to deal with conflict must be made with a completeness and finality never before required.

Will it be that in times of conflict we fight to win
with whatever means are available? If that should be our decision, civilization will not long endure.

Will it be to suppress all conflict with a superimposed
order enforced by all the devices and sanctions available
through modern technology? If that should be our decision,
all the great values of life distinctively human will fade out
of our existence.

Over against these two alternative ways of using technology to deal with conflict there is a third way. In this
third way, physics and chemistry, biology and psychology,
economics and all the social sciences may be applied to find
out how the conflicting demands can be met by modification,
reorganization, and new discovery. But this cannot occur
unless our lives are ruled by commitment to this way of
dealing with conflict.

The institutions of religion can come to appreciate
more clearly from the scientific community how open, conscious conflicts of ideas can be creative of better ideas and
ways of living. In their limited problem areas, scientific
communities have demonstrated ways in which open conflicts
of ideas can be resolved by killing bad ideas with reason and
evidence rather than by killing the scientists who hold them.
Scientists have learned how to express openly, rather than
suppress, conflicting ideas and, by this method, how to
reach new levels of enriched understanding and concensus.
Why cannot this same richness of creative conflict be applied
to religious ideas to engender the ruling commitments to the
total requirements for the life of the total interdependent human community? Could we not thus keep our precious free-
doms and value differences while at the same time avoiding
the hatred or destruction of our fellowmen and sister cultures with whom we are now interdependent?

THE GREATEST GOOD

Perhaps no idea is subject to greater diversity of
meanings than <u>greatest good.</u> Yet nothing determines the
course of human living more profoundly than what men choose
as the greatest good. We shall treat the idea under the head-
ings of freedom and love. These also are words of many
meanings, but it may be simpler to seek clarity and some
agreement on these than on the more comprehensive concept
of greatest good. But we must say something about the good
in general before we discuss these major forms of it.

Any limited goal-seeking activity viewed apart from
all other activities is experienced as good when it successfully attains its goal. Therefore, a successful goal-seeking
activity is the elementary unit of good.

But no limited goal-seeking activity can be separated
from other activities. The goal of every activity is further
activity. Also, the individual self is a vast complexity of
goal-directed activities, both those concerned with internal or
individual behavior and those relating to other individuals.
This can be extended indefinitely.

Therefore, the good I experience can never be limited
to any one activity, no matter how successful, but to the totality of all those with which I identify myself; and these in
turn are dependent on other activities of which I have no
knowledge. Therefore, it is impossible to estimate the good
of life by computing the success of all the activities with
which I am identified. Where and how, then, can I find the
greatest good?

This brings us back to the creativity discussed throughout this argument. There is a creativity running through the
whole of human existence, selecting some activities, rejecting some, and transforming others in such a way as to carry
through all of human life the maximum possible community of
mutual support and the historic continuity of the community.
To the degree that I can identify my good with this creativity,
to that degree do I experience the greatest good. This is
true if we define the good as any goal-seeking activity attaining its goal to whatever maximum degree is possible. The
only activity involving the total self that can do this is this
creativity.

The only good that I, as a total self, can experience is a good that involves the total self. To the degree that I identify my total self with this creativity running throughout the whole of human history and all society, to that degree do I experience the greatest good.

We can now look at freedom and love. We shall find them to be nothing other than forms of this greatest good.

Freedom in terms of a single activity is that activity attaining its goal. Freedom of the total self is that self attaining the one supreme unifying purpose for which it lives. If the self claims to have no one supreme unifying purpose but many purposes, either these obstruct and defeat one another or they support one another in some degree. To the measure that they obstruct and defeat one another, the individual is not free if we define freedom as any activity attaining its goal. To the measure that they support one another, the individual has freedom. But to the measure they support one another, they are implicitly parts of a single unifying goal. So our definition of freedom stands. The individual's consciousness is free only to the measure that he identifies himself with some one form of activity which is successful and which he prizes so highly that all his defeats, frustrations, rejections, and ignominies count as nothing against the success of this one ruling activity.

The individual may be imprisoned, frustrated, and defeated in many of his limited activities. He may even be killed, but if he can in some way make his limited frustrations, defeats, and death contributory to the one supreme form of activity for which he lives, he finds his freedom in the success of that activity. We have seen that the one activity that triumphs over all others and always makes for the greatest good when and where and to the degree it triumphs is the creativity we have been considering. Therefore, the individual and the community find fullest freedom to the measure that they commit themselves to this creativity.

There is objection to this from many who hold other forms of religion. Some will say there is a cosmic activity that goes on after human existence disappears. Only he has fullest freedom who identifies himself with the total cosmic process. Others will say that even this falls short of fullest freedom. Only he who identifies himself with the creative ground of all being can find fullest freedom, because this will continue when the cosmos disappears.

My reply is in the form of questions. Is it true that the total cosmos carries on any activity beyond human existence with which the human person and human community can truly identify without ascribing to the cosmos something pertaining to human existence?

Is it true that the ground of all being carries anything with which men can identify unless it involves potentialities of human existence?

It seems to me those questions answer themselves. Only by way of illusion can a human being identify himself with anything except the potentialities of human existence. He can identify himself with the destructive potentialities or with the constructive potentialities or with some mixture of these. But it would seem to be a self-contradiction to say that he can without illusion identify with anything that is not the potentiality of human existence. This excludes the sub-human cosmos except as it supports human existence; and the same applies to the ground of all being.

One may identify himself with the destructive potentialities of human existence, and if these win over the constructive he may be said to have attained his freedom. But one cannot attain fullest freedom in that way, because goal-seeking activities that cease cannot have as much freedom as goal-seeking activities that continue indefinitely attaining their goals.

Finally, let us say that if it be true that the total cosmos or the ground of all being is one single unified goal-seeking, then fullest freedom is found by identifying oneself with that activity, supposing one is able to know what it is. But, even so, he must find it in human existence, because that is where he is, and if he cannot find it there he cannot find it anywhere in such form that he can identify with it.

Love is generally considered to be a form of greatest good. But this word, like other words in common usage, is either highly ambiguous or else carries little meaning until carefully examined.

There are many kinds of love. We here wish to distinguish that one kind that has greatest value. The word "agape" has sometimes been used to distinguish this kind of love, but we shall not use it, because we believe it also is confusing. In our judgment, agape is not the kind of love

that carries greatest value unless it is identified with what
will here be defined as having this superior character.

Love, like all forms of value, is one kind of goal-
seeking activity. When love is identified with sex, as it often is, the goal-seeking activity is obvious. The kind of love
here to be distinguished as having greatest value can be sexual in the sense that sex may be one ingredient. But it need
not be sexual except as sex may be involved in response to
the total self.

Love of the kind that carries greatest value is that
response of one person to another (or to a community) that
has two distinguishing characteristics: (1) it engages the total self more fully than any response other than the religious
can do; (2) it unites what is good for the self with what is
good for another self (or selves) to make a total good which
is their summation. Yet this summation of all the goods is
not merely their addition. This summation is the weaving of
the goal-seeking activities of the two or more into a total
unity such that each component activity is more effective in
attaining its goal than it could be outside the co-operative
system. Also, each component activity carries the value of
the whole system. Furthermore, the creativity that weaves
the activities of the two or more lives together operates to
expand their community by weaving into their joined lives the
activities of other people, expanding indefinitely into the economic, the political, the educational, the artistic, the interpersonal, and all the other activities of life.

When this kind of love takes the sexual form and creates a family, this indefinite expansion of activities weaving
an ever wider system of support is obvious. But communities of various other kinds can be formed in this way. They
exemplify love to the degree that (1) they engage the total
self in response to others and (2) these responses create a
common good of interwoven activities. The religious community aims at this kind of fellowship and under the leadership of great religious personalities has approached it. Also, the family has at times approximated it. Perhaps we
should say that the great majority of religious institutions
and families do not, but the religious community and the family community are based on principles more specially fitted
to engage the total self than other communities. Also, in
principle they are fitted to extend their community to bring
more individuals and more causes and more values into the
system of mutual support and common concern.

While this kind of love is of the highest order, some qualifications must be added. It was defined as engaging the total self more fully than other interests can do. But the words "more fully" must be emphasized. There is reason to think that the total self is never completely and perfectly engaged. Always there are unconscious regions of the self that are withheld from the response. This is a matter of degree, in some cases much more, in other cases much less. Love may engage the total self more fully than any other response, yet in some cases no response may engage the self more than fragmentarily. Thus the response might be one of love and still fall far short of engaging the total self. Hereafter, when we speak of this kind of love engaging the total self, it should be understood that we mean to a higher degree than any other response can do except the religious. Whenever we speak of love as the "greatest," we mean to except the religious, unless the two merge into one, as is often the case.

Also, they who seek the way of love are perhaps more commonly addicted to illusions than when pursuing many other interests of human life. One may think that he is responding with his total self when that is very far from what actually happens. A passion that absorbs the conscious mind does not necessarily bring all the interests of the total self into action. There is the further illusion of thinking that one is responding to the other person or community when in truth he is responding to what he mistakenly thinks the other to be. In such a case, he is responding to some construction of his own imagination.

All of life is infected to various degrees with this failure to understand one's own self and the true selves of other persons. But, to the degree that that kind of love prevails which has the greatest content of value, sensitivities and intuitions are awakened to enable each to understand himself and the other more profoundly than is possible in any other relation.

One may think that he is loving with this superior kind of love when his love is really of a different sort. There is the kind of love that lavishes compassion and care on the other person without understanding the other person's true needs or responding to his true personality. Rather, in this kind of love the other person or the community is sub-ordinated to the interests of the lover's own self. Instead of creative interchange, in which each creates the community of their

shared lives, the other is treated as though he were a beloved piece of property and not truly another self. With this
kind of love, one dominates and controls the other.

        Then there is the opposite kind that might be called
servile love. One subordinates himself to the other as a
servant or a slave. The hidden desire in this case is to
cast off responsibility for one's own activities, to have another take the responsibility. In the higher kind of love,
each assumes responsibility for that united life made of the
activities of the two meshed together to form a united life.
But in servile love the individual assumes no responsibility,
either for himself or for the other.

        Then there is that kind of love in which each seeks
the company of the other for the pleasure he gets out of it.
This may be sexual, but not necessarily so. It may be the
wit and charm of the other that gives the pleasure; it may
be the fun they have together in games and at parties; it may
be the glamor or fame of the other which one feels is re-
flected on himself by the association. There are many ways
in which one may gain personal satisfaction from a relation
called love which is not love of the highest order.

        When we say that the love of greatest value is a
weaving together of the diverse activities of the total selves
of two or more individuals in mutual support to form a single life, we do not mean that this weaving together is done
by the conscious control and direction of the participant individuals. This they could not do any more than one can
create the living cells in his biological growth or direct the
detailed operations of metabolism by which the organism
lives. One can provide the conditions for this growth, but
he cannot create and direct the operations of the million
cells which are the growth. So also one cannot consciously
direct the million subtle, complex, often unconscious impulses, sensitivities, and intuitions which create the community of two or more lives. This is the work of that creativity which has been our central theme. We can serve it, we
can live for it, we can seek always to meet its required
conditions. But if we tried to do by direct conscious control what this creativity does, it would be like trying to make
the flower grow by direct control of the process of growth.
We would kill the flower if we tried. So also love of the
highest order is killed if we try to shape it to serve our
present purposes rather than letting it creatively transform
our purposes into a community of purposes.

Love is one of the supreme creations of this creativity, but love is not its only creation. To develop human existence, creativity is always operative at some level, whether conscious or unconscious. It is even present in hate. Hate has some kinship with love. Hate arises when individuals rebel against, and try to break, the bonds of interdependence which unite them. To the degree that people are independent of one another, they may be indifferent toward one another or feel contempt or disgust, but they do not hate. Hate arises when they fight against the interweaving of their diverse activities that create a life shared together. Hate can obstruct this creativity but cannot eradicate it completely.

There is a kind of love called the love of all mankind. There is no community of all mankind in the sense that every individual responds to every other individual of the millions on earth or shares the culture of every other. What, then, can it mean to love all mankind?

To love all mankind means to be fully committed to the creativity that creates a shared life between individuals and peoples whenever association makes it possible. It means to be always in readiness to respond to every individual or community of individuals in a way that creates a community of value whenever conditions permit. It is also readiness to participate in a community of mutually sustaining individuals.

This participation in a community is also a form of love. This readiness to love may not always be actualized when one comes into personal contact with individuals and communities. The other person or the community of persons might use every approach you make serve the ends of hostility. But insofar as one is fully committed to the creativity that creates love when that is possible, one does in an indirect way love all mankind.

This love for all mankind requires a most complete commitment to the creativity that weaves the activities of diverse individuals into a system of mutual support. Only when this commitment to creativity is most profound can obstacles in some cases be overcome. But sometimes they cannot be overcome. Perhaps only a few persons throughout human history have given themselves to creativity with such a measure of completeness as to be able to love all mankind. But, like all such matters, this can be approximated to various degrees. According to the standard here adopted, this love for all mankind is the supreme attainment of human life and merges with the religious when fully developed. This kind of love is not a potentiality for all men, but it is a potentiality for human existence in the sense that it will be created where conditions permit.

In summary, the greatest good calling for religious commitment can be conceptualized thus: The greatest good is experienced when one is most fully committed to that creative interchange which integrates diverse activities into an expanding system, absorbing new activities when encountered, controlling conflicts and diversities in ways that are mutually sustaining, and endowing each participant activity with the value of the total expanding system. Even when this creativity is obstructed and beaten back we experience the greatest good to the measure we are fully committed to it, because this creativity carries the potentiality of all the great values ever to be experienced in human existence. This is religious commitment of the kind to be joined with science.

Notes

1. Ian G. Barbour, Issues in Science and Religion (Englewood Cliffs, N.J.: Prentice-Hall, Inc., 1966), p. 178.

2. John Wharton, "En Route to a Massacre?" Saturday Review, November 4, 1967, pp. 19-21.

KNOWLEDGE, RELIGIOUS AND OTHERWISE*

Most of the time we live sustained and guided by physiological processes equipped with unthinking habit and impulse
and the undiscriminated flow of felt quality. Out of these
arise knowledge and belief. Knowledge and belief are meager
compared to the massive continuity of physiological processes
and the flow of felt quality. They play only a small part in
sustaining and guiding our lives. Yet, limited and fallible as
they are, knowledge and belief are indispensable at the level
distinctively human. Furthermore, their share in the conduct
of human living increases rapidly with increase in social complexity and with growth of science and technology.

In our time dependence upon knowledge has become so
great that civilization cannot continue if knowledge is not
more clearly distinguished from forms of conscious awareness which are not knowledge. In the sciences this distinction is clearly defined and well established in practice. But
outside the sciences, where knowledge must deal with values,
the confusion of knowledge with other forms of consciousness
has become a danger which threatens disaster. By no means
does the good and evil of life depend entirely upon knowledge.
But the part which knowledge must play increases to the point
where the use of pseudo-knowledge to do the work which
knowledge must play increases to the point where the use of
pseudo-knowledge to do the work which knowledge alone can
do is causing trouble which mounts as time passes.

The most fateful task to be accomplished in any life,
whether that of the individual or that of society, is to find
the way to escape from major evil and the way of access to
greater good. But what is evil and the way of escape from
it? And what is the greater good and the guide thereto?
Knowledge is required to answer these questions correctly.
"Morality" and "religion" are the names we give to that area

*Reprinted from The Journal of Religion, Vol. XXXVIII: 1
(January, 1958), pp. 12-28.

of concern where men struggle with this problem. Yet precisely in the field of morality and religion and values generally the greatest confusion reigns concerning the distinctive character and rightful function of knowledge. If this were merely a matter of theory, it would not be so urgent. But it is not merely a question of theory. As life becomes more complex, everything for which men live and die increasingly depends upon the proper understanding and use of knowledge in distinguishing better and worse, right and wrong. The question distinctively religious which calls for an answer by means of knowledge is this: What transforms man as he cannot transform himself to save him from evil and lead him to the best that human life can ever attain, provided that he give himself over to it in religious faith and meet other required conditions?

I think that it is generally agreed among students of the subject that knowledge must present itself in the form of statements. We can have all manner of experiences, some of greatest value, which cannot be articulated in the form of statements. Therefore these experiences are not in themselves instances of knowledge. But we may be able to make statements about them, and these last can be instances of knowledge.

Of course not all statements are knowledge. Many are rationalizations, fantasies, deceptive devices, and serious beliefs held without the kind of supporting evidence required to give them the status of knowledge. When these beliefs are used as though they were forms of knowledge, we expose ourselves to dangers.

A statement is an instance of knowledge if, and only if, we (1) have an insight variously called "hypothesis," "theory," or "innovating suggestion"; (2) have put this suggestion into the form of a statement with terms unambiguously defined; (3) have developed the implications of this statement into a logical structure of propositions of such sort that some of these propositions specify what must be observed under required conditions if the statement is to be accepted as knowledge; and (4) have made the observations under the specified conditions to discover if the data do appear in the order required to warrant accepting the statement as having met the tests of probability.

The precision and elaboration with which we apply these tests to propositions varies enormously, depending on

the kind of knowledge we are seeking. At the level of common sense this process of testing is very simple compared
to the practices of science. Also what I have said about the
features distinguishing knowledge might be made more precise and elaborate. But my purpose here is not to investigate the complex structures of knowledge. I wish only to
distinguish knowledge in general from other forms of human
experience.

If we follow correctly the rules of inquiry, the resulting statement is valid knowledge even though it may not be
true. The demand that knowledge be infallibly true is a demand which would make it impossible to use the word "knowledge" to refer to any statement ever made by any human being. Even in pure mathematics the human mind is subject to
error. It is much more subject to error in statements about
concretely existing situations where all the values of life are
experienced, including the value of pure mathematics, since
an individual must exist in a concrete situation to experience
the value of mathematics.

Knowledge based on probability to the exclusion of logical certainty should not be confused with faith. When faith
is identified with the element of probability which enters into every instance of knowledge about concrete existence, confusion arises. Faith is not to be identified with knowledge.
Neither should it be identified with belief when belief means
nothing more than intellectual assent to a proposition. Faith
is something other than knowledge and something other than
belief, although it may be equipped either with knowledge or
with belief. Faith is commitment. Commitment means that
we give ourselves over to something or other so that we conduct our lives in dependence upon that to which we have thus
given ourselves. This something or other to which we have
thus committed ourselves may be specified by statements
which have met the tests of knowledge. In that case faith is
equipped with knowledge. On the other hand, this something
to which we have given our lives in dependence and devotion
may be specified by beliefs which have not met the tests of
knowledge. In that case faith is equipped with beliefs which
are not knowledge. But a faith equipped with knowledge only
and excluding beliefs other than those of knowledge is none-
theless faith. I shall try to show that faith equipped with
knowledge and repudiating beliefs which are not cases of
knowledge is a more worthy faith than one which depends upon beliefs which are not knowledge. The latter, I shall try
to show, is a source of corruption becoming increasingly

dangerous in our civilization.

"The joy of believing" can be one of the greatest obstacles in the way of getting knowledge concerning issues of
supreme importance for the conduct of human living. The
joy, the peace, the profound sense of security, derived from
a belief which is not knowledge, blind us to the error in such
a belief. Beliefs held in this way are likely to be concerned
with the most important decisions, fateful in determining the
greatest good or the greatest evil ever to enter human life.
But the joy and sense of security experienced by holding the
belief exempt from doubt and beyond the reach of cognitive
tests corrupt the mind with dishonest affirmations. Knowledge, fallible as it may be, is the best guide we have in making decisions and in the ultimate commitment of faith. Yet
the very expression "commitment of faith" suggests to most
people a commitment not guided by knowledge. This identification of faith with belief which is not knowledge is the
mounting danger threatening the world community with disaster.

If our best knowledge should indicate that we cannot
know what to choose in making our major decisions, then we
should make our decisions without belief, because belief which
is not knowledge kills that alertness by which evidence might
be discovered and error acknowledged.

Knowledge of other minds is not different in essential
features from any other kind of knowledge. I test my intuition about what is in the mind of the other person by observing what he says, his gestures and tones of voice, and all
the complex physiological expressiveness of the human organism. If these appear in the form and order in which they
should if my belief is true, then I accept it as knowledge.
Later observations may lead me to revise my beliefs about
the other person; but he who refuses to test and revise his
beliefs about others by sensitive observations made as accurate as possible becomes a dangerous person spreading false
ideas about his associates. It is true that human beings often
seem to have a rapport enabling them to understand one another by intuitions with amazing correctness and comprehensiveness. But this correctness of intuition, like correctness
of intuition in any other area, must be developed by long experience devoted to testing and correcting intuitions which
were often mistaken in their original form.

Knowledge of the past is like knowledge of the pres-

ent and future in this respect. We test the rightness of
memory by observing what must be present here and now if
the memory is correct. We test our theories about remote
times and places by observing relics from the past which
must display a certain form and order if the theory can be
called "knowledge." Constructive imagination is always required in attaining knowledge, whether it be in physics or in
history or in knowing the mind of the other person. Genius
appears in developing constructions of the imagination which
can meet the tests of knowledge.

One serious difficulty in the way of getting knowledge
in any area but most of all in religion can be illustrated by
a single example taken from a book by C. I. Lewis.[1] The
example is a very simple experience, much more simple
than the difficulties involved in religious inquiry. But the
principle is the same whether the problem be simple or complex. Simple cases serve best for illustration.

The example is the experience of looking at a white
wall and seeing a spot of red paint, so it seems. The spot
is in truth not red paint but an after-image of red projected
on the wall by an established reaction of the psychosomatic
organism. Impulsively, inevitably, beyond my power of control, I project the red image as though it were a spot of
paint. While my seeing of the red paint on the wall cannot
be corrected because of the established propensity of my organism, my believing that it is a red spot can be corrected.
I can test the correctness of my perception by following the
rules for reaching knowledge as these were above described.
In like manner I correct my perception of the earth as flat
and my perception of things behind the mirror when I look
into it.

May I now take another illustration, this time involving religious belief. Suppose the tradition in which I have
been reared has established another propensity of the psychosomatic organism to react to certain data in conscious awareness. This time, however, the data are not afterimages projected on a white wall. This time the data are certain feelings and certain perceptions which I impulsively and automatically have, causing me to project upon the man Jesus Christ
the image of a supernatural person identical with God. I
cannot help having this perception, just as I cannot help having the perception of a red spot on the wall. While I cannot
help having the perception, I can in both cases correct the
belief if I follow the procedures which produce valid knowledge.

May I take another illustration. Suppose that I am a
Nazi living in Germany when Hitler is at the height of his
power. Suppose that I am a young man of eighteen and, having been subjected during my formative years to Hitler's ora-
tions and other Nazi propaganda, that my psychosomatic organism impulsively and beyond my control reacts to the sight
of a Jew in such a way that I see him to be a demon. I
cannot help having this perception if my psychosomatic organism has been conditioned after the manner mentioned. But I
can correct the belief if I subject it to proper tests.

May I take still another illustration. Suppose under
certain special conditions I look at a tree or at a person and
have an ecstatic experience in which I automatically and beyond volitional control interpret the experience as one in
which I and the tree or I and the other person are merged
into a blissful unity in which there is no longer any distinction between myself and the tree or myself and the other person but all are merged in "Reality." I cannot help having
this mysterial experience; but my belief about it can be corrected by following the rules for distinguishing between true
and false beliefs.

When deep-laid habits and powerful passions create in
us false perceptions and when these false perceptions are
shared by others to whom we are bound by the imperative
needs of personal security, we may be coercively impelled to
select only the data which seem to support our cherished belief. We ignore or argue away the evidence which would reveal the error of our belief.

May I quote again from C. I. Lewis from the book
previously mentioned:

> No inductive conclusion is well taken and justly
> credible unless the obligation to muster all the giv-
> en and available evidence which is relevant to this
> conclusion has been met.... If pertinent evidence
> has been ignored or suppressed, then any probabil-
> ity on the premises specified...does not represent
> a warranted conclusion or a rationally justified be-
> lief.[2]

Lewis goes on to note that this demand, namely, to consider
all the evidence hostile as well as favorable to my cherished
belief, reveals a moral quality involved in intellectual inquiry. Will we be honest enough to recognize evidence

against our cherished belief as well as what supports it? Or
will we suppress the contrary evidence? This moral quality
is, I think, most flagrantly lacking in the field of religious
belief and religious propaganda. I use the term "propaganda"
because propaganda in its most pernicious form means the
proclamation of beliefs supported by evidence which has been
selected to support the beliefs and excluding contrary evidence.

Turn now to a second point often neglected in religious
inquiry. It has to do with what is called "insight" or "vision" or "innovating suggestion." An insight or intuition,
mystical or otherwise, is not knowledge; but intution is the
raw material out of which all knowledge is made. By intuition I mean a new idea emerging in the mind combined with
a feeling that it is true. To confuse insight or intuition
with knowledge is a gross error, even though insight or intuition is absolutely indispensable to the attainment of further
knowledge. We cannot test a new idea if we do not have a
new idea to test. The new idea may enter the mind with
compelling conviction that it is true, like the red spot on the
wall, like the demonic character of the Jew for the Nazi,
like the ecstatic vision of fellow man for Martin Buber.
Without these new ideas or perceptions, no advance in knowledge is possible. But the new perception must be tested.
The intuition of the Nazi that the Jew is a demon has contributed considerably to our knowledge, since it has stimulated research into cultural differences, thereby demonstrat-
ing more thoroughly than ever that diverse moral qualities
cannot be identified with diverse peoples. So with other new
perceptions. But the new perception, intuition, vision, suggestion, or theory is not knowledge until it has been subject
to the proper treatment. This applies as imperatively to
Martin Buber's intuition as it does to the Nazi's or to any
other you wish to mention.

As the personality of the Nazi was conditioned by living in a society surcharged with propaganda so that he intuitively discerns the demonic character of the Jew, so likewise the Christian is conditioned by living in a society surcharged with propaganda about Jesus so that he intuitively
discerns in Jesus the embodiment of the supernatural Deity.
But the one conviction is no more based on the correct procedures for getting knowledge than the other. Jesus may
embody a supernatural Deity, but we do not have knowledge
of it until the belief has been subjected to the treatment
whereby a belief becomes knowledge.

One distinctive feature of religious inquiry is that it must be passionate. By "passionate inquiry" I mean a concern to find the truth when the concern is so strong that we cast our whole self into the inquiry in such wise that we are in a state of readiness to recognize our own distorting prejudices and pride and the conditioning which falsifies our intuitions and perceptions. In passionate inquiry as I here use the term I mean a zeal for valid knowledge which drives us to search out our own desperate clinging to certain beliefs for the sake of personal security, thereby blinding ourselves to contrary evidence. In passionate inquiry we search our souls to uncover those corrupting biases which creep in to mislead the mind when the inquiry is about matters which profoundly shape the course of life.

There is a second sense in which inquiry must be passionate if it is to achieve religious knowledge. After we have achieved knowledge in the sense of fair treatment of all the evidence, including logical coherence of propositions, we must cast our whole self in religious commitment of faith under the guidance of this knowledge, not because this knowledge is necessarily the truth, but because inquiry is not religious unless it includes commitment of faith in the form of action and decision shaping the course of life. In this way error may be discovered if error is sought; but error will not be discovered if we hold our belief tenaciously for the sake of security.

Since religious inquiry must be passionate in this second sense, namely, in the sense of casting our lives in devotion under guidance of the best knowledge we can discover, religious knowledge must be intensely practical. It must be knowledge which points out the direction of all our striving. Therefore, knowledge about ultimate reality and the Being of being and the cosmic process and First Cause is not properly religious knowledge unless, and insofar as, such knowledge marks out a distinctive and transforming course of action in dealing with family and friends, our jobs, our sicknesses and health and immediate conditions of human existence. I am not saying that all metaphysical knowledge is outside the bounds of religious knowledge. I am saying that it is outside those bounds when and if it fails to indicate rather clearly a distinctive way of life for man to which he can give himself quite completely in conducting his daily affairs.

Since passionate inquiry is one of the essential features of the method by which religious knowledge is attained

and without which no genuine religious knowledge can be had,
I shall try to illustrate what I mean by passionate inquiry as
a form of action. I am indebted to William James for the
illustration which I shall use, although I am rejecting his
doctrine about "The Will to Believe." Also I am modifying
the illustration to serve my own purpose.

Suppose a group of men are on a mountaintop caught
in a blinding blizzard. They know that they will die if they
do not descend the mountain, but they have lost their sense
of direction. They know that there is a safe way down, but,
if they go in the wrong direction, they will fall to their
death over a precipice. They gather all the evidence they
can and make careful estimates until they conclude that the
probabilities indicate one direction to be the right one for
avoiding the precipice. They then proceed in single file, one
man in the lead so that, if he falls over the precipice in the
blinding storm, the others will be warned and may turn back.

In making this venture, the leader believes he is moving in the right direction but at the same time recognizes his
liability to error. He is guided by knowledge in the form of
probability, since he has subjected his belief to every available test. His inquiry is passionate in the sense that he exposes himself to destruction in order to discover the way of
salvation. Only when we commit ourselves in a way to be
destroyed, if necessary, can we be liberated from the clutch
of those beliefs which possess us or grasp us. We are liberated because in this way we find our security not in our
beliefs or in our knowledge but in the completeness of our
commitment to the reality which saves, no matter how different it may be from our beliefs about it, accepting destruction if that should reveal this reality in its true character.
Then, and only then, are we able to examine critically our
religious beliefs and test them to find what error may be in
them, even though this testing lead to our own defeat or other loss. Perhaps the illustration should be completed by saying that the leader fell over the precipice but that some of
his followers were saved.

In religion in contrast to the sciences the beliefs to
be tested very often sustain our total being in a way of life
to which we have committed ourselves. Herein lies the
source of corruption and self-deception so prevalent in religion. We cannot truly detect the error in our beliefs if the
beliefs are indispensable to our ultimate security as we see
it. For this reason religious inquiry must be passionate with

a passion stronger than the religious way of life to which we
have given ourselves when the religious way is defined by accepted beliefs. Not in Christianity must we find our ultimate
security if we are to escape the corruption just mentioned.
Christianity may well be the religion which guides our commitment, because Christian doctrine is the best guide we have
been able to discover, and it may be the best we shall ever
discover. But our ultimate security must be found not in
these beliefs and doctrines which define the Christian way of
life. Rather our ultimate security must be found in what
does in truth operate in human life to transform man as he
cannot transform himself to save him from evil and lead him
to the best that human life may ever attain. If this transforming power should differ from the specifications about it
laid down in "biblical faith," then it is to this transforming
power that man gives himself in ultimate commitment, different though it be from his beliefs which rest on probability
only.

    Unless we recognize that the beliefs by which we live
may lead us to the precipice, and unless we accept this possibility as a necessary feature of the inquiry, finding our
blessedness not in the rightness of our beliefs but in the
rightness of our devotion, only then can we be free of the
corruption which rises out of religious faith. In such case
we use our beliefs to shape the course of our lives, ending
at the precipice if that must be; we also use them to guide
our search and to be corrected by further evidence if such
evidence emerges. But we must not use them to provide the
ultimate source of our security. Our security is found in
the completeness of our devotion to what we seek, not in the
certainty with which we hold the beliefs shaping our present
way of life. Unless we do this, we will not detect the precipice when we draw near it; or, supposing it impossible for
us to detect the precipice in time to save ourselves, our followers will not recognize it even when we fall into it, if they
find their security in affirming a belief about the right way
rather than seeking evidence concerning what is in truth the
right way.

    This illustration must not be overworked. Of course
the right religious way may call for self-sacrifice to the
point of death, and many other disasters may be encountered.
But the issue should be clear. Either it is possible to get
some knowledge concerning the way of man's salvation or it
is not. If any knowledge can be gained, security sought and
found in beliefs which are not knowledge will block the in-

quiry by which such knowledge might be gained. Even when
security is based on knowledge, this kind of security will
block the way to more reliable knowledge. The saving reality itself which we seek to know and not our knowledge about
it calls for the ultimate commitment.

Theories in the natural sciences are not, as in religion, wrought into the organization of personality at such a
depth that any great change in them requires a reorganization of the personality. In fact, this reorganization of personality is precisely what occurred in the historically famous
conversions of religious beliefs. That of Paul on the road
to Damascus is the classical example. Our personalities
from infancy may have been organized about the religious convictions of communism, or about the conviction that the white
race is ordained of God to rule over the Negro, or that capi-
talism is identical with the will of God and any deviation
therefrom is sin, or that the Japanese race from its origin
has been in process of preparation for the high mission of
ruling the earth.

You and I, of course, are very sure that the religious
convictions reaching down to the roots of selfhood in us do
not require the sort of correction demanded of these other
faiths. It is conceivable, however, that our complacency is
ill-founded. It is not ill-founded in the sense of requiring
us to adopt one of these other faiths; but our complacency
does not justify us in refusing to devote ourselves to religious inquiry with the kind of passion here described as one
distinctive feature of search in the field of religion. We may
not cease to be Christian, but we should cease to be compla-
cent Christians.

Passionate inquiry is especially important in taking the
first step toward getting religious knowledge. This first step
is insight, otherwise called "intuition." It is an innovating
suggestion emerging in the mind. It should be of such character as to lead to fruitful inquiry. Commitment to passionate inquiry produces a state of mind in which fruitful intuition is most likely to break through the barriers of pride and
conditioning. This is so because passionate inquiry means
religious living which does not depend for its ultimate security upon accepted beliefs held exempt from doubt and the
search for error.

After the emergence of promising intuition comes the
second step in getting knowledge. This is accurate defini-

tion of terms and statements. Take, for example, the idea
of God. Many say that God cannot be defined. Now definitions apply only to words and other signs and symbols which
convey meaning. Chair and table cannot be defined except
in the sense of defining the meaning of the words "chair" and
"table." Therefore when we say that God cannot be defined,
either we are affirming a triviality, since the same can be
said of every existing thing down to tables and chairs and
knives and forks, or else we are saying that the word "God"
cannot be defined. If we are saying that the word "God"
cannot be defined, we are saying that the word has no meaning. We are saying that this word is as meaningless as a
grunt. To be sure, a grunt has meaning in the sense of indicating a physiological disturbance; but I am sure that believers in God do not mean that the holy name signifies nothing more than a grunt.

It is impossible to conduct religious inquiry or any
other kind of inquiry unless the words employed, including
the word "God," are so defined that it is possible to gather
evidence to indicate the truth or error of the proposition under consideration.

May I suggest a definition of what we seek to know
when we seek to know what God is. In seeking God, we
seek to know what operates in human life to transform man
as he cannot transform himself to save him from evil and
lead him to the best that human life can ever attain, provided that man commits himself in faith to this reality and meets
the other conditions demanded.

Please note that, when we seek for God, we are seeking to know what actually operates in human life to transform
man as he cannot transform himself thereby saving him from
evil and leading him to the best. What actually operates in
human life after this manner might conceivably be the ultimate reality on which all existence depends, sometimes called
Being with a capital B. It might be the First Cause or the
Highest Perfection. It might be omniscient, omnipotent, and
have any other attribute you wish. But it need not have any
of these characteristics. The one essential is that it be
found actually operating in human life to transform man as
he cannot transform himself when and if he commits himself
to it in religious faith and meets the other conditions which
must be met to the end that its saving and transforming power can operate effectively. Therefore it must first of all be
a process occurring in human life, because process means

anything whatsoever which occurs in our lives.   Another
word for process is "occurrent" or "event."

        For reasons stated, religious inquiry must first of
all be directed to what is going on in human life to find what
operates in the way mentioned.   After we have found the saving and transforming power at work in human life, we may
go on to inquire whether it is identical with, or otherwise
connected with, ultimate Being.   But to reverse the procedure is to miss the point entirely.   If we start with inquiry
about ultimate Being, we will almost certainly fail to find
the process which saves and transforms, because ultimate
Being is a mystery, as Tillich and many others assert.   The
great exemplars of religious personality, such persons, for
example, as Jesus, Socrates, Paul, Martin Luther, and
Gandhi, were not metaphysicians.   When and if metaphysical
problems engaged them at all, these problems were quite
peripheral to their central questions.   The primary question
for every one of them was the question about man's salvation and what operates in human life to accomplish it.

        This brings us to the third step in the procedure
leading to knowledge.   The first step was the emergence of
an insight or intuition leading to fruitful inquiry.   The second step was unambiguous definition of the concepts involved.
The third is logical coherence.   Any statement rightly called
"knowledge" or reliably leading to knowledge must be logically coherent with respect to its several parts and coherent
with other statements known to be true.

        A statement may yet be true even when contradicted
by all the knowledge we have.   This is so because the human mind is not infallible in what it claims to know.
Therefore a statement, contradicting what I claim to know,
might be true.   But that is not the point.   The point is that
I cannot know a statement to be true if it is contradicted by
other statements held by me to be true.   Neither can I know
a statement to be true if it contains substatements which contradict one another.   This is so because the achievement of
logical coherence is one of the steps in the procedure yielding knowledge; and, without it, we cannot know what is true
and what is false.   He who claims to know the truth while
rejecting this test which fallible minds must use in seeking
knowledge is displaying an inexcusable arrogance and claiming to have a god-like power of knowing which no human
mind possesses.

In the form of paradoxes containing contradictory statements religious doctrines are often proclaimed as somehow true. In honesty and humility we must admit that by some wild chance one or more of these contradictory statements may be true. But no human mind is justified in claiming to <u>know</u> that they are true until the statements have met the tests which statements must meet before they can be called "human knowledge." It may be true that fairies are now dancing on the roof of this house; but I am not justified in claiming to know that they are, because any statement to that effect is contradicted by many other statements which make up our knowledge about the world. Paradox may be legitimately used as a rhetorical device. Also it may serve to indicate an area of mystery where knowledge cannot reach. But in neither case is the paradox a confirmed statement.

What is said about paradox applies also to myth. A myth may guide us in dealing with some kind of important reality, but we cannot know what that reality is until we have defined the meaning of our statements and combined them into a logical structure and applied this system of propositions in a way to make the required observations. Otherwise any claim to know what the myth is about is a false claim no matter how useful the myth may be as a guide to some important reality.

A logical structure by itself alone gives us no knowledge of anything except the logical structure itself standing in bare abstraction. To give us knowledge of anything beyond itself, the logical structure must be applied in such a way as to yield predictable consequences under specified conditions. The predictable consequences must be certain selected data entering conscious awareness when the specified conditions are present and not entering conscious awareness when the specified conditions are not present.

In carrying out this fourth step, the human mind is most liable to error. It is very easy for the human mind to fabricate the data of conscious awareness in a way to support a desired belief. If a man's personal security depends upon seeing a red spot on the white wall, if an ancient tradition has taught him that the red spot is there, if his associates see the spot, and if fellowship with persons beloved by him requires that he see the red spot as they do, he will most likely see it. All the predictable consequences which might correct his error will be distorted in a way to support his claim that the after-image is truly a red spot on the wall.

Nevertheless, while the human mind is most liable to error
in taking this fourth step, there can be no valid knowledge
until this test of predictable consequences has been applied.
Hence the need for passionate inquiry as described above to
avoid so far as possible the distortions and perversions of
conscious awareness which fabricate the data sought as evidence.

We immediately ask: "What kind of predictable consequences or their absence must be encountered before we
can rightly claim to have religious knowledge?"

Before attempting an answer to that question, let me
name some of the predictable consequences falsely alleged to
be the tests yielding valid religious knowledge. The feeling
of personal security, sometimes called "peace of mind," may
be the predictable consequence of holding a belief. But all
manner of wild illusions can give the feeling of personal security and peace of mind. Indeed, one of the chief causes
driving men to resort to wild illusions is the desire for the
personal security which these illusions provide.

I believe it is possible to define personal security and
peace of mind in such a way that it might be a test of knowledge; but such a definition would require a great amount of
psychological information penetrating deep into the subconscious levels of human personality. (This is the first statement I have made indicating the contribution of the social sciences to religious inquiry and religious knowledge. It is my
first statement, but it comes at a crucial point where religious inquiry is most likely to go astray. It is precisely at
this fourth step in looking for predictable consequences that
we must turn to the social sciences for help in seeking religious knowledge.)

No appeal to divine revelation in Christ or the Bible
or the church or the Judeo-Christian tradition can save us
from idolatry when the appeal is made to evade the demand
for rigorous and passionate inquiry to discover just what is
true and what is false in all the statements attributed to
Christ, Bible, church, and tradition. Even if it should be
granted that in Christ the whole saving reality which answers
the religious question can be found, still any statement which
we make about this saving reality and any interpretation of
symbols referring to this saving reality of Christ are the
statements and interpretations of our fallible minds. Until
we have subjected these statements and interpretations to the

rigorous tests of inquiry, we have arrogantly refused to seek
the reality and have insisted instead that our ultimate commitment be given to these affirmations of our own minds
which, since they have not been rigorously tested, are much
more likely to be in error than those which have been.

There is another obstacle in the way of getting religious knowledge which I have not yet mentioned. The religious question is often formulated in such a way as to render impossible any inquiry which might lead to an answer.
For example, if we define religion as ultimate concern for
ultimate reality and then formulate the religious question by
asking, "What is ultimate reality?" we have misdirected the
search. As said before, we must first seek what actually
and observably operates in human life to save from evil.

Some say that the standard for judging what is better
and worse for man and for judging what kind of transformation moves in the direction of the best possible can never be
discovered by any kind of rational and empirical inquiry.
Good and evil, better and worse, right and wrong, are otherwise discerned, they say. This opens a complicated contro-
versy which cannot be entered here for lack of space. I
have discussed these questions in my "Intellectual Autobiography" to be published in the volume devoted to my thought
in the series entitled "Library of Living Theology." Here I
can only briefly suggest the kind of empirical evidence for
distinguishing good and evil and the greater good from the
lesser. The theory and the evidence supporting the theory
are taken from the social sciences, chiefly from the various
branches of psychotherapy. Evidence can also be gathered
from observation in daily life and from records of the past
pertaining to religious living to the origins of Christianity and
other sources.

The theory can be stated thus: When required conditions are present, a kind of interchange going on between individuals does two things: (1) it creates appreciative understanding of the unique individuality of one another and (2)
what is thus learned by each from the other is progressively
integrated into the unique individuality of each. This I shall
call "creative interchange" to distinguish it from other kinds
of interchange.

I intend to designate by "creative interchange" what
creates in the infant progressively that system of experience
which distinguishes man from every other kind of animal in-

sofar as this system develops and preserves its wholeness. There is another kind of interchange also characteristic of the human being which breaks this system of experience into conflicting parts of such sort that the satisfaction experienced by one of these parts conflicts with satisfaction of the other parts. This second kind of interchange has been given various names, such as "security operations," "defense mechanisms," and other labels. To the measure that this second kind of interchange prevails, the individual cannot appreciate and approve anything with the wholeness of his being but rather finds every satisfaction at one level of his being frustrative and dissatisfying at other levels.

The question before us is this: What predictable consequences are evidence that commitment to creative interchange will save from evil and produce the best that human life can ever attain? This question cannot be answered until we define what we mean by the words "good" and "evil."

By "good" I shall mean the experience of being satisfied. This requires something which is satisfying and a self being satisfied. The greatest possible good for any individual is satisfaction of the self in the wholeness of its being and not merely satisfaction at one level which frustrates other levels of the total individuality. Empirical evidence indicates that this kind of satisfaction must be progressive in the sense of expanding more or less continuously the range of what can be appreciated, understood, and controlled by the total unified self; increasing the depth of appreciative understanding which we can have of other individuals; and enlarging the capacity to learn appreciatively from the experience of others across the barrier of diversity and estrangement.

To distinguish these developments from other kinds, I shall call them collectively the "creative transformation" of the individual in the wholeness of his being. If creative interchange as above defined produces creative transformation of the individual, then the observation of this consequence is empirical evidence that creative interchange is the greatest good and the saving power in human life.

At the risk of repetition, I again note that perfection in this respect is not asserted but that it can be approached in varying degrees.

Creative transformation by way of creative interchange cannot occur to any great measure unless a certain defect in human beings is to some degree corrected or neutralized. This defect has already been mentioned. It has been given the name of "security operations" by Harry Stack Sullivan.[3] Theologically, it can be labeled "original sin." It is the development in the individual of devices by which he protects his self-esteem in terms of a false idea of himself. Self-esteem satisfied in this way prevents satisfaction of the self in its true character and wholeness, because esteem of a false idea of one's self demands for its satisfaction what cannot satisfy the self in its true character. Thus, when we are dominated by security operations, satisfaction at one level--the level of security operations--creates dissatisfaction at other levels of the total self. This is the opposite and contradictory of satisfying the individual in the wholeness of his being. So long as this inner conflict prevails, the individual cannot find satisfaction for his individuality in its wholeness, because he lacks wholeness and because he seeks what could not satisfy that wholeness.

This condition is evil because it prevents satisfaction of the individual in the wholeness of his being, and what prevents the greater good is evil relative to that greater good. What saves from this evil condition is the kind of interchange which creates appreciative understanding of the unique individuality of one another. This creative interchange saves because we are helped to know ourselves as we truly are by seeing ourselves as others see us when they see us with appreciative understanding of our true individualities. Also when we encounter appreciative understanding of our true individualities, we no longer feel it to be necessary to develop a false front and conceal ourselves from ourselves and from others. Absence of creative interchange develops self-identification with a false front, and consequently the evil condition of self-frustration and self-defeat, anxiety and loss of any sense of meaning in life which satisfies the whole self.

These predictable consequences of good when creative interchange is more or less continuously dominant and these predictable consequences of evil when creative interchange is not dominant are the predictable consequences to be observed. If they are observed, we have evidence that creative interchange is what saves man from evil and saves him unto the greatest good when he gives himself over to it in religious commitment of faith.

Creative interchange is obstructed by many counter-processes going on in human life. But, when conditions are favorable so that it can operate effectively, observations in psychiatry and clinical psychology, in other sciences devoted to the study of man, the observations of common sense, and the records of religious conversion seem to indicate that creative interchange is what calls for the commitment of religious faith, because it saves from evil and transforms man as he cannot transform himself to reach the greatest good ever attainable in human existence.

When I speak of this transformation of man as a kind of creativity, I do not mean the creative work of man whether in art or science or social organization or technology or in any other area of human achievement. Not man's creative work but the creative transformation of man himself is what I mean. I cannot here attempt to describe in all its fulness what this transformation is, but I can specify four features by which it can be distinguished from the many other changes which occur in human life. These four are not separable; they involve one another and are aspects of a single process.

1. This creativity is an expanding of the range and diversity of what the individual can know, evaluate, and control.

2. It is an increasing of one's ability to understand appreciatively other persons and peoples across greater barriers of estrangement and hostility.

3. It is an increasing of the capacity of the individual to integrate into the uniqueness of his own individuality a greater diversity of experiences so that more of all that he encounters becomes a source of enrichment and strength rather than impoverishing and weakening him.

4. It is an increasing of the freedom of the individual when freedom means one's ability to absorb any cause acting on one's self so that the consequences resulting from it express the character and fulfill the purpose of the individual himself. The way Socrates died is an example. His death expressed the character and fulfilled the purpose of Socrates and not of those who caused his death. The way Jesus absorbed everything done to him in such a way that his own individuality determined the ensuing consequences rather than allowing these to be determined by the character of the cause acting on him is another example of what is here meant by freedom.

This all-too-brief statement indicates the kind of consequences which should be observed in seeking knowledge of
the way man is saved from evil and saved unto the greater
good. The greater good is what satisfies the individual progressively in the wholeness of his being and in conjunction
with others who also find in the same process the progressive satisfaction of unique individuality in the wholeness of
its being.

All Christian symbols can apply to this creativity,
such as the living Christ, God, Holy Spirit, the power of salvation by faith, and others. Commitment means that the demands of creative interchange shall take priority over every
other demand whenever we can choose among alternatives.

One of the major obstructions to the saving power of
this creativity is the shared experience of groups when this
shared experience is attained by forms of interchange which
do not create appreciative understanding of unique individuality. For example, the Nazis had the shared experience of
hate for the Jew and the shared conviction that the Aryan
race was destined to conquer and rule the world. This gave
them a tremendous dynamism but did not create appreciative
understanding of the unique individuality of persons brought
into interchange with them. Many white people have the
shared conviction that the Negro is inferior and should be
kept in place of servitude under the dominance of the white
man. Millions of Americans, it would seem, have the
shared experience derived from comics and cheap movies,
giving them a false picture of human life and leading them
to misunderstand their own personalities as well as the personalities of other people. Propaganda of many sorts produces experience shared by multitudes. Hysteria and hate
sweeping a nation are shared experiences. Therefore, when
I speak of the kind of interchange which creates appreciative
understanding of unique individuality and of the needs and
problems of groups other than one's own group, I am not
speaking of shared experience produced in any other way than
by creative interchange.

When religious knowledge is under consideration,
something should be said about divine revelation. In speaking of revelation, I shall use the word "God" to designate
whatever in truth operates in human life to save from evil
and unto the greater good, no matter how this process of
transformation may differ from every idea ever formed of
a divine Being. This process of transformation as it oper-

ates in its true character is here given the name of God because of the salvation it actually achieves for man and not
because it conforms to any idea of God which human beings
may hold to satisfy their "security operations." This distinction between conforming to a pre-established idea and conforming to an actual process is crucial for any inquiry leading to knowledge.

God understood in this way is revealed when the process of transformation saving man from evil and to the greater good appears in such conspicuous and obvious form that it
cannot be missed except by those who base their ultimate security upon mistaken beliefs about it. In Jesus and his early
fellowship I think that we see the kind of interchange which I
have identified with the saving and transforming power at
work in human life and which should be called God, because
it does save by transforming man as he cannot transform himself. In Jesus and his fellowship this kind of interchange appears in a form so conspicuous that none can miss it except
those driven by the need of personal security to believe that
God must be a supernatural Being and not a natural process
of interchange.

This saving power is revealed in Jesus not necessarily because it is more powerfully present in his fellowship
than anywhere else in history. It is obvious and conspicuous
in that fellowship because of the way historical developments
have lifted that fellowship to a mountaintop, so to speak.
All subsequent ages in Western culture can see and feel this
transforming power in Jesus and his early followers because
of the social and psychological conditions then and there prevailing combined with the way great streams of social development converged upon, and radiated from, that time and
place. In this sense it can be said that history has made
Jesus the revelation of God to Western man.

I am not now speaking of what has been called the
"Christ of faith" in contrast to the "Jesus of history," when
Christ of faith is what later generations have believed about
Jesus. I am not talking about belief, although of course belief in the form of knowledge enters into the picture. What
we can know about the matter seems to indicate that this
man and his little group did display the power to transform
lives from evil to good. There is the further historic fact
that this transforming power has been caught up by massive
social developments in such a way that it shines like a beacon light, or, to quote an ancient gospel song, it appears

"towering o'er the wrecks of time."

It must be emphasized that revelation is not knowledge. Revelation is the conspicuous presence of the saving power in human life. Knowledge of what this power is, how it operates, what conditions must be present in order for it to operate most effectively--all this must be discovered by the social sciences, including the kind of knowledge going by the name of "common sense." We already know something of the conditions which must be present for this creative interchange to operate effectively in saving men from evil and to do good. The traditional church, by observation and experimentation, has gathered considerable knowledge of the required conditions. For example, repentance is one of the required conditions. Much more knowledge is now being gained by studies in inter-personal relations, psychiatry, and clinical psychology.

I can see nothing but folly and sin in the distress which some religious people seem to feel over any knowledge which can be gained by historical or psychological or other research which helps us better to understand how this saving power operates and what its required conditions may be.

Let me summarize the argument of this paper.

I have tried to show (1) procedures by which knowledge is achieved; (2) what valid knowledge is when achieved; (3) what specifically is the question which religious inquiry seeks to answer, thus distinguishing the area of religious knowledge from other areas; and (4) how religious knowledge should be sought, namely, by passionate inquiry. At the end I have tried to bring it all together by suggesting very briefly how the social sciences might contribute to our knowledge of the revelation of God in Jesus Christ.

In pointing to the paramount importance of religious knowledge in our time to supplant religious belief which is not knowledge, I am not suggesting that any man acquires belief which is not knowledge, I am not suggesting that any man acquires his religious faith by way of knowledge or by exercise of reason. He does not any more than he acquires his native language and his culture by rational appraisal of diverse languages and cultures leading him to choose one and not the others. Man acquires his religion as he acquires his culture. In Christianity this particular culture transmitting a faith is under the supervision of the church thus dis-

tinguishing it from the culture in general.   But this fact that
we acquire our religion without the use of reason makes all
the more imperative that we use reason to examine critically the faith by which we live to purge it of error and evil so
far as we are able.   Every traditional form of religion is infected with error and evil, and in some cases the evils and
illusions become monstrous.

The tradition which brings us Christianity cannot be
discarded even if we wished to do so.   Our minds have been
shaped by this tradition.   Our insight, our religious consciousness, our way of life, and our resources for religious
inquiry must for the most part be found in this tradition.
Whether for better or worse, and whether we like it or not,
such is the case.   All this is so obvious that it would be
foolish to deny it, and I certainly do not deny it.

In this statement about the way to religious knowledge
I am not discarding Jesus Christ, the Bible, the church, and
the Judeo-Christian tradition.   Neither do I deny the importance of faith, insight, mystic vision, divine grace, the obstructive and blinding fact of sin, the imperative need to confess and repent of sin in order to conduct religious inquiry,
and the indispensability of insight and divine grace for any
success in seeking religious knowledge.   It is true that I have
interpreted sin and evil in such a way that they apply to good
Christian people and to church leaders and theologians.   This
may render the interpretation quite unsatisfactory.

Notes

1.   The Ground and Nature of the Right (New York: Colum-
       bia University Press, 1955).

2.   Ibid., p. 32.

3.   The Interpersonal Theory of Psychiatry (New York: W.
       W. Norton & Co., 1953).

BIBLIOGRAPHY

The reader should consult this bibliography as supplementary to the one in The Empirical Theology of Henry Nelson Wieman, Robert W. Bretall, editor (Carbondale and Edwardsville: Southern Illinois University Press, 1969), pp. 399-414. This bibliography lists: (1) works of Wieman that have been published since the cut-off date of 1961 in Bretall, namely, one new book, four books reprinted, and essays and articles in journals and periodicals; (2) works of Wieman that went unreported in Bretall; and (3) works by others on Wieman's thought. It should be noted that this bibliography is limited and selective; is not intended to be exhaustive.

I. BOOKS BY WIEMAN

1963

Man's Ultimate Commitment (Carbondale and Edwardsville: Southern Illinois University Press), paper reprint edition. First published in 1958.

1964

The Source of Human Good (Carbondale and Edwardsville: Southern Illinois University Press), paper reprint edition. First published in 1946 by University of Chicago Press.

1968

Religious Inquiry: Some Explorations (Boston: Beacon Press).

1970

Religious Experience and Scientific Method (Westport, Conn.: Greenwood Press). Hardbound reprint edition. See next entry.

1971

Religious Experience and Scientific Method (Carbondale and Edwardsville: Southern Illinois University Press), paper reprint edition with a new preface by Wieman. First published in 1926 by The Macmillan Company, this 1971 reprint edition was published by arrangement with Henry Nelson Wieman, who renewed the copyright in 1954.

Normative Psychology of Religion (with Regina Westcott Wieman) (Westport, Conn.: Greenwood Press). Hardbound reprint edition. First published in 1935 by Thomas Y. Crowell Company.

II. FOREIGN PUBLICATIONS OF WORKS BY WIEMAN

1956

"The Religious Need of Our Time," in Humanism, Art and Religion, Ichiro Hara, editor (Tokyo: Sekkei-Syobo Press). This essay is an excerpt of "The Promise of Protestantism-- Whither and Whether," which first appeared in The Protestant Credo, Vergilius Ferm, editor (New York: Philosophical Library, 1953). Humanism, Art and Religion also contains an essay on "humanism" by Julian Huxley and an essay on "art" by Herbert Read.

1959

Man's Ultimate Commitment (Tokyo: Sekkei-Syobo Press), edited, with notes by Ichiro Hara. This publication contains only "Introduction" and the chapters "From Drift to Direction" and "Living Richly with Dark Realities" from Man's Ultimate Commitment (Carbondale: Southern Illinois University Press, 1958).

1961

Intellectual Foundation of Faith (London: Vision Press Limited).

1962

Industry and Organization (Tokyo: The Hokuseido Press), edited, with notes by Ichiro Hara. This volume contains two chapters, "Industry" and "Organization," which are the chapters "Industry Under Commitment" and "Organization Under Commitment" in <u>Man's Ultimate Commitment</u>.

1968

<u>Creating a New Age</u> (Tokyo: The Hokuseido Press), edited, with notes by Ichiro Hara. This volume contains three chapters, "What Is Creativity?", "Creativity of History," and "The Decision Required of Us," plus a lengthy "Supplementary Essay" by Wieman especially for this volume. The chapters are reprints of "Introduction," "History Under Commitment," and "The Decision Required of Us" in <u>Man's Ultimate Commitment.</u>

III.   ESSAYS, ARTICLES, AND REVIEWS BY WIEMAN

1930

"What's the World to Me," <u>Ventures in Belief,</u> Henry P. Van Dusen, editor (New York: Charles Scribner's Sons).

1935

"Types of Theism," review of <u>God in These Times</u> by Henry P. Van Dusen, <u>God and the Common Life</u> by Robert Lowry Calhoun, <u>God</u> by John Elof Boodin, and <u>God and the Social Process</u> by Louis Wallis, in <u>Christendom,</u> I, pp. 198-203.

1937

"New Directions in Religious Thought," review of <u>The Nature of Religious Experience: Essays in Honor of Douglas Clyde Macintosh</u> by J. S. Bixler et al., in <u>Christendom,</u> II: 4.

1941

"Theology and the Philosophy of Religion: A Comparison and A Contrast," <u>Journal of Liberal Religion,</u> Vol. 2, pp. 163-175.

1954

"Bernhardt's Analysis of Religion," <u>The Iliff Review,</u> Winter issue, pp. 48-57.

1957

"Toward an Analysis of Ethics for Rhetoric" (with Otis M. Walter), Quarterly Journal of Speech, XLIII:3.

Intellectual Autobiography, original version, mimeographed and privately circulated (Carbondale: Southern Illinois University), 57 pages. The essayists of The Empirical Theology of Henry Nelson Wieman had access to this version.

1959

"The Problem of Mysticism," in Mysticism and the Modern Mind, Alfred P. Stiernotte, editor (New York: The Liberal Arts Press).

1961

"Speech in the Existential Situation," Quarterly Journal of Speech, XLVII:2.

"Concerning the Intellectual Foundation of Faith--An Exchange of Views" The Iliff Review, Fall issue, pp. 51-53. (See entries for Charles S. Milligan in section IV below.)

1962

"The Structure of the Divine Creativity, An Exchange of Views," The Iliff Review, Winter issue, pp. 37-42. (See Milligan in IV below.)

"The Ways of God with Man," The Iliff Review, Spring issue, pp. 37-41. (See Milligan in IV below.)

"Commitment for Theological Inquiry," Journal of Religion, XLII:3.

"A Waste We Cannot Afford," Unitarian Universalist Register-Leader, CXLIII, (November).

1963

"Intellectual Autobiography" (shortened and revised version) and "Replies," in Robert W. Bretall, editor, The Empirical Theology of Henry Nelson Wieman (New York: The Macmillan Company).

"Reply to My Critics," Religion in Life, XXXII:3. (See entry for John B. Cobb, Jr. in IV below.)

"The Divine Creativity in History," Religion in Life XXXIII:1.

"Purpose and Discipline in Education," The Education Forum, March, pp. 279-288.

1966

"Commentary on Theological Resources from the Social Sciences," Zygon, I:1.

"Empiricism in Religious Philosophy," in Philosophy, Religion, and the Coming World Civilization: Essays in Honor of William Ernest Hocking, Leroy S. Rouner, editor (The Hague: Martinus Nijhoff).

"Science and A New Religious Reformation," Zygon, I:2.

"Comment on 'The Death of God'," The Radford Review, 20, Fall issue.

"The Problem of Religious Inquiry," Zygon, I:4.

1967

"Salvation as Creative Evolution," Religion in Life, XXXVI:2.

"Reinhold Niebuhr," in The Encyclopedia of Philosophy, Volume 5, Paul Edwards, editor in chief (New York: The Macmillan Company and The Free Press).

1968

"Co-operative Functions of Science and Religion," Zygon, III:1.

"Religious Humanism and Theism Rejected," Religious Humanism, II:4.

1969

"The Promise of A Naturalistic Theology," Action-Reaction (San Francisco Theological Seminary), II:2.

"Conflict and Creativity," Interchange (Center for Creative Interchange, Des Moines, Iowa), February.

"The Revolution of Our Time," Interchange, March-April.

"Intellectual Autobiography" and "Replies," in Robert W. Bretall, editor, The Empirical Theology of Henry Nelson Wieman (Carbondale and Edwardsville: Southern Illinois University Press), paper reprint edition.

"Creativity and the Universe," Interchange, May.

"Rebellion and the New Generation, Interchange, Summer.

"Response," in William S. Minor, editor, Charles Hartshorne and Henry Nelson Wieman (Carbondale: The Foundation for Creative Philosophy, Inc.).

"Organization for Power: Its Danger and Corrective," Interchange, September-October.

"Transcendence and 'Cosmic Consciousness," in Herbert W. Richardson and Donald R. Cutler, editors, Transcendence, (Boston: Beacon Press), reprint of Chapter II in Religious Inquiry: Some Explorations.

1970

"What Is Creative Interchange?" Interchange, January.

"On Rearing Children," Interchange, Spring.

"Religion, Science, and Philosophy Combined," Interchange, Summer.

"The Universe and Creative Interchange," Interchange, Fall.

1971

"The Ruling Commitment for Human Existence," Journal of Social Philosophy, II:1.

"Sex and the Valuing Consciousness," Interchange, "Issue No. 10."

"The Question to Answer," Interchange. "Issue No. 11."

"The Human Predicament," in Ewert H. Cousins, editor, Process Theology (New York: Newman Press), excerpts from chapter II of The Source of Human Good.

1972

"The Axiology of Robert S. Hartman," in John W. Davis, editor, Value and Valuation: Axiological Studies in Honor of Robert S. Hartman (Knoxville: University of Tennessee Press).

IV. PUBLICATIONS DEALING SPECIFICALLY WITH WIEMAN'S THOUGHT

Bernhardt, William H. "The Metaphysical Orientation of Wieman's Thought," The Iliff Review, Spring 1951, pp. 57-72.

Bretall, Robert W., editor, The Empirical Theology of Henry Nelson Wieman (Carbondale and Edwardsville: Southern Illinois University Press, 1969), see especially Part II, "Essays of Interpretation and Criticism of the Work of Henry Nelson Wieman," by nineteen authors.

Brooks, D. M. "Toward a Synthesis of Creative Communication in the Philosophy of Henry Nelson Wieman," (Doctoral thesis, Southern Illinois University, 1968).

Cauthen, Kenneth. The Impact of American Religious Liberalism (New York: Harper & Row, 1962), chapter 10, "Theological Naturalism: Henry Nelson Wieman."

Cobb, John B., Jr. Living Options in Protestant Theology (Philadelphia: Westminster Press, 1962), chapter 4, "Henry Nelson Wieman."

Conlon, F. Allen. "A Critique of the Neo-naturalistic Philosophy of Henry Nelson Wieman in Light of Thomistic Principles," (Doctoral thesis, The Catholic University of America, 1958).

Farley, Edward. The Trenscendence of God (Philadelphia: Westminster Press, 1960), chapter VI, "God as Supernatural Event: Henry Nelson Wieman."

Future of Empirical Theology, The. Edited by Bernard E.

Meland (Chicago: University of Chicago Press, 1969), _passim_.

Gilham, W. R. B. "The God-World Relation in Whitehead, Hartshorne, and Wieman," (Doctoral thesis, Princeton University, 1964).

Henderson, James G. "Henry Nelson Wieman: His Theology and His Aesthetic Theory and Their Bearing Upon Modern Literature," (Doctoral thesis, Union Theological Seminary, NYC, 1973).

Hepler, Cedric L. "Introducing a New Generation to Henry Nelson Wieman," St. Luke's Journal, X:3, March 1967.

_____. "H. N. Wieman: His Work Perpetuated," Christian Century, LXXXVI:34, August 20, 1969.

Howie, John. "Creativity in the Thought of William Ernest Hocking and Henry Nelson Wieman," (Doctoral thesis, Boston University, 1965).

King, Martin Luther, Jr., "A Comparison of the Conceptions of God in the Thinking of Paul Tillich and Henry Nelson Wieman," (Doctoral thesis, Boston University, 1954).

McBride, Robert E. "A Study of the Philosophy of History in Selected Contemporary Theologians with Special Reference to the Writings of Reinhold Niebuhr, Henry Nelson Wieman and the Process Theologians," (Doctoral thesis, University of Chicago, 1960).

Maher, Paul J. "A Critical Exposition of the Notion of Commitment in the Works of Henry Nelson Wieman," (Doctoral thesis, The Catholic University of America, 1971).

Meland, Bernard E. The Realities of Faith (New York: Oxford University Press, 1962), _passim._

Milligan, Charles S. A review of Intellectual Foundation of Faith, in The Christian Advocate, August 17, 1961.

_____. "A Rejoinder to Professor Wieman," The Iliff Review, Fall, 1961.

_____. "Broader Than the Measure of Man's Mind, But ...," The Iliff Review, Winter, 1962.

Minella, Mary J. "The Eschatological Dimension in Henry Nelson Wieman's Theology of Creativity," (Doctoral thesis, The Catholic University of America, 1974).

Minor, William S., editor. Charles Hartshorne and Henry Nelson Wieman (Carbondale: The Foundation for Creative Philosophy, Inc., 1969).

_____. "Creativity in the Thought of Henry Nelson Wieman," (Doctoral thesis, University of Chicago, 1971).

Mow, J. B. "Redemption and the Demonic in the Historical Process: A Study of the Theological Ethics of C. H. Dodd, Paul Tillich, and Henry Nelson Wieman," (Doctoral thesis, University of Chicago, 1964).

Peden, W. Creighton. "Wieman's View of Religion," The Iliff Review, XXIII:2.

_____. "Wieman's Scientific Method," The Redford Review, XX:3.

_____. "Wieman's Alternative to the Death of God," Anglican Theological Review, L:4.

_____. "Henry Nelson Wieman: A Dialog," Religious Humanism, IV:3.

_____. "Reflections: A Dialogue with Henry Nelson Wieman," The Journal of Religious Thought, XXX:1.

Peters, Karl E. A review of Wieman's Religious Inquiry: Some Explorations, in Union Seminary Quarterly Review, XXIV:1.

Rich, Charles Mark. "Henry Nelson Wieman's Functional Theism as Transcending Event," (Doctoral thesis, University of Chicago, 1963).

Smith, Gerald B. A review of Wieman's Religious Experience and Scientific Method in Journal of Religion, VI:4.

Smith, Huston. "Mr. Wieman's The Source of Human Good," a review, in The Iliff Review, Spring issue, 1948.

Terry, R. Franklin. "The Problem of Evil and the Promise of Hope in the Theology of Henry Nelson Wieman, Religion in Life, XXXIX:4.

Thomas, Owen C.   "Radical Reinterpretation," a review of
Wieman's Religious Inquiry: Some Explorations in Christian
Century, December 25, 1968.

Thompson, W. B.   "Faith and Reason in the Theology of Henry Nelson Wieman," (Doctoral thesis, University of Michigan,
1971).

White, Hugh Vernon.   A review of The Empirical Theology
of Henry Nelson Wieman in Religion in Life, XXXIII:1.

Williams, Daniel Day.   A review of Intellectual Foundation
of Faith in Theology Today, XIX:1.

_____.   "The Philosophy of Henry Nelson Wieman," chap-
ter 5 in Charles Hartshorne and Henry Nelson Wieman, William S. Minor, editor.   (Carbondale: The Foundation for
Creative Philosophy, Inc., 1969).

INDEX

Absolute, the: and creativity 150; Wieman and Hocking on 150

Absolute goal: definition of 151; Wieman and Hocking on 152

Absolute good: empirical route to 150, 151

Alexander, S. 48, 49

"All-knowing mind": contradiction of term 158

America: democracy and Christian faith 206; faith of, and European thought 207; power and Christian faith 208; and Russia and China 207

Appreciable activity: defined 95, 97, 105; not appreciated activity 102; and meaning 96-100; and purpose 97; and value 8-10

Appreciative consciousness: and creative interaction 167; and value 152

Aristotle 139

Art: and the unknown 81

Asiatic peoples: and the world situation 209, 210, 211

Atomic energy: and the world situation 209, 211

Authority: in religious traditions 238

Axial period of history: and religious creativity 227

Barbour, Ian 254, 255

Belief: and empirical and rational evidence 162; and use of power 162

Bertocci, Peter 129

Better and worse: standard of 146

Biological processes: and human existence 259-260

Biological survival 237

Boulding, Kenneth 231

Brightman, E. S. 129

Carnell, Edward 129

Christian faith: Americanized 207

Church: and nameless community of creativity 203

Coherence: and human existence 151; as work of "whole

305

idea" 151

Cold war: and the world situation 209, 210

Commitment: in worship, and empirical inquiry 135; to creativity 230

Communication: in modern society 184; and unknown 81; spoken and written 191; and television 184

Community of creativity: is nameless 202

Concept: defined, 45; and logical categories 46; and objects in nature 45-46

Consciousness: and life 146

Creative conflict: and human existence 261-263

Creative education: nine methods of attaining 219-221; integration of benefits and methods of 221-223; threats to 212; ten benefits of 214-215

Creative interaction: and absolute good 169; inertias against 168, 169; nature of 168-169; and persons 173

Creative interchange: analyzed 136-140, 228-231; and conflict of interests 186-187; and creation of the mind 156, 157; as creator of the universe 139; and culture 139; and existential situation 185; and good and evil 186; and the greater good 187; and "hidden persuaders" 189; and history 139-140; and human existence 139; and human self-destruction 187, 191; not an ideal 185; and predictable consequences 288; and propaganda 188; as revelation of God in Jesus Christ 138; and salvation of the person 140; and the sense of good and evil 182; three elements of 182; and three-fold aim of education 211-212; and traditional concept of God 11; and transcendence 11; two-fold work of 287; and unconscious resources of 189-190; as Word of God 138

Creative interest 19; as organized conflict of minds 23-24

Creative transformation 288

Creativity: and Christ 153; and Christian symbols 291; as "divine presence" in human life 8, 244; as equivalent expression for creative interchange 228; and feeling awareness 244; four-fold analysis of 242; and human conflicts 263; and human existence 264; and human interests 19; as natural process 3, 11; not human achievement 290; operative in human life 230; a process with a structure 244; and propaganda 291; religious expressions for 229; sovereignty of 174; and traditional theology 2, 13; understandings of 230-231; and "unknowable God" 12; and unknown dimension of 11; and valuing consciousness 1, 229, 232

Creativity of God 166-171; and created goods 200-201;
     meaning of 203-204; and the New Testament 205;
     not peculiar to Christianity 170; and orders of life
     199-200; and personal stability 199-203; self-confi-
     dence and ideals 200; and social stability 195, 206
Crucifixion of Jesus 174
Cultural problems: their bearing on philosophy of religion
     121-127
Culture: and human existence 188

"Death of God": symptom of rapid change in religion 241
Democracy: individual worth and world purpose 149
Descartes 236
Dewey, John 55-70 *passim*
Divine presence: and creativity 8, 244
Drucker, Peter F. 216, 218

Education: and cultural heritage 213; and generation gap
     117-118; and knowledge 213; moral and spiritual val-
     ues in 211; and unknown 81
Educational Psychology (Thorndike) 33, 34
Einstein, Albert 139
Empirical method: and knowledge 5
Empirical philosophy of religion 152-153, 162-163
Enjoyable activity: not enjoyed activity 105
Evil: defined 289; and supreme good 82-83
Existential situation 182
Existentialism: rational alternative to 237-240
Existentialists: irrational methodology of 236
Experience: defined 40
Experiment in Education (Hocking) 148

Faith: as commitment 274
Forgiveness of sin 165, 173-177
Freedom: as fulfillment of goal-seeking activity 265; and
     human existence 266
Freudian psychology 22

Gandhi 284
"Generation gap": and education 117-118
Goal-seeking activities: and unit of good 264
God: and abstract order 88; as all-knower 158; con-
     cepts of 158; defined 283; and level of sensation

158-159; and mystery of being 162; original source
of knowledge of 157; and possibility 73-75; and process 71, 73-75; as structure of supreme value 71,
88; and symbols 87; two meanings of 142-143; and
the unknown 78-80; as unlimited growth of connections
of value 109-111; and value 83, 109-111
God's love: and creativity 170
God's wrath: defined 170
Good: defined 169-170, 288; as fulfillment of any interest
19, 20
Good and evil 133; ontology of 14, 142; predictable consequences of 289; standard of judging 13-14, 141-142,
183, 287
Graham, Billy 129
Grapes of Wrath (Steinbeck) 204-205
Greatest good 19; and creativity 264; and freedom 265;
and love 266
Ground and Nature of the Right, The (Lewis) 276, 277

Hate: its kinship with love 270
Heidegger, Martin 236
Herrick, C. J. 34
History: and human existence 188
Hocking, William Ernest: philosophy of, discussed 148-164
passim
Holy Spirit: and creativity 153
Human existence: analysis of 259-263; and creativity 243
Human interests: adaptive 26-27; classification of 25-
39; creative 28-30; and creativity 19; coordinated
by harmony, rejected 22-23; instrumental 27-28;
organization by conflict of tendencies, proposed 23-24;
organization of 19-20; three types contrasted 29-33
Human judgment: relativity of 133
Human organism: and knowledge 4
Human predicament 192

Ideals: subordinate to creative interchange 185, 186
Individualism 238-239
Instrumentalism: defined 59; and philosophy of John Dew-
ey 55-70 passim; perverse uses of 55-58
Interpersonal Theory of Psychiatry, The (Sullivan) 289n
Introduction to Neurology (Herrick) 34
Intuition: and creativity of God 204; and "passionate in-
quiry", 282; the raw material for knowledge 278
Issues in Science and Religion (Barbour) 255

James, William 280
Jaspers, Karl 226, 227, 236
"Joy of believing": as obstacle to religious commitment
     275

Kant, Immanuel 236
Kierkegaard, Søren 236
Knowable world: definition of 160;   limited by finitude of
     human organism 160
Knowledge: abstracted from physiological process and felt
     quality 4, 5;   analysis of processes of 276-277;   ele-
     ments of 89;   and felt quality 272;   and meaning 256;
     of nature, self and others 156;   of other minds 275;
     and physiological process 272;   and probability 161,
     274;   and statements 273;   three dimensions of 156;
     and value 257;   Wieman's theory of 3-8
Knowledge of God: and creativity 156;   and knowledge of
     persons 159

Language: and human existence 188
Lewis, C. I.   276, 277
Life: defined 41-42;   and mind 41
Lippmann, Walter 198
Love: and abstract terms 71;   contrasted with "agape"
     266;   and creativity 269;   as goal-seeking activity 267;
     perverse forms of 268-269;   two characteristics of
     267;   and the unknown 81
Luther, Martin 284

Mass organization and production: and creative interchange
     218;   and education 217;   as transformer of modern
     life 216
Meaning: and appreciable activity 96-100;   defined 99-100
Meaning of God in Human Experience, The (Hocking) 149,
     150, 155
Meaning of the 20th Century, The (Boulding) 231
Mechanized communication 184
Metaphysics: and religious inquiry 284
Mind: five cultural developments of 237-241;   defined 43;
     and life 43;   and physical nature 41
Mystery of being: and universe 160, 161
Myth: and religious knowledge 285

Nature: and the self and other minds 158; as temporal
    and spatial structure 40
Nature experience; and religious experience 155, 157
Nature of man: and creativity of God 199-200
New Society, The (Drucker) 216, 218-219
Newton, Isaac 139

Origin and Goal of History, The (Jaspers) 226

Paradox: and religious knowledge 285
Perry, R. B. 21
Personal stability: and adaptation 198; and idealism 197;
    not a human structure 203; and orders of life 195;
    and self-confidence 196; and the "way of faith" 197-
    198
Personality, reorganization of 282
Philosophy: defined 84; function of 259; and perverse in-
    strumentalism 57
Philosophy of religion: challenges of 127-128; contrasted
    with theology 114-116; and cultural problems 121-
    127; and social change 116-119; task of 114
Post-civilization, analyzed 231-233
Power: ontology of 14, 142
Practical knowledge: and religious inquiry 279
Preface to Morals, A (Lippmann) 198
Probability: and knowledge 161
Process: defined 71; and God 71
Process of progressive integration 72-73, 78

Religion: analysis of function of 244-250; defined 229,
    251; devotion to unknown best 60; function of 82-84,
    243; Hocking's definition of 148; and knowledge 60;
    perverse forms of 84-88; and perverse instrumental-
    ism 57-58; and philosophy 84; a problem to be
    solved 233, 234, 235-236; responsibility of in post-
    civilization 232; and science 85-86; supreme devo-
    tion and knowledge 226; and use of power 162; and
    value 69-70, 82-83
Religious commitment 251; and creativity 258; and great-
    est good 271
Religious faith: and community 251, 252
Religious inquiry: and discovery of error 279; and meta-
    physics 284; as "passionate inquiry" 279-281; and

values 89-90
Religious knowledge: accurate definitions in 282-283; and
    intuition 282; and logical coherence 284; and predict-
    able consequences 285-286
Religious reformation: conditions necessary for 233, 234;
    issues to be avoided 234-235
Resurrection of Jesus 175, 176
Revelation: as creativity operative in history 291-293;
    and religious inquiry 286-287

Sartre, Jean-Paul 236
Science: analysis of 254-259; and experience 7; function
    of 243; and knowledge and power 226; and religion
    85-86; responsibility of in post-civilization 232; tech-
    nique of 50; and unknown 80-81
Scientific control: and creativity 258
Scientific knowledge 255; creativity in 257, 259
Scientific method: defined 49; and experience 50-52; and
    knowledge 5
Security: and religious devotion 281
Security operations 288; and creative transformation 289
Self: and openness to correction 134; and ultimate com-
    mitment 134
Self-consciousness: and human existence 260-261
Self-sufficiency: denied for universe, mind and knowledge
    160-161
Sin 166; confession and repentance of 177-180; defined
    171; and specific goods 172
Skepticism: and knowledge 256
Social change: and education 118; and life styles 118;
    and philosophy of religion 116; and religion 117; and
    science 117
Social experience: and religious experience 155, 157
Social heritage: and unknown 81-82
Social psychology 167
Social reconstruction: and unknown 81
Social sciences: and religious knowledge 286
Social stability: and the American way 206
Socrates 284
Sophistication: defined 119; and philosophy of religion
    119, 121; and psychology 119; and religion 119, 120,
    121; and science 120
Space, Time and Deity (Alexander) 49n
Statements: and knowledge 273
Structure: defined 71; and experience of value 83; and
    God 71, 83

Structure of integration 72-73
Subjective knowledge 256
Sullivan, Harry Stack 289
Supernatural intervention: notion of 262
Supreme value: as one process among many processes in
    nature 75-78; defined 71-72
Symbol: defined 44-45; and God 87

Theology: and philosophy of religion 114-116; task of
    114
Thorndike, Edward L. 33, 34
Tillich, Paul 129, 236, 284
Total self: and creativity 264; freedom of 265; and love
    268
Traditional religions: their loss of power to inspire 227
Tree Grows in Brooklyn, A (Smith) 190
Truth: and designating concept 47; and logical categories
    48; and strict logic 49

Ultimate being: and religious inquiry 284
Ultimate commitment: and beliefs 145; and certainty 146;
    and Christian religion 143-144; and fallibility 146-147;
    and Jesus Christ 144; and ontology of good and evil
    142; as religious faith 1; two levels of 1, 87, 140-
    141, 142
Universe: different structures of 160; and human imagi-
    nation 161; and "mystery of being" 161; self-suffici-
    ency of, denied 161
Unknowable mystery 239-240
Unknown, the: and God 78-80; not the unknowable 80

Value: and abstract principles 94; and appreciable activ-
    ity 94-97; and biological patterns 92-93; and coher-
    ence 152; and connection of activities 101-102, 105;
    defined 152; and the emotion 91; empirical principles
    of 66-67, 103-105; and empirical reality of creativity
    152; empirical system of 9, 10, 11; and enjoyment
    101-106; as goal-seeking activity 228; greatest pos-
    sible, analyzed 76-77; and ineffable experiences 93-
    94; and intelligence 92; and meaning 88; as mean-
    ing of enjoyments 64; order and purpose 93; and
    personality 93; and possibilities 108-109; a process
    in nature and existence 63; process of 10; and proc-
    ess of communication 68-69; and process of interaction

63; relativity of judgment of 133-134; and religion 69-70; and society 93; test of 106-108; three alternative systems of 228; unit of 105; and universe 83, 108-109; Wieman's empirical study of 8-12

Values: and discovery of error 182, 183; empirical observations and operations of 61; and existential situation 183; and power of communication 192; and religious inquiry 90; plural processes of 61-63

Valuing consciousness: and creativity 1, 229, 232

"Way of faith": and modern man 198

Wharton, John F. 258

"Whole idea": Hocking's concept of 148

Worship: Hocking and Wieman on 154-155; and empirical evidence 133; and human fallibility 130; and modern life 131-132; objective of 130; perversions of 130-131; and rational inquiry 133

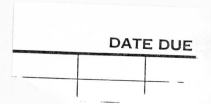

DATE DUE